The Elephants and the Grass

A Study of Nonalignment

The Elephants and the Grass

A Study of Nonalignment

CECIL V. CRABB, Jr.

FREDERICK A. PRAEGER, *Publishers*
New York • Washington • London

FREDERICK A. PRAEGER, Publishers
111 Fourth Avenue, New York 3, N.Y., U.S.A.
77–79 Charlotte Street, London W. 1, England

Published in the United States of America in 1965 by
Frederick A. Praeger, Inc., Publishers

Library of Congress Catalog Card Number: 65-15653

Printed in the United States of America

To Cele and Van

Contents

Introduction

Nonalignment, or neutralism, as it is sometimes called—the dominant diplomatic philosophy of the Afro-Arab-Asian world—has never received the attention from informed students of international affairs which its importance deserves. It is both a widespread and an increasingly influential ideology. Any successful Western effort to understand and to establish lasting rapport with societies whose governments desire to avoid Cold War entanglements demands systematic, dispassionate, and continuing appraisal of the diplomatic philosophy to which these societies are committed.

This analysis of nonalignment is predicated upon an assumption that is contrary to the premise underlying much of the contemporary Western, particularly the American, response to neutralism. This is that officials at the head of neutralist governments are fully as intelligent, as politically astute, as capable of weighing foreign-policy alternatives realistically, and as sensitive to significant global developments as are their counterparts in the West or in the Communist bloc. Once this assumption is accepted, it follows that their decision to remain nonaligned vis-à-vis Cold War power groups must be explained on a more rational and penetrating basis than is customary with most Western observers.

For far too many years, the Western view of nonalignment has been compounded chiefly of irritation and
pique, mystification and bewilderment, suspicion and
mistrust. Neutralism, Western reactions suggested, was a
kind of foreign-policy aberration; it arose because of the
failure of the normal process of foreign-policy decision-
making from west Africa to east Asia. Thus, Western explanations of the neutralist phenomenon have implied
that its adherents failed to recognize the "true nature"
and gravity of the Communist menace to global peace
and security; or that neutralism reflected a seemingly inexplicable anti-Western prejudice on the part of certain
countries, leading them erroneously to "equate" Western
and Communist objectives in world affairs; or that it
stemmed from a kind of Machiavellian opportunism that
led them to "seek the best of both worlds" in their relations with East and West; or, at worst, that it indicated
that countries dedicated to this ideology either had become, or were becoming, *de facto* members of the Communist bloc.

In brief, Western explanations of neutralism have largely
consisted of little more than clichés, stereotypes, crude
value judgments, and plain factual errors. In many instances, the very concept of nonalignment was not understood correctly. And even when it was, little effort was
made to fathom its origins or to deal dispassionately with
its implications for the diplomatic goals of the Western
alliance.

In part, this tendency may be attributed to a long-
standing Western conviction that neutralism was a transitory movement, a passing phase in the history of international affairs. Neutralist countries, a prominent American
declared recently, were "trying to make up their minds"
about which Cold War camp to enter. Neutralism, in other
words, was essentially a manfestation of diplomatic in-

decision and equivocation. Once nations finally "decided" whether they really "belonged" to the East or to the West, the neutralist movement would largely disappear.

In common with many other Western judgments about nonalignment, this one has been discredited by events. Neutralism has not only failed to disappear; but in spite of (or, in some respects, because of) traumatic experiences like the Himalayan clash between India and Red China, it has become both a remarkably durable and an expanding global force. Latin America is the next area in which we may expect an increasing interest in the concept of nonalignment and a growing sense of "identification" with the neutralist community. And, spurred by the crisis on the island of Cyprus, the government of Greece —hitherto an unswerving member of the NATO system— is actively seeking more cordial relations with Communist Bulgaria, a move induced in part by Greek disaffection with Western policies toward Cyprus. Across the Iron Curtain, Romania is also endeavoring to loosen the ties of its former tight "alignment" with the U.S.S.R., both by cultivating more intimate relations with France and by endeavoring to "normalize" its relations with Communist China. And for policy-makers in Washington, Gaullism— with its emphasis upon *la dignité* and *l'indépendance* as cardinal elements in the new French role in global affairs—has brought the tendency toward diplomatic nonalignment into the center of the Western alliance.

These provide merely a few indications that nonalignment is firmly established as a foreign-policy credo and that it will confront Western officials and students of international affairs with a challenge for some time to come. The purpose of this study is to make the nature of this challenge more intelligible and to provide a more satisfactory basis for appraising it than mere dislike of neutralism or the belief that neutralist governments have simply abandoned the normal process of diplomatic decision-making. In an attempt to avoid preconceived value judgments, our analysis endeavors to present the case for non-alignment, as advocates of the idea understand and justify it. It is, quite frankly, a sympathetic study of the neutralist credo, both because many of the arguments (particularly the strategic-military arguments) have seldom been objectively evaluated in the West and also because giving the neutralist side the benefit of the doubt may at least have the virtue of raising the level of discussion in the West above the plane of emotionalism and moralistic condemnations. For even if Western observers continue to reject many of the tenets of the neutralist credo, they will be obliged to refute them with more persuasive and rational arguments than they have used thus far in their relations with neutralist countries.

The author wishes to express his appreciation to the Rockefeller Foundation for supporting the research upon which this study is based. He is no less grateful to the Faculty Committee on Research and the administration of Vassar College in providing time and financial assistance which made the study possible.

A large number of officials and citizens from neutralist countries generously contributed their time to discuss the nature and implications of the neutralist movement. During the course of my research, I endeavored to interview officials from nearly all neutralist governments. These interviews were conducted at U.N. headquarters in New York and at embassies in Washington, D.C. Always, I found such officials cooperative, interested, and frank. Since most of these interviews were "off the record," no effort has been made to identify the officials concerned or to cite the interview record in the documentation. Special thanks are owed to the Embassy of India in Washington, whose officials were unusually helpful in making available their file of Indian journals and periodicals.

The staffs of the Vassar College Library, the Johns Hopkins University Library, and the New York Public Library provided invaluable assistance and access to materials, particularly microfilms.

Miss Cynthia Hewitt, a political science major at Vassar, gave generously of her time and her outstanding talents as research assistant as well as critic during 1963–64. For her expert typing skill and her helpful editorial suggestions, I am deeply indebted to Mrs. Lester F. Tubby.

As always, my wife, Harriet, served unstintingly and capably as critic and editor. If at times she became weary of serving as an "average reader," she has the consolation of knowing that her role was indispensable, for an author in the throes of producing a manuscript runs the risk of losing sight of the reader. She endured the research, writing, and revision with far more equanimity than I had any right to expect.

Naturally, the generosity of others in no way deprives the author of full responsibility for the contents of this book. Errors of fact and judgment are mine alone.

Cecil V. Crabb, Jr.

Poughkeepsie, New York
August 11, 1964

The
Elephants
and the
Grass

A Study of Nonalignment

When two elephants fight, it is the grass that suffers.

—AFRICAN PROVERB

Nonalignment: Theme and Variations

Strongly criticizing President Johnson's foreign-aid program, on June 1, 1964, a minority on the House Foreign Affairs Committee lamented the fact that "After 10 years and $370 million in aid, Cambodia has asked us to pick up our marbles and go home." This minority was no less distressed that "Indonesia, with $870 million of our money, continues to threaten freedom-seeking Malaysia." [1] These are merely two examples of the fact that since the emergence of "neutralism" as a global force, following the Afro-Asian Conference of 1955, official and public commentators in the West have tended to view neutralist conduct in global affairs with deep suspicion, skepticism, hostility, mystification, and uneasiness.* Beneath these reactions, it has long been apparent, has lingered a pervasive ignorance about the meaning and implications of "nonalignment" and about the specific goals and tactics of countries espousing this philosophy of foreign relations. All too often, in evaluating the neutralist phenomenon, official and unofficial interpreters have relied chiefly on

---

* For reasons that will become apparent, this analysis uses "neutralism" and "nonalignment" synonymously. Following neutralist practice, it avoids other terms—especially "neutral" and "neutrality"—which have connotations unacceptable to nonaligned countries.

3

clichés and stereotypes seriously inhibiting intelligent understanding of the origins, nature, and consequences of the neutralist movement. Nonaligned countries have been accused of "straddling the fence" diplomatically, of opportunistically seeking the "best of both worlds," or of merely endeavoring to "play off Washington against Moscow (or Peking)."

The tendency for epithets to replace enlightened judgments in Western appraisals of neutralism is to some extent engendered by the philosophy itself and by the behavior of individual nonaligned nations. A rich, confusing, not to say contradictory, multiplicity of terms and phrases surrounds the neutralist movement. An Arab commentator declares that Arab states are committed to a policy of "active independence" and "neutralism." Premier Ben Bella characterizes Algeria's policy as "dynamic, independent, and disinterested"; Algeria belongs to the camp of "nonengaged" countries and champions "constructive neutrality." Officials in Egypt, along with those in leading African states like Ghana and Guinea, espouse "positive neutralism." Yet when Egypt merged with Syria in 1958, the new United Arab Republic committed itself to "an independent neutral course" in global affairs. On another occasion, these two countries joined with Jordan in supporting a "policy of active neutrality." Morocco, on the other hand, has identified its policy as one of "nondependence" in global affairs. A Sudanese official has said: "We . . . are not positive neutralists; we just want to be neutral." Israel prefers the term "nonidentification." Nigeria, according to one official, takes "an independent view, which is not the same as neutralism." President Sékou Touré of Guinea has used the phrase "active formal neutralism" to describe his country's policies. On the eve of independence, the African state of Malawi (formerly Nyasaland) proposed to follow a policy of "discretional alignment and neutralism." Officials of Afghanistan and Cambodia, on the other hand, prefer the terms "neutral" or "neutrality" to characterize their foreign-policy orientations. Indian officials have repeatedly insisted that "nonalignment" is the only correct designation for their country's policy toward the great powers. Nearby Nepal has similarly endeavored to remain nonaligned in great-power discords—and to maintain a delicately balanced position of "neutrality" toward the conflict between India and Red China. In 1954, the great powers sought to "neutralize" the tiny Asian kingdom of Laos. And in 1964, French President de Gaulle advocated a plan of "neutralization" for the whole of Southeast Asia.*

Two points should be made with regard to this apparent semantical and philosophical confusion. First, there is an underlying consensus among countries professing nonalignment with respect to its dominant elements. Second, despite this consensus, there is disagreement and uncertainty about the ideological and policy ramifications of

---

* As we shall see, neutralism and nonalignment must be carefully distinguished from the closely related but essentially different concepts of "neutrality" and "neutralization." Since neutrality is discussed at a later stage, here we will only note that there have been two outstanding instances of "neutralization" in the postwar era—Austria and Laos. In both cases, the Cold War power blocs concurred in drawing up a treaty or settlement whereby the terms of neutralization were made explicit. Under these terms, neither country was permitted to enter into military alliances; great powers were to refrain from intervention in the internal affairs of the country concerned; neither country was to allow its territory to serve as a military base for a great power. Neutralization was thus a policy _imposed_ by outside powers upon Austria and Laos. In Austria's case, particularly, it encouraged Vienna to pursue a cautious and carefully guarded course between East and West—a position that nonaligned countries reject. Since "neutralization" was the price of independence for Laos and Austria, it entailed a much greater limitation in the policy alternatives open to these states than does a policy of neutralism, or of nonalignment. For the details of the neutralization of Laos, see _Asian Recorder,_ VIII (February 12–18, 1962), 4421–22. Interesting insights into Austrian neutralization are provided in Alfred Verdross, "Austria, Neutrality and the United Nations," _India Quarterly,_ XVI (January–March, 1960), 24–31.

neutralism. Let us examine the implications of these general observations more fully.

Dominant Motifs in the Neutralist Refrain

Because of the presence of many deeply embedded misconceptions in the Western mind about the concept of nonalignment, let us begin by examining briefly what the doctrine does *not* entail. Throughout the neutralist zone, a basic consensus exists that a policy of neutralism or nonalignment must be carefully distinguished from a position of "neutrality" in global affairs. A desire to highlight this distinction has prompted spokesmen like President Nkrumah of Ghana to assert: "Ghana does not intend to follow a neutralist policy in its foreign relations, but does intend to preserve its independence to act as it sees best at any particular time."[2] Arab sources have repeatedly deprecated use of the term "neutrality" to describe a policy of neutralism or nonalignment. Neutrality implies that a country has been reduced merely to the role of a spectator in global affairs, that it is "isolated from the events taking place in the rest of the world," and that its policies are based on indifference to global issues. Arab commentators recognize many gradations of "neutrality" under international law. But neutrality essentially means "keeping out of war. It is the condition of those who remain at peace while others are fighting." Thus, neutrality can legally exist "only in connection with war and during an armed conflict." Indian spokesmen have repeatedly emphasized the distinction between "neutrality" and "neutralism" in their moral-ethical connotations.[3] Labeling the Western belief that India's foreign policy was synonymous with neutrality a "total misapprehension," the late Jawarhalal Nehru once called neutrality an expression of a bad odor; it means a person who sits on the fence and who cannot decide between right and wrong. India is certainly not neutral, and her policy of nonalignment is anything but a neutral policy. She believes in nonalignment because she feels that the only way to achieve peace is to extend the climate of peace and to prevent the Cold War spreading into other parts of the world.

On another occasion, Nehru declared: "One cannot be neutral to right or wrong." [4]

Advocates of nonalignment thus see several fundamental differences between their foreign-policy credo and neutrality. Neutrality has traditionally defined the relationship between nonbelligerents and belligerents—a posture that has no relevance in the absence of overt military hostilities among great powers. Rather than admit that the Cold War is analogous to a global military contest, which a position of neutrality would imply, nonaligned countries seek to mitigate Cold War tensions and to *prevent* the outbreak of a military conflagration between East and West. Advocates of nonalignment also categorically deny that neutrality implies diplomatic "fence-sitting," insensitivity to moral and ethical issues, or adherence to a philosophy of moral relativism that requires (or gives rise to) a midway position between rival Cold War contentions.*

* Nomenclature, as we have indicated, is far from uniform among countries eschewing alignments with Cold War power blocs. From time to time, advocates of nonalignment themselves use terms like "neutral" or "neutrality" to describe their policies—as when Syria and Egypt, in 1958, jointly pledged themselves to "an independent neutral course" with respect to Cold War antagonists; when Saudi Arabia, in 1958, espoused a policy of "positive neutrality"; or when Sudan, in 1961, described its role as that of a "friendly neutral" between East and West. Yet on such occasions, the reservations we have described above apply; what is meant is a policy of diplomatic nonalignment or neutralism. Thus Switzerland—the nation exemplifying "neutrality"— and countries like Ireland, Sweden, Finland, and Austria, have played little or no role in the "neutralist" movement. They were not, for example, invited to the Belgrade Conference of 1961.

2   This leads to a second dominant misconception about
nonalignment: that it implies a policy of "noninvolvement," "nonengagement," isolationism, or passivity in international affairs. From West Africa to East Asia, governmental leaders are agreed that nonalignment is not tantamount to a policy of "isolationism"; nor does it signify the
absence of a foreign policy. A desire to highlight this fact
accounts for such designations as "positive," "active," or
"dynamic" to describe the kind of neutralist role that nations throughout the Afro-Asian world are determined to
play. Ghana, Nkrumah has said, does not "choose to play
the role of silent spectator in world affairs, or in matters
which affect our country's vital interests and the destiny
of the African peoples. Our policy of positive neutralism
is not a passive or neutralist policy. It is a positive policy
based upon our firm belief in positive action." [5] Similarly,
the Government of Morocco has emphasized that its policy of "nondependence" did not "mean that Morocco
seeks to remain in isolation. On the contrary, Morocco in-
tends to maintain friendly relations with all countries." [6]
Israel has equated its policy of "nonidentification" with
"an independent foreign policy prompted by the necessity
for the State to recognize its responsibilities . . . for making
its own contribution toward the preservation of international peace." [7] A key element in Indonesia's "active and
independent" policy is the determination to "do our utmost
to prevent a next war which we believe will only result in
the extinction of human civilization." [8] The pervasive belief that nonalignment in no sense entails diplomatic passivity or quiescence stems from an underlying conviction
we shall examine in greater detail in Chapter 2. This is the
belief that nonaligned countries are in a peculiarly advantageous position to ameliorate Cold War conflicts and
to make "peaceful coexistence" a reality.

A third prevalent misapprehension about the concept of

nonalignment is underscored by a Cambodian official's insistence that neutralist countries ought not "to form another monolithic group" that would sooner or later become "another bloc—a third bloc, which has already been termed, rather paradoxically, 'the Neutral Bloc.'" [9] The Prime Minister of Nigeria has agreed that "It is a pity . . . that nations who are members of the United Nations have constituted themselves into blocs." [10] President Nasser has emphasized that in following a nonaligned policy, Egypt did not "belong to any bloc." In nearby Sudan, an official described his country as a "friendly neutral"—not only with respect to Cold War belligerents, but with regard to controversies among "nonaligned" countries as well.[11] Proponents of nonalignment thus widely disclaim any desire to form a "neutralist bloc." On the contrary, a cardinal goal of the neutralist movement is the *elimination* of tightly cohesive, antagonistic diplomatic blocs. Not only do nonaligned nations disclaim any intention of creating a neutralist bloc; they are fully aware that the basic policy divergencies among them place insuperable obstacles in the path of achieving this goal. One Western observer characterized neutralist diplomatic maneuvering at the Belgrade Conference:

> Some are busiedly inclined to favour one of the two super powers; others are involved in cold wars of their own—the Arabs against Israel, India and Afghanistan against Pakistan, Ghana against Togo and Ivory Coast, Iraq against Kuwait and Saudi Arabia, and so on.[12]

Another commentator concluded on the basis of the Belgrade proceedings:

> A bloc implies some organization, some measure of joint agreement, among its members before any action can be taken. Nehru's diplomacy would be subject to the veto of

Somaliland. Nasser could not act unless all the Arab powers agreed. . . . They are not united on anything except anti-colonialism and their fear of war.

He added that the influence of neutralist nations collectively "may well be lost if they try to act as a body." [13] Admittedly, from time to time advocates of nonalignment refer to what an Arab source has called a "common non-aligned purpose" and a "common approach to the basic issues confronting the world today" [14] that provides cohesiveness to the neutralist community, and it is generally referred to as a "third force" on the global scene. Yet despite the underlying affinity between neutralist countries in their relations with Cold War power groupings, it cannot be said that they have achieved that degree of mutual diplomatic cooperation and cohesiveness required to fuse African, Arab, and Asian nations into a "neutralist bloc" that could rival the Western or Communist coalitions.

A fourth misconception about nonalignment widely prevalent in the West has repeatedly been pointed to by Yugoslav spokesmen. A position of nonalignment may lead a neutralist country "to an attitude which sometimes draws closer to, or even coincides with, that of one or another country included . . . in any of the [Cold War] blocs." Accordingly, Yugoslav commentators have emphatically rejected the idea that genuine neutralism required its advocates to "steer a middle course between East and West—a course at the same distance from both." Such diplomatic equidistance is deplored by proponents of nonalignment as an attempt to apply canons of traditional "neutrality" to present-day neutralism. Neither philosophically nor in the actual conduct of their foreign relations do nonaligned countries accept the obligation of equidistance. Instead, they overwhelmingly agree with the Yugoslav contention that the influence of a neutralist country increases when its policies coincide with those of one or the other Cold War power bloc.[15]

Our analysis of prevailing misconceptions about the neutralist credo has already suggested certain positive elements common to its African, Arab, or Asian manifestations. In general, it may be said that above all neutralism or nonalignment implies *diplomatic freedom of action and choice* with respect to Cold War contestants. The crux of nonalignment, according to Egyptian President Nasser, is that "our voice in international forums is not counted as an automatic one attached to a particular bloc." Crown Prince Faisal has said that a neutralist policy means that Saudi Arabia proposes "to deal with every state in the world in accordance with its interests and . . . general Arab interests." For the government of Ghana, "positive neutralism" means pursuing "a policy that is not committed ideologically nor militarily to any particular power or power bloc." Following this policy, Accra proposes to "act as it sees best on any issue" in the light of Ghana's diplomatic interests and obligations. A position of nonalignment, Prime Minister Nehru once said, meant "an independent nation functioning according to its own lights" diplomatically; diplomatic alignment, on the other hand, meant "being regimented to do something which you do not like and thereby giving up a certain measure of your own independent judgment and thinking." A communiqué issued after talks between Yugoslavia's President Tito and Egypt's President Nasser declared that in pursuing "nonalignment," these two countries "have resisted every pressure, and decided to conduct an independent policy. . . . We have resisted outside influence with stubborn firmness in order to preserve our independence and freedom." A neutralist course for Afghanistan signifies that the country is "not the satellite of anyone. We are free and independent—and we intend to remain so." Two of the newest states

in the family of nations have supplied their own definitions of nonalignment. For Premier Ben Bella of Algeria,
the policy signifies that "we are aligned with nobody, not
even with nonalignment. . . . We are convinced that we
shall not be able to please everybody, and we don't even
intend to try." And from the Prime Minister of Malawi has
come what is perhaps the most succinct formulation of the
doctrine available: "When the West is doing what I think
is right for Malawi, I will align with the West. When the
East is doing what is good for Malawi, I will align with
the East." [16]

These formulations suggest several corollaries implicit in
the doctrine of nonalignment. A basic one (to which we
shall devote greater attention in the next chapter) is the
intimate relationship between nonalignment and national
independence. Particularly for countries emerging from
colonialism, a policy of nonalignment is viewed as both
the hallmark and the prerequisite of independence.
Nonalignment also precludes any permanent or "automatic" diplomatic or military identification with either
East or West, as poignantly expressed by the Arab, "rejection of demands that the Arab states commit themselves
in advance—often without their own consultation—to policies which would involve the Arab countries in global
issues, the implementation of which would demand sacri-
fices from the Arab countries." Expressing a conviction
that serves as a common denominator of neutralist policy,
this same Arab source declared: "The Arab countries are
unwilling to play the role of 'junior partner.'" The same
logic governs neutralist viewpoints toward military pacts.
His country, said Crown Prince Faisal, had "joined no
foreign pacts because of its belief that accession to foreign
pacts conflicts with Arab interests, and that pacts should
arise from the Arab states themselves." [17] Like other neutralist countries, Saudi Arabia had no objection to mili-

tary pacts in principle; still less did it, or any other non-aligned state, equate neutralism with nonviolence, pacifi-cism, or an indifference to the role of military force in international affairs. What the neutralist nations do oppose is *permanent diplomatic or military identification with great powers.*

It follows that nonalignment, which defines the posi-tions of its adherents toward the great powers, does not attempt to prescribe the relations of neutralist countries with each other. The doctrine neither seeks to, nor does it, guide Morocco's relations with Algeria, Ghana's with the Ivory Coast, Egypt's with Iraq, or India's with Burma. Similarly, it neither prohibits nor requires neutralist mem-bership in regional groupings like the Casablanca and Monrovia groups in Africa, the Arab League, or other as-sociations unrelated to the Cold War.

Four basic alternatives are thus open to nonaligned countries in their approach to global issues. Neutralist states may (1) agree wholly with the West; (2) agree wholly with the Communist bloc; (3) agree partially with each bloc; or (4) formulate distinctly "neutralist" posi-tions of their own.*

* It must be recognized that, in view of the growing "polycentricity" characterizing both the Western and Communist blocs, neutralist rela-tionships with nations identified with the East and West may in practice be more complex than this. General de Gaulle's proposal for the "neutral-ization" of Southeast Asia—a move firmly opposed by the United States—obviously commands wide support among nations in the neutralist zone. Similarly, Soviet and Chinese policy-makers take radically differing views on neutralism; and neutralist countries in turn assess Soviet and Chinese policies in Laos very differently. The complexity that the trend toward multipolarity introduces in neutralist relationships with East and West is highlighted by India's policies since 1962. India is obviously no longer "nonaligned" with respect to Red China, but adheres to nonalignment with respect to the Soviet Union and the United States.

Neutralism in Major and Minor Keys

Addressing an audience in Seattle on November 16, 1961, President Kennedy declared: "We find some who call themselves neutrals, who are our friends and sympathetic to us, and others who call themselves neutralist, who are unremittingly hostile to us." In the same period— a few weeks after the close of the Belgrade Conference of Nonaligned States—an Indian observer noted the tendency of State Department officials to classify neutralist countries as "positive" or "negative," depending on the extent to which their viewpoints and policies (as revealed at gatherings like the Belgrade meeting) coincided with those of the United States. Several months earlier, the *Egyptian Gazette* had deplored the distinction made by President Kennedy between "genuine neutrals" and countries that "don the mask of neutralism to exploit world conflicts to enhance their own power." [18] Other observers have alluded to a conviction in the State Department that some neutralist states were more "truly nonaligned" than others, to an official belief that at Belgrade the neutralist countries had felt a "need to move toward Moscow's viewpoint" on global issues; still other American officials distinguished between two kinds of neutralism—an acceptable "independent" variety and a "dependent" variety that intentionally or unintentionally supported the Communist cause.

For many years, the broad diversity of viewpoints and policies identified with a host of countries professing diplomatic nonalignment has posed an intricate problem for policy-makers and students of international affairs. Secretary of State John Foster Dulles' widely quoted dictum that neutralism was "immoral" tended to obscure the fact that Dulles was fully aware of the complexities and subtleties inherent in the concept of nonalignment. In spite of his apparent distaste for the doctrine, Dulles specifically exempted certain countries (such as India) from his blanket indictment. In 1957, he further qualified his views by saying that the Middle Eastern nations were "not neutral toward international Communism. They are mostly strongly opposed to Communism. There is no neutrality of spirit at all . . . in that area." [19] Former Vice President Nixon also differentiated between a form of neutralism that springs from the desire to avoid participation in military alliances and one that "makes no moral distinction between the Communist world and the free world. With this viewpoint, we have no sympathy." On another occasion, Nixon distinguished between what he called "military neutralism" and "economic neutralism," on the one hand, and "moral neutralism," on the other. Referring to moral neutralism, he said that the American people were "getting a bellyful of so-called neutralism" and that they were "fed to the teeth with some neutral leaders" who "try to blackmail us" and who refuse to judge Western and Communist conduct by a "single standard." Voicing a widespread American complaint, Nixon charged that advocates of moral neutralism often "take our economic assistance eagerly and then proceed to kick us in the teeth diplomatically." [20]

Official attempts to distinguish among the varieties of neutralism continued in the Kennedy-Johnson period. American policy in Asia, one official declared, ought to strive to have countries professing neutralism remain "really neutral"; if they are, they "require our protection as well as support." Despite public and legislative misgivings about Sukarno's policies, officials believed that "Indonesia at this time is not aligned with the Communist bloc nor is it aligned with us." Tiny Cambodia was designated both an "aggressive neutralist" (in its determina-

tion to *remain* nonaligned) and an "effective neutral."
The neutralism practiced by Nasser's Egypt was held to be
"restrained" and was commended for its "moderating influence" on Middle Eastern affairs. Yet American officials
believed that Algeria's policy of nonalignment was
"marked by pro-Communist influence." The neutralism of
such African states as Zanzibar, Mali, and Ghana similarly
revealed a pronounced "pro-Communist" orientation.[21]

These examples focus attention upon what is surely one
of the most complex, important, and inescapable problems
posed by the emergence of neutralism as a global force:
the twofold challenge of *classifying* the manifold varieties
of neutralist thought and conduct, and of *formulating*
policies that take account of evident differences among
these varieties. The problem poses formidable and continuing difficulties for policy-makers in Washington, London, and Paris, in Moscow and Peking—and, increasingly,
in Accra, Cairo, Baghdad, New Delhi, and Djakarta. However diverse the judgments about neutralism in these capitals, this much would command wide agreement: As an
Indian observer put it, neutralism is a "many-splendored
and many-mirrored thing, depending upon which looking-
glass one peeps into at a particular moment." Nothing
perhaps testifies more eloquently to the complexity of the
problem than the Indian query: "It would be interesting to
know . . . what exactly is meant by nonalignment. Could
somebody enlighten us?"[22]

Almost any major development involving a neutralist
country since the Bandung Conference of 1955 would
serve to illustrate the heterogeneous character of neutralism. Anti-American demonstrations erupt in Ghana;
Chou En-lai, the Foreign Minister of Red China, is accorded an enthusiastic reception in Arab and North
African countries; former Premier Khrushchev visits
Egypt, where he extends new loans to Nasser's govern-

ment, and where the official Egyptian communiqué dealing with his visit points to the congruence of Egyptian and Soviet views on a host of global issues; Iraq vigorously denounces "British imperialism" on the Arabian Peninsula; India purchases Soviet MIG aircraft and receives a loan from Moscow to construct a jet-aircraft factory; Burma severs its foreign-aid ties with the West and nationalizes foreign corporations within the country; President Sukarno tells the United States to "Go to Hell!" with its foreign aid and vows to carry out his proclaimed military "encounter" with the new state of Malaysia; Cambodia accuses the United States of "aggression" at the United Nations; the Belgrade Conference adopts a series of resolutions heavily weighted against "Western colonialism" and conspicuously silent on Communist-instigated threats to peace and national independence. Such episodes are guaranteed to produce laments in the West that the neutralism of some nonaligned countries is in fact pro-Communist and bogus, or that these countries practice a type of "dependent" neutralism amounting to *de facto* subservience to the Communist bloc.

Quite different events naturally engender different verdicts. Tito's government concludes a foreign-aid agreement with the United States (and, in the same period, militantly proclaims Yugoslavia's "independence" from both Moscow and Peking); Guinea expels Soviet diplomatic officials and sends the Soviet Union a strongly worded protest about Communist machinations against President Touré's regime; Nkrumah's government tones down its anti-American propaganda and assures Washington of its continued "friendship" with the United States; the Ivory Coast and other former French West African possessions announce their desire to continue an "association" with the European Economic Community, in the face of other African denunciations of EEC as a "neocolonialist plot";

Zanzibar merges with Tanganyika in order to avert a Communist takeover; Algeria concludes a new foreign-aid agreement with France and points out that most of its foreign assistance comes from the West; Arab leaders condemn Communist intrigues in the Middle East as incompatible with "Arab nationalism"; India urgently calls upon Britain and America for military aid in its Himalayan encounter with Red China; Djakarta strongly condemns Peking's support of the Chinese minority in Indonesia. It may safely be predicted that such developments will engender official and unofficial accolades in the United States commending the "pro-Western" orientation of individual neutralist countries, discussing the extent to which such countries are "genuinely and truly nonaligned," or underscoring the fact that, in the last analysis, the desire of such nations to remain nonaligned accords with the diplomatic interests of the United States.

Before dealing with the problem posed by attempts to classify disparate neutralist behavior, we may profitably begin with certain general observations. In the United States and other countries, policy-makers must perforce make some *de facto* distinctions among neutralist states. It is obvious that all versions of neutralism are not alike and that all are not equally compatible with American, Soviet, or even other neutralist foreign-policy goals. Perhaps the only thing worse than the tendency to classify varieties of neutralism on the basis of impromptu and emotionally dictated criteria would be to pretend that there are *no* differences among varieties of neutralism, or to operate upon the premise that neutralism is monolithic. At the same time, it is a regrettable, if perhaps inevitable, temptation for policy-makers to attempt such classifications on the basis of the latest (often quite ephemeral and trivial) international development receiving widespread publicity and demanding some immediate response from the President, the Secretary of State, or other public officials.

The student of international affairs is apt to find little or no consistency or continuity in official and public attempts to differentiate among neutralist countries. *Ad hoc* judgments tend to be the rule; neutralist nations are classified episodically, individually, and with little apparent regard for the over-all pattern of the neutralist movement. United States officials have either tended to declare categorically that there are "no clear-cut tests of alignment and nonalignment and no clear-cut test of neutralist policy," or they have shown the mystification and uncertainty apparent in Secretary Rusk's remarks in 1961:

> Insofar as our attitude toward neutrals are [*sic*] concerned, this is getting into something of a quagmire because there are many neutrals; and there is nothing very solid about the only thing they seem to have in common, and that is they do not happen to be aligned either to the Sino-Soviet bloc nor to the so-called Western bloc. So there are many shades of opinion and attitude among the so-called neutrals.[23]

As Rusk's comment suggests, American officials do not appear to have a typology of neutralism that provides a basis for evaluating the viewpoints and diplomatic conduct of individual nonaligned countries.

This leads to another closely related general tendency. Official and public attempts to classify neutralist countries are almost invariably based on criteria that are neither explicit nor articulated. State Department officials must and do differentiate among varieties of neutralism; but it is seldom apparent *why* such differentiations are made, why they are changed (as they frequently are changed), how officials compare one version of neutralism with another, or what order of priority officials establish among varieties of neutralism, in terms of their compatibility with American foreign-policy goals.

Such failings are in no way a reflection upon, nor are they limited to, policy-makers in Washington. To a substantial degree, they are an inevitable concomitant of a complex and inordinately difficult problem. The very nature of the neutralist ideology—and of attempts to translate it into specific patterns of national diplomatic behavior—probably foreordains that there can be no universally applicable typology of nonalignment, no one scheme acceptable to policy-makers in the West, in the Communist bloc, in the neutralist zone, as well as to authorities in the field of international relations. Any typology offered will involve at least four major variables, each of which in turn may be a product of several subvariables. Judgments about the relative importance of each major variable, and about the precise interaction among them, will yield highly divergent conclusions about identifiable varieties of neutralism.

Neutralist Typologies and Categories

First of all, assessments about the precise character of any country's neutralism—and particularly about its orientation toward East or West—will be affected by the extent to which implicit or explicit value judgments infuse the inquiry. Value judgments may be overt and crude, as illustrated by Secretary Dulles' public denunciation of neutralism as "immoral," Vice President Nixon's labeling of "moral neutralism" as "bunk," or Soviet Premier Khrushchev's declaration that "while there can be neutral nations, there can be no neutral men."

More subtle value judgments are apparent in the classification scheme proposed by Hans J. Morgenthau, who purports to discern one variety of neutralism representing nothing more than "escapism pure and simple," another characterized by "moral indifference" to global issues, and still another that amounts to "surreptitious alignment with the Soviet bloc." [24] Ignoring the Dullesian overtones in this system, the root problem here is that Morgenthau's classification rests upon some underlying conception of an "ideal" or "pure" type of neutralism that serves as a standard by which deviant types are measured. With Morgenthau, as with many other commentators on the neutralist movement, this standard is never explicitly set forth. This in turn illustrates a general tendency that is frequently deplored by advocates of nonalignment: the inclination of observers in the West (or in the Communist bloc) to postulate their own conception of what nonalignment ideally *ought* to entail and to categorize deviations from this norm with labels like "so-called neutralism" or "surreptitious alignment with the Soviet bloc." In the neutralist view, this practice exemplifies the very state of affairs—the formulation of foreign policy goals *for* neutralist countries by outsiders—that a policy of nonalignment seeks, above all else, to avoid.

In the second place, any scheme to classify discernible varieties of neutralism is inevitably a function of time. The crucial influence of the time interval is illustrated by developments in Guinea since 1958, when this key African nation received its independence from France. In the months immediately following independence, President Touré's foreign policy was cited in the West as a model of specious or "pro-Communist" neutralism. As a flood of Communist economic and military aid, accompanied by expanding numbers of Soviet "technicians," threatened to inundate the country, Western commentators depicted Guinea as the "first Communist bridgehead" in Africa. Then, in late 1961, the picture changed abruptly. Confronted with mounting Communist intrigues against his regime, President Touré abruptly dismissed the Soviet Ambassador, drastically reduced his economic and military dependence upon the Soviet Union, and in time moved to "normalize" his relations with the West, and ultimately with France itself.[25]

Yugoslavia is perhaps the classic example of the crucial importance of time. For Western observers, plotting Tito's erratic course between the Cold War power giants—and calculating his precise diplomatic position between East and West at any specified time—is a challenge that is as difficult as it is apparently irresistible. As Belgrade alternately "normalizes" its relations with Moscow and Washington, as it joins other neutralist states in denouncing Western "neocolonialist" plots and at the same time concludes a new foreign-aid agreement with the United States, attempts to categorize Tito's version of nonalignment become little more than a series of superficial epithets or momentary commendations. The extreme subjectivity of judgments like "pro-Communist neutralist" when applied to Tito is highlighted by the fact that to Red China, Tito is an "imperialist agent" whose "neutralism" results from his subservience to "the NATO bloc." Amidst Tito's frequent and often abrupt changes of diplomatic course, there is one polestar: his unswerving determination to maintain Yugoslavia's independence and diplomatic freedom from *both* East and West. Accordingly, as with nearly all other versions of nonalignment, only one point about Yugoslavia's neutralism possesses continuing validity: The essence of Tito's foreign policy is pro-Yugoslav neutralism, and his contacts with East and West are designed to make it, and keep it, a reality.

The purpose that classification schemes are designed to serve constitutes a third significant variable inevitably affecting the kind of pattern prevailing among species of neutralism. Official American reactions to the behavior of particular neutralist countries afford numerous illustrations. In 1961, when the United States sought to generate maximum support for its disarmament proposals—in the face of Indian criticisms directed at the sincerity of its dedication to arms reduction—American officials publicly accused Indian spokesmen at the U.N. of "pro-Soviet and anti-American neutralism." Yet when Secretary Dulles made a good-will tour of Asia in 1954, he declared no less frankly: "I do not find that India is neutral on the question of democracy versus totalitarianism in the world." On the contrary, India was endeavoring to "promote democracy and to prevent the spread of totalitarianism in the world." And in seeking to justify foreign-aid requests before congressional committees congenitally skeptical about neutralism, executive officials have almost invariably taken the view that India is "a country . . . trying to develop under institutions of freedom," that it is engaged in "competition with the efforts of the Chinese Communists," and that the United States must "help to see to it that the free methods of India produce better results than the police state, collectivist totalitarian methods of Communist China." [26]

Both advocates of nonalignment and observers outside the neutralist zone have been heavily influenced by the purpose to be served in identifying and classifying varieties of neutralism. Prolonged diplomatic maneuvering, for example, was required to agree upon the invitation list to the Belgrade Conference in 1961. This involved no mere dispute over diplomatic protocol, for the invitation list would in turn largely determine the agenda, tone, and results of the conference. Two schools of thought were in sharp conflict. Militant neutralist nations like Indonesia, joined by Guinea, Mali, and Cuba, favored a "narrow" conception of nonalignment that would, in effect, exclude countries like Nigeria, the Ivory Coast, Tunisia, and Malaya. The result (if not the intention) at Belgrade would almost certainly have been vocal neutralist condemnations of Western "colonialist" and "neocolonialist" intrigues, coupled with minimum attention to the diplomatic sins of the Communist bloc.

By contrast, Nehru's India, supported by Burma, Ceylon, Cambodia, and (in the end) Egypt and Yugoslavia, advocated an extremely "flexible" and permissive definition of nonalignment that would impart a global character to the Belgrade proceedings and would well-nigh compel the assembled neutralists to concentrate upon transcendent international, as distinct from local and regional, issues. Above all, Nehru insisted, the Belgrade conclave should strive for "constructive" results and refrain from bogging down in negative and futile fulminations against "Western imperialists" or other targets of neutralist ire. Eventually, Nehru's conception prevailed. The sponsoring countries adopted broad criteria for defining nonalignment that were capable of accommodating highly diverse manifestations of the neutralist credo.*

* Five criteria were agreed upon for determining which countries were "nonaligned" and which were not. In essence, these were that countries attending the Belgrade Conference pursue an "independent" foreign policy; that they accept the principle of peaceful coexistence; and that they support the "national liberation" of still dependent peoples. Ideally, nonaligned countries were not supposed to have military ties or agreements with either of the great-power blocs. Literal application of this test, however, would have excluded countries like Saudi Arabia, Yugoslavia, Libya, and Cuba; the loophole was left, therefore, that if military agreements existed, they should have been concluded outside the context of Cold War disputes. As if these standards were not sufficiently flexible, it was left for countries desiring invitations to interpret the extent to which their own policies accorded with specified criteria. The result was that almost every country wishing to attend the neutralist conclave at Belgrade sooner or later received an invitation.

Participants at the conference were: Afghanistan, Algeria, Burma, Cambodia, Ceylon, Congo, Cuba, Cyprus, Ethiopia, Ghana, Guinea, India, Indonesia, Iraq, Lebanon, Mali, Morocco, Nepal, Saudi Arabia, Somalia,

The fourth variable determining existing versions of nonalignment is at once the most crucial and complex of all. If attempts to classify divergent species of neutralist behavior had to contend with this one variable alone, the task of identifying and classifying varieties of neutralism would remain formidable. This variable arises out of the fact that for neutralist (as for all) countries, foreign relations constitute a mosaic. In the case of any given nonaligned nation, the resulting neutralist image is, in turn, a product of (1) the pieces that are chosen for inclusion in the mosaic, and (2) the manner in which these pieces are arranged, so that some inevitably receive more conspicuous notice than others. Thus, during any specified time interval, India might be markedly pro-Western in its ideological leanings, roughly balanced between pro-Western and pro-Soviet inclinations in its economic affairs, more pro-Western than pro-Soviet in its military relations, and more pro-Soviet than pro-Western in its diplomatic orientation. For Ghana, the pattern might be: more pro-Soviet than pro-Western in internal political and ideological affairs, more pro-Western than pro-Soviet in its economic

---

Sudan, Tunisia, United Arab Republic, Yemen, and Yugoslavia. Observers were sent by Bolivia, Brazil, and Ecuador. Significant omissions from this list of nonaligned states were Israel (still confronted with implacable Arab opposition), Malaya (believed to be too pro-Western), Nigeria (which did not conceal its ideological links with the West and its opposition to the views of militant African states like Ghana), and the states of former French West Africa (which continued to maintain intimate ties with France). Yugoslavia was the only European state deemed "nonaligned," as distinct from being "neutral" or (as in the case of Finland and Sweden) from being a *de facto* member of a Cold War power bloc. Counting "observers," the Belgrade list showed the following breakdown: seven neutralist states from Asia, seven from sub-Saharan Africa, eight from North Africa and the Arab world, four from Latin America, and one from Europe.

For discussions of preliminary efforts to define "nonalignment" in preparation for the Belgrade session, see the following issues of the *Times of India:* May 23, June 15, June 26, and September 4, 1961.

ties, neither notably pro-Western nor pro-Soviet in its military affairs, and more pro-Soviet than pro-Western in its diplomatic orientation.

Given the fact that the foreign relations of neutralist countries are multidimensional—that diplomatic freedom of choice may be and is exercised in several areas of policy simultaneously—an almost infinite number of possibilities exists for local and regional variations in the neutralist credo. And when this fact is coupled with another to which we directed attention earlier—that the Western and Communist blocs themselves are increasingly losing their diplomatic cohesion—the range of possibilities in neutralist relations with individual countries in the Cold War groupings becomes virtually incalculable. Let us examine the complexities present in the problem by focusing upon four major dimensions of neutralist foreign policy.

Take first the *ideological* realm. Here we may visualize a scale, with one end represented by pro-Communist Yugoslavia and the other by pro-Western, democratic India. Close to Yugoslavia might be grouped neutralist states like Ghana, Guinea, Mali, Algeria, Burma, and Indonesia, which variously espouse "African socialism" or some other ideology that draws significantly from Marxist sources. Close to the middle of the scale might fall most of the nonaligned Arab states, which often categorically reject "Western" democracy, but which are no less militant in rejecting the principal dogmas in the Marxist creed. At the other end of the spectrum, close to India, can be found countries like Tunisia, Lebanon, Malaya, and Ceylon, whose "moderate" political ideologies draw more heavily from Western than from Communist sources. There remains a group of neutralist countries—notably Liberia, Ethiopia, Saudi Arabia, and Afghanistan—whose political ideologies continue to be overwhelmingly traditional.

In all instances, however, the dominant fact that

emerges is that whatever their degree of overt ideological dependence upon or leaning toward East or West, neutralist states are determined to compound their own ideological "mix" from alien and indigenous sources. From Morocco to Indonesia, nonaligned countries are united in opposing the importation of foreign ideologies or the imposition of alien doctrines, whether applied externally or by foreign-supported subversive movements. Just as Tito's government is resolved to fashion its own version of "national Communism," India, Malaya, and Tunisia are equally unwilling to adopt indiscriminately "democratic" institutions and patterns of thought marked "Made in the West."

A second major dimension of neutralist foreign policy is economic affairs. The specific character of India's or Iraq's or Morocco's "neutralism" in this sphere might be judged by (1) the nature of its internal economic institutions, (2) its foreign-aid ties with great powers, and (3) the pattern of its foreign trade. So far as its international economic institutions are concerned, the controlling fact about neutralist countries is that all of them are *underdeveloped, capital-deficient nations*—a condition virtually necessitating active and massive state control over economic activities. In this sense, not one such state could be called pro-capitalist in its neutralism; the great majority is dedicated to some form of socialism. At the same time, it is almost everywhere *non-Marxist* socialism. Its models tend to be Great Britain, France, Sweden, and Israel—along with "pre-colonialist" customs and traditions engendering "communalist" patterns of economic cooperation.

In the realm of foreign aid, neutralist relations with East and West present a more variegated pattern. Some neutralist countries—chiefly Afghanistan, Ethiopia, Guinea, Ghana, Indonesia, Iraq, Mali, Nepal, Somalia,

Syria, Egypt, and Yemen—have received most of their foreign assistance from the Communist bloc, primarily from
the Soviet Union. Yugoslavia, Cyprus, Tunisia, Nigeria, a
large group of newly independent states in former French
West Africa, Liberia, Libya, Jordan, Lebanon, Israel, India, and Malaya have leaned more heavily upon the West.
In some instances (as in former French possessions in West
Africa, or in former British territories like Tanganyika and
Kenya), ex-metropoles have supplied, and will likely continue to supply, the bulk of the outside assistance extended
to these countries.

Despite a widespread tendency in the United States to
believe otherwise, the quantity of foreign aid per se extended by America, Russia, or some other country to neutralist nations signifies very little about the character of
the recipient's neutralist position between East and West.
Much more crucial are two other questions: How has the
foreign aid been used? And to what degree has it created
an economic dependence upon the great power that provides it? Paradoxically, the great majority of neutralist
countries benefiting heavily from Communist assistance
have thereby added to their ability to *remain* nonaligned,
to preserve their diplomatic freedom of choice. To the extent that such aid has enabled nationalist leaders to solve
deep-seated and pervasive internal problems, it has simultaneously strengthened the country's ability to withstand
Communist or Western efforts to "align" it forcibly with
the Cold War power constellations. Nor is there any convincing evidence, periodic alarms in the United States to
the contrary, that acceptance of economic aid from the
Communist bloc inherently compromises the independence of nonaligned nations or reduces them to a position
of *de facto* Communist satellites. Proponents of nonalignment have long deplored an American tendency to under-
estimate their attachment to national independence and

to derogate their political adroitness in the face of efforts by both East or West to undermine their nonaligned position. In Belgrade, in Conakry, in Accra, in Fez, in Cairo, in Baghdad, in Rangoon, in Djakarta, and in nearly all other neutralist capitals, nonaligned governments have thus far refused to permit economic aid programs from the great powers to foster *de facto* political or diplomatic subservience. In fact, certain nonaligned Arab states have accepted massive foreign aid from Iron Curtain countries and Red China, while simultaneously outlawing the Communist Party internally and denouncing Communist intrigues in the Middle East. This pattern has been widely copied in Africa and in Asia. There is thus no evidence that the scope of economic aid programs extended by East and West affords a meaningful basis for classifying neutralist countries.

Usually, patterns of trade are even less significant. For most of the reservations we have noted about foreign aid as an index of neutralist orientations apply equally to trade relations. If the over-all tendency of neutralist countries has been to *expand* their trade with the U.S.S.R., Red China, and other Communist countries, we must remember that before independence very few nonaligned countries carried on *any* trade with Communist nations. In the case of Red China, much of its trade with Asian neutralists is merely a continuation of age-old Chinese trade patterns. Moreover, such trade is greatly facilitated by lingering Asian mistrust of Japan. Note must also be taken of the determination of most neutralist countries to alter fundamentally the long-dominant colonialist character of their trade with the West. This entails demonstrating both actually and symbolically that they are now free states, capable of negotiating the most advantageous trade terms available. For example, the United States has refused to buy Ceylon's rubber or to sanction its sale to Red

China. Not unexpectedly, Ceylonese officials refused to accept such Western dictation in their economic affairs; they took the only course open in preserving economic viability, selling their rubber to Peking. Neutralist nations have also been establishing trade ties within an international environment of *expanding* East-West trade generally. The American-Soviet wheat agreement in 1963–64 is merely one example of growing trading across the Iron Curtain. Another indication of the same tendency is the fact that the American-led effort to maintain an economic embargo against Red China has all but collapsed—owing primarily to the opposition encountered from the other Western allies.

A third major aspect of neutralist foreign policy is their *military* relationship with East and West. As we have emphasized, nonaligned African, Arab, and Asian states view formal and continuing participation in Cold War military alliances or defense agreements as incompatible with a neutralist position. Within this general limitation, however, neutralist countries maintain a broad range of military ties with Cold War power groupings, including Yugoslavia's "association" with NATO; Tunisia's and Malaya's willingness to make naval bases available to the West in time of war; Tanganyikan and French West African reliance upon the troops of former metropoles to deal with internal political crises; Syrian, Iraqi, Indonesian, and other neutralist acceptance of military aid and advice from the Communist bloc; Cambodia's threat to arrive at a military *détente* with Red China if America's powerful Southeast Asian allies (South Vietnam and Thailand) continued to jeopardize Cambodian security. In attempting to discover general patterns amidst this tangled web of military relationships, let us focus upon two kinds of military ties between neutralist states and countries associated with the Western and Communist blocs: military aid programs and reliance upon great powers during periods of military crisis.

Much that has been said about economic aid programs applies also to military aid. Neutralist countries recognize no limitation upon their right to purchase arms or to accept military advice from any quarter. Nor is there any creditable evidence, despite a tendency in the West to believe otherwise, that neutralist countries relying heavily upon the Communist bloc for arms aid and military advice (such as Yugoslavia, Algeria, Egypt, Syria, and Indonesia) have passed into the Communist orbit diplomatically or have in any significant way compromised their independence. As with economic assistance, many of these neutralist countries (several Arab states and Indonesia are conspicuous examples) initially requested military aid *from the West,* and were denied such aid, before they turned to Moscow or Peking. Moreover, in several cases neutralist countries began military build-ups only when neighboring countries (like Israel or South Vietnam) had begun to acquire new quantities of Western arms. Experience has afforded no evidence for questioning the neutralist conviction that the acquisition of arms constitutes a commercial transaction implying no diplomatic inclination toward the great power involved.

Does neutralist reliance upon great powers during periods of military crisis signify any departure from, or abandonment of, nonalignment? The classic case is afforded by India, after its encounter with Red China in 1962. Nasser also relied upon the threat of "Soviet volunteers" in Egypt during the Suez crisis of 1956. And Tito's regime has at least implicitly relied upon its links with NATO to safeguard its security during periods of tension with the U.S.S.R. Cambodia has also invoked the threat of a military *rapprochement* with Red China to counter hostile moves by its neighbors. In each case, neutralist countries have differentiated between accepting arms aid and military advice from great powers, on the one hand, and accepting foreign *troop commitments* or other forms of direct military intervention on the other.* Neither during nor in the months that followed military crises did neutralist countries seek to enter military-alliance systems sponsored by the Cold War power blocs. Nor did temporary military reliance upon a great power create a discernible diplomatic dependence that radically altered voting patterns in the United Nations or at conferences like the Belgrade meeting. Indeed, leading neutralist nations like Yugoslavia, Egypt, and India have attempted to balance their military ties with East and West, in order to avoid both the appearance and reality of total military dependence on one Cold War power bloc.

Most significantly—and herein lies a major difference between nonaligned countries and Western satellite nations like South Vietnam and South Korea—leading neutralist nations have in no instance looked to great powers to save them from external threats. Throughout the Sino-Indian conflict, for example, officials in New Delhi repeatedly emphasized that, in the last analysis, India had to save itself from Chinese aggression. This would be greatly facilitated by preventing a great-power military confrontation on Indian soil; that is to say, it would be promoted by the extent to which India continued to remain nonaligned. Massive military intervention in India,

---

* This has not been true of certain African states which have asked Britain and France for military intervention to deal with *internal* political crises. Thus Britain intervened to suppress a military mutiny in Tanganyika in 1964; de Gaulle's government has repeatedly sent French troops into Togo, the Congo Republic (Brazzaville), Gabon, and other former French African territories to put down political disorders against established (and pro-French) governments. This is unquestionably one reason why most neutralist countries did not regard the members of the pro-French Brazzaville group in West Africa as *bona fide* members of the neutralist community.

even during the country's darkest hour in the Himalayan
contest, was still viewed as highly prejudicial to national
security. Neither during the crisis nor later did India or
other neutralist nations abandon the strategic principle
embodied in the African proverb: "When two elephants
fight, it is the grass that suffers." *

A fourth, and highly important, dimension of neutralist
policy is *diplomatic* relations between nonaligned countries and members of the Cold War blocs. The same wide
divergencies in neutralist behavior can be discerned in
this area of policy as in the others. The Belgrade Conference adopts a series of resolutions criticizing the West;
the neutralist countries in the U.N. reject Khrushchev's
troika proposal; Nasser and Khrushchev label Israel a
"tool of Western imperialism" and pledge their joint efforts to "liberate" Palestine; Nigeria cooperates with the
U.N. Congo operation, in the face of other neutralist-led
efforts to disrupt it; Guinea praises Soviet support for anti-

---

* The author has discussed many of the military implications of nonalignment, especially during eras of crisis, in "The Testing of Non-Alignment," *Western Political Quarterly*, XVII (September, 1964), 517–42;
"An 'Agonizing Reappraisal' for Nonalignment?" *Christianity and Crisis*,
XXIII (July 8, 1963), 128–31; and "Himalayan Crisis: Moment of Truth
for Nehru—and Ourselves," *Vassar Alumnae Magazine*, XLVIII (June,
1963), 10–16. Although we shall reserve detailed treatment of most of
the policy implications of nonalignment for the United States for Chapter 7, it might be worth noting here that Indian sources were careful to
base their continued support for nonalignment upon something more
logical and durable than mere reiteration of established doctrine. The
Himalayan crisis, said the *Times of India*, in no way altered India's case
for "rejection of military alliances" or its right "to judge every issue on the
merit in the light of the nation's interests." (*Times of India*, January 30,
1963). For that matter, Indian sources widely interpreted America's willingness to extend arms aid to the leading exponent of nonalignment as
a "significant change" in American policy, indicating that American
policy-makers differentiated much less sharply between "aligned" and
"nonaligned" countries than had been supposed previously. (See *Indian
Express*, January 16, 1963.) This view was fostered by President Kennedy's comment: "We have gone to the aid of imperiled nations, neutrals
and allies alike. What we do ask—and all that we ask—is that our help
be used to best advantage."

colonialist measures; violent demonstrations erupt in Moscow against Baghdad's suppression of the Iraqi Communist Party; Laotian Premier Souvanna Phouma denounces Communist (chiefly Red Chinese) efforts to subvert his neutralist regime; Indonesia terminates American foreign aid and castigates Washington's support of Malaysia.

Which of these diplomatic moves testifies accurately about the true character or orientation of particular neutralist countries? Which provide policy-makers in America or elsewhere with satisfactory criteria upon which to base official responses to neutralist behavior? Manifestly, the answers are likely to vary widely among competent observers, and the process of formulating answers is likely to entail the exercise of often highly arbitrary, subjective judgments. In evaluating such daily and weekly occurrences, however, a few basic considerations offer some guidance in distinguishing between purely transitory, often trivial indications of neutralist conduct and more lasting and significant diplomatic behavior that must be assessed in any attempt to classify species of neutralism.

So far as the coincidence between neutralist and Communist diplomatic positions is concerned, it has long been apparent that neutralist countries tend to be *congenitally anti-Western on several global issues*. Neutralist countries almost invariably oppose the West, for example, on colonial issues and questions of racial discrimination. This is not *because* they are "neutralist"; rather they are "neutralist" because they are anti-Western, as expressed in the nationalist movements that brought them freedom from Western political control. Yet they are not anti-Western because the Communist bloc opposes the West on these and other such issues; their positions diverge from the Western position either in spite of Communist policies or because neutralists welcome Communist support for their own positions. As an outgrowth of the nationalist ferment gripping the Afro-Arab-Asian world since World War II, neutralism might be expected to become less overtly anti-Western with the passage of time. Experience has tended to confirm this generalization. Many neutralist countries experienced a period of militant xenophobia directed against the West, during which, as a British observer noted, "It is political death for any African leader to become labeled as a pawn of the West." [27]

Even during the brief period of time in which most African countries have experienced independence, however, African neutralism has "matured" and has lost much of its anti-Western cast—at least in its official, if not always in its public, manifestations. Today, in such countries as Guinea and Algeria—where the struggle for independence left unusually bitter anti-Western legacies—incumbent governments have led the way, sometimes in the face of evident public opposition, in normalizing their relations with France and other prominent Western nations. Similarly, in the early 1960's, Nasser sought to heal the deep wounds left by the Suez crisis and to arrive at a *modus vivendi* with Britain and France.

Another consideration that must be constantly borne in mind in evaluating headlines like "Egypt Follows Soviet Lead in U.N.," or "Belgrade Conference Takes Pro-Communist Line," is this: The Soviet Union and its satellites (if not Red China) have endeavored much more than the Western bloc to win and hold the goodwill of nations in the neutralist zone. When studies show a high incidence of neutralist nations voting with the Communist bloc at the U.N., it must always be asked: Who is "following" whom? On most global issues, there is at least as great a probability that the Communist bloc is seeking to ingratiate and "identify" itself with the neutralist world as the reverse. To put it differently: There is no evidence that Ghana or Syria or Indonesia would be any less opposed to perpetuation of colonial administrations, or to apartheid in South Africa, or to continued nuclear testing if there were no Cold War and no Communist threats to Western security.

This suggests another fact about the neutralist movement that has been insufficiently grasped by Western observers. Experience since the Bandung Conference has shown a fundamental difference between the way neutralist and Western (especially American) policy-makers tend to appraise the diplomatic goals and tactics of the Communist bloc. From one end of the neutralist zone to the other, there is visible reluctance to accept the idea that Soviet diplomatic intrigue in the Middle East or Red Chinese expansionism in the Himalayas can be explained by reference to the machinations of "international Communism" or to the "Marxist global conspiracy." Before the Chinese attack upon India, Prime Minister Nehru declared: "Ideologies are less important than national interests. We see major power blocs armed to the teeth and cracking among themselves. Talk of Communism and anti-Communism as governing the world no longer holds good." [28]

Nehru held to this conviction even after Peking's Himalayan aggression. Similarly, neutralist countries tended to interpret the Cuban missile crisis of 1962 primarily as a clash of rival American and Soviet national interests, rather than as a conflict between competing ideologies or a contest between two ways of life.

Believing that historical and national, much more than ideological or philosophical, influences determine the diplomatic moves of the great powers, neutralist nations also believe that the policies of rival Cold War blocs are susceptible to change and adaptation in the light of internal and external developments. Neutralist states have thus been much more prone than the United States to believe that Khrushchev inaugurated a new era in Soviet foreign policy, chiefly because the Kremlin, in the interests of Russian security, has accepted the implications of nuclear stalemate between East and West.

Neutralist states are fully aware that the great powers often vote with, or support, the position of nonaligned countries for reasons of diplomatic expediency. Policymakers in Algiers, Cairo, and Baghdad are by no means ignorant of the fact that the Kremlin supports Arab neutralism largely as an anti-Western force; nor are they unmindful that the United States within recent years has sought to win neutralist goodwill by its decision to condemn Portuguese colonialism publicly, its efforts to conclude an East-West test-ban accord, and its willingness to rely upon the U.N. at the time of the Cuban missile encounter.

Western policy-makers and observers are also obliged to recognize what is surely another key fact about neutralism. This is the widespread belief—reflected in, fully as much as it is caused by, the emergence of neutralism— that Western policies have tended to become sterile and stagnant in dealing with international issues likely to affect global peace and security. Neutralism thus represents a kind of diplomatic emancipation from rigid and outworn policies identified with the West, which have long prevented an effective dialogue between hostile blocs espousing divergent ideologies.

If statistics of voting behavior in the U.N. sometimes reveal that neutralist countries vote more often with the Communist bloc than with the West, this may consequently prove nothing at all about the basic orientation of neutralist nations vis-à-vis East and West. It may prove a great deal, however, about (1) the growing influence of neutralist states within the U.N., and about their ability to focus the organization's concerns upon issues deemed vital to nations in the neutralist zone; (2) the ability or inability of the West and the Communist bloc to adapt their own policies to an increasingly "multipolar" global environment; and (3) the inability of the great powers to accept, and to base their policies upon, fundamental changes in the global context, which the emergence of neutralism has symptomized fully as much as it has caused.

The Wellsprings of Nonalignment

By the 1960's, the doctrine of diplomatic nonalignment was embraced by governments representing between one-third and one-half of the human race, depending upon how the doctrine was defined. The global tendency toward nonalignment had thus become a mighty stream, profoundly altering the familiar "bipolarized" international landscape long dominated by the United States and the Soviet Union. As new nations in Africa joined the neutralist community, as General de Gaulle repeatedly disrupted the cohesiveness of the Western alliance, as a growing tendency toward greater independence in foreign affairs was evident throughout Latin America, and as the Sino-Soviet dispute, along with diplomatic restiveness in countries like Poland and Romania, shattered the unity of the Communist bloc, nonalignment appeared to be the diplomatic wave of the future.

Western observers, including many informed students of world affairs and public officials, were prone to attribute the growth of the neutralist movement to causes that were as simple as they were often disheartening. The appearance and growing influence of neutralism as a diplomatic credo were explained by reference to the "lack of realism" displayed by neutralist policy-makers in evaluating global issues, or to a deeply embedded moral obtuseness that prevented them from differentiating between the motives of the West and the Communist bloc, or to the desire of some nations to get the best of both worlds by soliciting foreign assistance from the East and the West, or to an ingrained anti-Western predisposition that gave the Communist bloc the benefit of the doubt on a host of international issues.

These are a few not untypical examples of explanations advanced by Western, particularly American, observers to account for the emergence and growth of the neutralist ideology. Unfortunately, such explanations seldom transcend the level of clichés, epithets, and crude value judgments. Westerners have usually been more inclined to condemn the neutralist idea than they have to understand its wellsprings and its implications. Moreover, appraisals of the origins of neutralism in the West reflect underlying assumptions that are highly unflattering to neutralist governments. More often than not, neutralism has been viewed as a kind of policy *aberration,* signifying the existence of a policy *vacuum* or *immobilism* on the part of its adherents. Western explanations imply that the process of formulating and carrying out foreign policy in neutralist states is fundamentally different from the process followed in Western, or even Communist, nations. Such explanations suggest that the principle of nonalignment is not arrived at through the normal processes of rational decision-making. Instead, this principle is allegedly adopted for extraneous reasons—emotionalism, ingrained prejudice toward the West, or diplomatic myopia—which prevent neutralist governments from engaging in the kind of sober, careful consideration of policy alternatives customarily associated with governmental decision-making. In short, Western criticism of neutralism suggests that governments embracing this credo are somehow incapable of defining their own national interests and of formulating policies that promote these interests.

Our discussion of the wellsprings of nonalignment will focus upon four fundamental influences inducing countries to accept nonalignment as the guiding principle of their foreign relations on Cold War issues.

The Legacy of Colonialism

In an article prepared for *Life* magazine in 1959, President Nasser explained his commitment to diplomatic nonalignment by saying:

> I feared alignment with any outside power because I know the Arab history and the Arab people. For hundreds of years they had been accustomed to look upon their governments with fear and suspicion as the agents of foreign powers, as governments which took their orders from ambassadors. . . . If defensive pacts are necessary in the Arab world they should be formed by the Arab countries alone, for the people must feel that they are really independent. They must feel that they are defending their own families, their own children, their own property—not British or American interests. . . . Such an alignment could open the door for the big power to become dominant, and to bring back imperialism and colonialism to the Arab lands.[1]

On another occasion, he dealt with the rationale invoked by the British Government to justify its long occupation of Egypt:

> They always said they were on the point of leaving, and always found an excuse to stay. At first they claimed they were in Egypt to protect the foreigners against the Egyptians . . . then they claimed they had to stay to protect the Christian and Jewish minorities against the Moslems. . . . The defense of the Suez Canal and the maintenance of their lines

of communication with India and their Far Eastern Empire
were further pretexts. When World War II came they said
they could not go because the Suez Canal was an important
base, and after World War II they explained that they had
to stay to safeguard the interests of the free world.[2]

These statements call attention to a relationship that is
crucial in explaining the origins of the neutralist movement. From West Africa to East Asia, nonalignment is
viewed as springing from, and being an integral part of,
the ongoing struggle against colonialism, to which almost
all neutralist countries are committed in their foreign relations. The policy of nonalignment is held to be both a
visible symbol of a nation's dedication to anticolonialism
and a method of inhibiting new colonialist tendencies.

Since we shall discuss contemporary colonial questions
in Chapter 4, let us here confine our discussion of colonialism to three aspects of the issue that are fundamental to
an understanding of the emergence of the neutralist mentality. The first is that colonialism is a force identified almost exclusively with the West. This was illustrated poignantly by an official publication of the Government of
Iraq in 1962, which declared:

> On colonial questions we are anti-Western. Our position re-
> garding colonialism is definite, we want the complete libera-
> tion of the colonial territories and of the new states from
> colonial rule and all the vestiges of the colonial system. . . .
> It must be pointed out that, at present, the West is on the
> wrong side of a social and political revolution which is
> sweeping all the underdeveloped areas of the world.

And a student of African affairs has asserted that the first
step in improving Western relations with newly emergent
African countries is to

> realize that in most of Africa "colonialism," with its connota-
> tion of a ruling European group and subordinate African

masses, is widely held to be *the* worst enemy. Communism is a secondary peril, and apartheid is to most Africans a greater danger than the dictatorship of the proletariat.[3]

For a variety of historical, legal, and philosophical reasons, neutralist governments do not as a rule equate Western colonialism with Communist control over Eastern Europe or with Chinese suzerainty over Tibet, a fact that frequently distresses Western observers and encourages them to accuse neutralist countries of applying a diplomatic double standard to East and West. In saying that neutralist spokesmen do not accept the concept of "Communist colonialism," however, we must interpret the neutralist viewpoint correctly. Proponents of neutralism do not necessarily imply that Communist domination of Eastern Europe is any less reprehensible than was Dutch colonialism in Indonesia or British colonialism in the Gold Coast. Nor do they countenance Communist occupation or absorption of weak societies. Nor do they disagree with the proposition that Communist subjugation of unwilling peoples ought to be terminated. They mean simply that a number of significant differences can be drawn between traditional colonial relationships and Soviet control over Bulgaria or Chinese control over North Korea.*

* We may summarize these differences briefly by saying that (1) colonialism traditionally denoted European domination over non-European societies; (2) in the vast majority of instances, it entailed international recognition of a dependent political relationship, demanding, for example, that American relations with India during its period of colonialism be carried on through the British Foreign Office; (3) it usually involved the domination of the white race over nonwhites; and (4) in theory, if not always in fact, the economic resources of the colonies were used primarily for the advantage of the mother country. Neutralists contend that Soviet occupation of Poland, for example, does not fit most of these customary criteria. Legally, Poland is an independent country, belonging to the United Nations; within recent years, it has acquired an increasing degree of *de facto* independence in its political and economic affairs. The Poles and the Russians are both members of the white race and of the European family of nations. Therefore, Soviet control over Poland can more accurately be compared, not with traditional "colonialism," but

Few facts are more decisive in predisposing countries throughout Africa, the Arab world, and Asia against formal diplomatic or military alliance with the West than the still vivid recollection that West European nations, rather than Soviet Russia or Red China, established and maintained the system of colonial control that has not yet been totally liquidated.

A second aspect of the relationship between colonialism and neutralism is the conviction of neutralist nations that although colonialism as a global force is waning, it is by no means dead or incapable of attempting to regain control over the affairs of once-dependent societies. "It is quite erroneous to imagine that colonialism is dead," said a recent publication of the Iraqi Government. "On the contrary, it survives and generates great trouble and danger. . . . Nevertheless, the fight against colonialism is still raging in parts of Asia, Africa, and Latin America." Colonialism, said the Foreign Minister of Ghana in 1961, is the "greatest evil in the modern world"; it is the "root cause of the desire to possess arms" and hence "the root cause of the arms race and the problem of disarmament." [4]

Westerners may well regard such judgments as extreme and naïve; not even all proponents of nonalignment accept them without serious qualification. One characteristic of India's "moderate" neutralism, for example, has been the extent to which New Delhi has sought to gain acceptance for the idea that the Cold War was at least as grave a threat to mankind's future as colonialism—a conviction that has met with only limited acceptance at neutralist gatherings like the Belgrade Conference. The dominant view remains the conviction expressed by officials of Iraq and Ghana and by an editorial in the *Egyptian Mail* in 1961. Imperial-

---

with the concept of the "sphere of influence," such as the British maintained in Persia in the nineteenth century and the United States maintains currently in countries like Turkey, Iran, and South Vietnam.

ism, said this Egyptian source, was a basic factor in the continuation of the Cold War or, at the very least, "the Cold War is frequently made the excuse for its continued existence." The overriding task of nonaligned countries, therefore, was to bring "imperialism to a rapid end." [5]

Anticolonialist feelings and the colonial experience support attachment to nonalignment in foreign affairs in yet another respect—i.e., the conviction that independence *in the sphere of foreign policy and national defense* constitutes the final, and perhaps the most bitterly contested, stage of the nationalist ferment against Western domination. This is perhaps one of the least understood forces supporting the neutralist ideology. Conscious of the fact that Western powers have granted freedom to more than forty dependent societies since World War II—and that the Soviet Union and Red China show little inclination to loosen their grip on their satellites—Western observers have little patience with the neutralist preoccupation with colonialism. To the Western mind, neutralists are far too concerned about the theoretical danger of Western control over their foreign and military affairs and too little concerned about the genuine risk of Communist domination in these spheres.

To understand the neutralist mentality on this point, however, we must re-examine the traditional colonial relationship. There were of course many varieties and gradations of colonialism. Some countries (e.g., India, Indonesia, and Indochina) were outright colonies. Others (Egypt and Morocco, for example) were protectorates of powerful European countries, and possessed considerably more internal autonomy than colonies. Still others (like Afghanistan, Iraq, and Saudi Arabia) were neither colonies nor protectorates, but were regarded as lying within the sphere of influence of Western countries. Technically, such countries were fully independent, and domestic affairs were in the hands of indigenous governments. Yet important decisions affecting their relationships with the outside world were invariably made in London, Paris, or Berlin. In many cases, native governments were obliged to accept such arrangements as a price for political survival and continued autonomy over internal matters.

However varied and unique the colonial arrangements may have been, they shared certain common elements: (1) the colonial powers exercised control over *diplomatic and military affairs,* although considerable freedom might be left for native societies to manage their domestic affairs; (2) colonial powers were more prone to relinquish control over the internal affairs of their dependencies than over their external affairs; (3) even after nominal independence was granted to dependencies, powerful Western nations resorted to various devices to perpetuate *de facto* control over the country's foreign and military relations, a practice that has continued into the present. Thus any attempts today to "align" neutralist countries with one great-power bloc or the other on disputes that do not directly involve the interests of newly independent countries are interpreted as merely new versions of very old tactics, whereby the foreign policies of weaker states are subordinated to the diplomatic and strategic requirements of foreign countries.

Official and public statements from neutralist sources clearly reveal the significance of the colonial heritage as a primary factor engendering the neutralist ideology. Under colonialism, Nasser observed in the excerpt quoted earlier, native governments were looked upon by their own citizens "as governments which took their orders from ambassadors." In the modern period, said a spokesman for Libya at the Bandung Conference in 1955, attempts to impose ideological or diplomatic conformity upon countries constituted "but another kind of colonialism more dangerous and of much stronger effect, since it embodies all the disadvantages of colossal colonialism, and, in addition, intellectual slavery." [6] The clearest example of the relationship we are describing here is furnished by the Government of Iraq. Iraq received its independence in 1930 and joined the League of Nations as a sovereign state. Yet from that time on, until General Karim Kassim's *coup d'état* on July 14, 1958, Iraq was firmly "aligned" with the West. From the nineteenth century to World War II, Iraq had been within the British "sphere of influence" in western Asia. During World War II, its loyalty to the Allies was assured (despite considerable pro-German sentiment within the country) by a massive Anglo-American military occupation of the country. After the war, as the United States assumed many global commitments formerly carried by Great Britain, Washington based its containment strategy in the Middle East on the premise that—perhaps alone among the major Arab countries—Iraq was linked firmly with the Western coalition. Under Dulles and Eisenhower, this premise was made explicit when Iraq became (along with Turkey, Iran, and Pakistan) a member of the Baghdad Pact system of military alliances, which was in turn linked with NATO in the west and SEATO in the east. Under its avowedly pro-Western leader, Premier Nuri es-Said, and in the face of violent Arab opposition to such pacts, Iraq became the keystone of the northern tier alliance against Communist expansionism.

Within a short time, however, events revealed that Iraq's formal alignment with the West added new fuel for a subsequent nationalist eruption that was to alter profoundly the country's internal and external policies. Nuri es-Said was widely regarded by Arab nationalists as a pliant tool of London and Washington, a political puppet who accepted Western directives even when these ran directly counter to the mainstream of Arab nationalist de-

mands. After 1955, Nuri's position in Iraq deteriorated
steadily. The long-expected political explosion came on
July 14, 1958, when a military junta headed by General
Kassim seized power. In the ensuing agitation, mobs
roamed the streets of Baghdad and other Iraqi cities, kill-
ing and destroying wantonly. When he was finally found,
Nuri es-Said was subjected to the most humiliating death
conceivable, a fate reserved for traitors and other hated
public figures: he was summarily executed and his body
dragged through the streets of Baghdad.

Although nominally independent for almost a genera-
tion, Iraqis celebrate July 14, 1958, as their "Independence Day."

To end what it called "dependency and partiality" in
foreign affairs, Iraq embraced nonalignment. This philosophy was officially justified as follows:

> Prior to the Revolution, the Iraqi foreign policy was merely a
> part of the imperialist design elaborated abroad and handed
> over to the prime ministers of the old regime for execution.
> These were tools for carrying out a policy that had nothing
> in common with the interests of the country. Neither did Iraq
> have . . . any say in defining its foreign policy and relations.
> It was necessary therefore, that the liberated Republic of
> Iraq should decide upon a new policy; one derived from the
> native land and in accord with the desire of all Arab people.[7]

The Search for Ideological Identity

In paying tribute to India's role in global affairs, the former Philippine diplomat and U.N. Assembly President,
Carlos P. Romulo, noted that until the emergence of the
neutralist movement,

> History . . . came to mimic the old morality play, the only
> active forces on the stage being Good and Evil or God and

Mammon, with poor humanity reduced to the passive role of an innocent pilgrim, pure in heart but almost stupid in his diminished power and his incapacity to assume an active role in the dialectics. The fate of nations, like the fate of Everyman in the old morality play—especially during the rigidity of the Cold War—was still decided by the Big Powers.

India had led the way in gaining acceptance for the idea that "contemporary nationalism is a cultural and political movement that transcends the orthodox dichotomies of East vs. West or of Democracy vs. Communism. It is a revolutionary movement that challenges thought as well as the structure of our own civilization, the philosophy of international relations and the rationale of our political actions." The concept of nonalignment had brought about a "loosening of the ideological straitjacket, as it were, of the Cold War" and had promoted the "spirit of criticism and free inquiry" on the international scene. The philosophy of nonalignment had gone far toward converting the international order into the "open society," where free inquiry, criticism, and ideological diversity might once again prevail.[8]

Romulo's observations call attention to certain forces nourishing the neutralist movement that cannot be measured statistically, reduced to lines on a graph, or tabulated for calculations by a computer. Yet they are among the most pervasive and significant influences sustaining the neutralist movement. At some point, nearly every apologist for nonalignment alludes to them, as when a Sudanese official asserts: "The great powers can no more believe in their divine power over the affairs of the world"; or when an official of Nepal affirms: "We have passed the age when smaller nations existed only as satellites of a Great Power or as buffer states preserved by international or regional agreements"; or when the President of Guinea declares that

freedom from French colonialism means: "We are ourselves again and will remain ourselves." But it was the
Prime Minister of Malaya who perhaps expressed the idea
most succinctly when he said: "We faced up to the fact
that with Independence, we should develop our Malayan
political point of view in foreign affairs." And on another
occasion he asserted: "Britain and the United States have
been doing our thinking for us for a long time. Sooner or
later we have got to stand on our own two feet and work
out our own salvation." [9]

Whatever their differences on specific issues, such as the
Berlin controversy, disarmament, or the conflict in South
Vietnam, neutralist countries are united in their belief that
nonalignment implies an *ideological and philosophical
emancipation* and that it promotes the quest for ideological and spiritual "identity" that is the hallmark of contemporary African, Arab, and Asian nationalism. Nonalignment, therefore, is the only conceivable principle of
foreign relations compatible with Afro-Arab-Asian nationalism. For freedom from overt alien political domination
must be accompanied by intellectual and ideological freedom as well. Emancipation from colonialism requires a
new state of affairs, whereby formerly dependent peoples
are permitted to formulate their own philosophical systems, to make their own ideological choices, and perhaps
above all, to assert their own spiritual values.

This demand for ideological "identity" provides a powerful motive force for the neutralist movement and has
both a negative and a positive dimension. Negatively, a
posture of nonalignment, as an Indian source expressed
the idea, prevents a nation from "being treated lightly or
with calculated disrespect." Neutralist governments, said
Nasser, were determined not "to accept the role of a satellite or allow our fate to be decided in a foreign country."
Or, as an Indonesian military leader declared in 1958:

As an ordinary Asian, I . . . feel that the West has hitherto dealt with Asia as an object of the East-West conflict and also as . . . propaganda material in the interest of the West's own unity in its conflict with the East bloc.

Societies rich in cultural traditions, and increasingly mindful of a past greatness often obscured by the many years of colonial rule, regard demands for alignment with either of the Cold War power blocs as offensive and un-appealing. For such demands come perilously close to an idea long invoked to justify colonialism. This was that backward societies lacked civilizations of their own, that they required political and philosophical "tutelage," and that their intellectual and spiritual "progress" would be dependent upon the successful operation of the colonial system. The neutralist mentality on this point was movingly expressed by Nehru, when he told the Bandung Conference in 1955:

> Are we copies of Europeans, Americans or Russians? We are Asians or Africans and none else. For anyone to tell us that we have to be camp-followers of Russia or America or any country in Europe is not very creditable to our new dignity, our new independence, our new freedom, our new spirit. . . .
> Are we, the countries of Asia and Africa, devoid of any positive position except being pro-Communist or anti-Communist? Has it come to this that the leaders of thought who have given religions and all kinds of things to the world have to tag on to this group or that. . . . It is most degrading and humiliating to any self-respecting people or nation. It is an intolerable thought to me that great countries of Asia and Africa should come out of bondage into freedom only to degrade themselves in this way.[10]

Yet the positive dimension of the neutralist demand for ideological identity is a no less powerful force attracting nations to the concept of nonalignment. Nonaligned countries believe that they are in a peculiarly favorable posi-

tion to contribute *positively and constructively* to the resolution of international conflicts and to the creation of an
international order based upon mutual respect for differing philosophical and political systems. Great powers are
therefore called upon to respect the desire of nations to
remain diplomatically nonaligned, not merely because
forced diplomatic association is deemed incompatible with
true freedom, but also because successful nonalignment
permits enrichment of the ideological environment by allowing ever more countries to contribute their own unique
viewpoints and experiences.

This idea was emphasized by an Ethiopian delegate to
the 1961 Belgrade Conference:

> We, the Asian-African countries, have a unique role to play.
> We find ourselves between two opposing worlds. Indeed, it
> is we, more than most, who, since the most remote times of
> history, have had to live intimately with groups of languages,
> races, and religions of the most divergent characters and who
> have had to cherish the sentiment of tolerance as a condition
> of national life.

This unique role has been variously described by proponents of nonalignment. President Sukarno once visual-
ized it as the duty to "inject the voice of reason into
world affairs"; on another occasion, he called upon neutralist societies to mobilize "moral violence" in behalf of
peace. A Ceylonese official conceived the neutralist role as
acting "as mediators in the dispute between the giants of
Communism and anti-Communism." Premier U Nu of
Burma believed that neutralist nations had an obligation
"to bring the East and West nearer." An Egyptian source
has called neutralist countries "a sort of incarnation of the
human conscience" in dealing with critical international
problems. Kwame Nkrumah has stated: "Throughout the
world there is a deep but often inarticulate desire for peace.

It is the duty of the countries which follow a positive neutralist policy to make this world opinion assert its full
weight." [11] However it is conceived, neutralist conscious-
ness of a unique role—not to say a kind of "mission" on the
world scene—must be regarded as a major force attracting
and holding nations to the concept of nonalignment.

What are the sources of this conviction? First of all,
there is the almost unanimous neutralist belief that although for many years the great powers have been endeavoring to resolve their differences, the result is still an
intractable Cold War deadlock. This affords an opportunity—neutralists would say, an obligation—for nonaligned
states to endeavor to break the impasse. A not untypical
expression of this viewpoint was the remark of Sir John
Kotelawala of Ceylon at Bandung:

> The nations on whom the responsibility [for peace] has
> hitherto devolved [namely, the great powers] are at a loss.
> They are hag-ridden by the demon of progress, the monsters
> of the scientists they have created. Neither their science nor
> their statesmenship can afford them any protection.

The protracted Cold War stalemate thus demands what
President Sukarno has labeled a "fresh approach" to the
problems of mounting global tensions and the omnipresent
threat of nuclear war.[12]

Then there is the further neutralist conviction that the
organization established to resolve international controversies and to halt the drift toward war—the United Nations—has too often been rendered ineffectual by the East-
West conflict. Neutralist countries enthusiastically support
the U.N. and seek to expand its influence in global affairs.
At the same time, they regard the organization as frequently dominated by the great powers, and they look
upon its structure as reflecting the distribution of world
power that prevailed at the end of World War II. Because

of these deficiencies, the U.N. can therefore do little or nothing to resolve issues like the crisis in Berlin and South Vietnam or disarmament.

Yet these considerations are subordinate to the strong conviction that the most valuable contribution neutralist states can make in the midst of a global ideological contest is to "cherish the sentiment of tolerance" in relations among nations. The necessity for ideological tolerance—or "coexistence"—infuses the psychology of nonalignment and is fundamental to it.*

Neutralist countries believe that they are uniquely qualified to play this role. For one thing, they feel their approach to crucial global issues is more *objective* than the approach of "aligned" countries. Said a Yugoslav source in 1961:

> it is not only the right but also the duty of the small and medium-size countries to be actively and directly concerned with the crucial world problems and to influence their solutions. In view of their objective attitude, as a result of which the nonaligned countries are not encumbered with any detrimental ballast from the past, these countries are capable of understanding the dangers threatening peace and the requirements of world development more clearly and comprehensively than others. It is essential that the uncommitted countries should take part in the solution of international problems if any progress is to be made.[13]

In whatever degree nonaligned states are committed to diplomatic goals of their own (as in the Arab conflict with

---

* In Communist (particularly Soviet) terms, "coexistence" means simply that the ultimate global victory of Communism does not require a military showdown with powerful non-Communist states. The reader is cautioned that there is a fundamental divergence between Communist and neutralist interpretations of "coexistence." The Western tendency to suppose that neutralist advocacy of coexistence merely follows the Communist line is deeply resented by the nonaligned nations. For a treatment of the two interpretations, see *Hindustan Times* (overseas edition), March 31, 1955.

Israel, the Iraqi claim to Kuwait, or the Indonesian opposition to Malaysia), they do not believe this fact prejudices their objectivity in dealing with dominant *Cold War* issues. In the neutralist view, the former issues tend to be local or regional, not *global,* do not normally involve ideological contests between great powers, and do not therefore entail the risk of endangering the future of humanity by unleashing nuclear war.

Even more fundamentally, neutralist countries have a sense of unique mission—particularly in mitigating ideological tensions likely to foment global war—because of their own cultural traditions and historical experiences. This is especially pronounced among certain Asian states —which believe the tendency toward world conflict to be endemic to *Western* (and, for this purpose, Soviet Russia is regarded as Western) diplomatic history. In 1956, Prime Minister Nehru told the United Nations:

> You have seen in the activities of European nations, in the last thousand years . . . a continent addicted to wars, more so than Asia—not that Asia has been very peaceful. But when I think of Asian history and European history, I am amazed as to the capacity for warfare that Europe has shown.

On another occasion, Nehru expressed a similar view about Russian Communism, a movement he believed to be in the ideological mainstream of European philosophy. An outstanding characteristic of Europe's philosophical development, to Nehru's mind, was its tendency toward ideological dogmatism and its unwillingness to tolerate differing belief systems, which produced fanatical wars and lesser social conflicts over religious and philosophical issues. He believed that the ideological militancy and rigid orthodoxy identified with Communism was an outgrowth of the European philosophical tradition.[14]

The peculiar qualification of nonaligned countries to

mitigate ideological differences has been a conspicuous
theme in the neutralism of certain countries. The Foreign
Minister of Morocco once emphasized his country's strategic location—its historical and cultural ties with Europe
and the Mediterranean, the Arab world, and Africa—as a
cardinal element supporting its policy of nonalignment.
Owing to its historical exposure to, and consequent assimi-
lation of, extremely diverse cultural and philosophical
systems, Morocco served as a link or bridge joining re-
gions with the most dissimilar value systems. Moroccan
society developed the ability to absorb radically different
belief systems and to create a stable social and political
order based upon mutual tolerance, or coexistence. Internally, all groups within the society benefited from this
process; externally, Morocco had much to offer a world
torn by clashing ideological rivalries and seeking a basis
for accommodating philosophical differences.[15]

For Arab countries, nonalignment is integrally fused
with the goal of creating—Arabs would say re-creating—
the "Arab nation" and bringing it once more to a position
of influence in world affairs. For the states of West Africa,
nonalignment derives logically from the effort to define
and assert the "African personality" on the continent and
the world scene. Thus the Accra Conference of Independent African States early in 1958 pledged the participants
to

> safeguard our hard-won independence, sovereignty, and ter-
> ritorial integrity, and to preserve among ourselves the funda-
> mental unity of outlook on foreign policy so that a distinctive
> African Personality will play its part in cooperation with
> other peace-loving nations to further the cause of peace.

Such concerns explain the tendency in the influential West
African state of Nigeria to describe its foreign-policy outlook as "Africanism," rather than neutralism, in order to

emphasize the distinctive and positive elements in its global outlook.[16]

Religious beliefs also often contribute to the conviction that nonalignment best allows its adherents to assert their own ideological identity and to make their unique contribution to international affairs. Hinduism, for instance, has unquestionably affected the Indian outlook toward Cold War ideological contests. The Indian subcontinent's dominant religion is syncretistic and highly personalized. In Hinduism, there is no priesthood, no creed, no standard of orthodoxy and—perhaps most pertinently—no impulse to proselytize. Inherent in Hinduism is an inclination toward compromise and toleration of widely divergent conceptions of truth, to an extent that would shock many rigidly orthodox Jewish, Christian, or Communist groups in other countries. India's dominant faith affirms the existence of many, often highly divergent, paths to ultimate truth, in accordance with the maxim that God "is but one, but the sages describe Him differently." Hinduism therefore insists upon no conformity among its adherents and is highly indulgent of differing theological systems.

For somewhat different reasons, the Buddhist faith also fosters an attitude of nonalignment in world affairs and encourages the search for ideological coexistence. In Buddhism, "there are no Armenians, Americans, British, Burmese, Chinese," or other national groups. Instead, Buddhism stresses the "fundamental sameness in all beings." National, racial, and ideological distinctions among mankind are held to be "superficial and not fundamental," "temporal and not everlasting." Conflicts throughout human society are attributed to an "excessive assertion of I-ness or egoism"; to counteract these tendencies, Buddhism prescribes "loving thoughts" and "magnanimity of heart." The result is a congenial philosophy of live and let live among culturally and ideologically dissimilar groups.

Prince Sihanouk of the Buddhist state of Cambodia has described his people's outlook in world affairs:

> They are not xenophobes. Their only two ideals are peace and freedom. . . . We came to neutralism as the most natural policy suited for us. We are no proselytes, no "fighters for neutralism."[17]

The Political Balance in Neutralist Societies

The national flag of the Union of Burma, which joined the family of nations in 1948, symbolizes a third major influence attracting and holding a large number of countries to a policy of nonalignment. In the upper left-hand corner are five small stars representing the nation's states and principal tribal districts—the Burmans, Karens, Chins, Kachins, and Shans. These are grouped around a larger star, signifying Burma's resistance movement. Throughout the postwar period, the transcendent political problem for Burma, as well as for a host of other newly independent countries, has been whether the Union's constituent elements would remain tied to the central government or whether centrifugal forces would tear the new nation apart, engendering political chaos and possibly anarchy throughout the country. For Burma, as for many other countries throughout the neutralist zone, the degree of political stability achieved is attributable in substantial measure to its policy of nonalignment, which provides what one observer has called a "broad national front behind which extremely divergent sections of the population are able to come together."[18]

To understand why this is the case, we must give brief attention to the principal factors in the political environment in those neutralist countries that have experienced nationalist revolutions. The dominant pattern is one of greater or lesser political instability, fostered by a variety of influences: the natural tendency of nationalist movements (often consisting of coalitions among several factions) to disintegrate into rival groups with the removal of the common enemy—the colonial power; a persistent undercurrent of mass disillusionment, once it becomes apparent that spectacular economic and social progress is not likely to accompany the achievement of independence; the difficulty of breaking the habit (acquired during the colonial era) of *opposing* the central government, even an indigenous one; the lack of a strong national tradition, fostering loyalty to the state and popular acceptance of the "rules of the game," whereby political contests can be kept within tolerable bounds; genuine disagreement among rival political groups over important internal and external policy questions confronting the government; natural exuberance and lack of inhibition in societies long denied management of their own affairs. In a number of countries (and the African continent abounds with examples), there is the even more crucial fact that the concept of "nationhood" possesses very little meaning. National boundaries were often drawn by colonial powers without regard for natural tribal or ethnic divisions. Many African nations have had to *create* a national union where none existed before, and where the inherent political tendency is for tribes and provinces to resist forcibly the imposition of a central governmental authority. The crisis requiring United Nations intervention in the Congo constituted merely an extreme case of the kind of political conflict that has been latent in many other African states. One authority has said that

> every African nation, large or small, federal or unitary, has its Katanga. . . . And so every African government knows that its first problem is how to hold the country together when it is threatened by wide disintegration.[19]

Three characteristics of the political environment in nonaligned countries have been fundamental in generating support for a neutralist outlook in foreign affairs. The first (upon which we have previously commented) is that the leaders and elites now holding the reins of governmental power only recently led the struggle against *Western control over their affairs.* Many of these leaders received their education and training in the West, and almost always they are attracted to at least some features of Western political ideology. In spite of these facts (or perhaps because of them), they must continually prove their independence from undue outside influence over their internal and external policies.

Second, prominent leaders of leading neutralist countries—like Nasser (Egypt), Nkrumah (Ghana), Touré (Guinea), Kassim (Iraq), Nehru (India), and Sukarno (Indonesia)—have tended to be considerably *less anti-Western* in their ideological and policy orientation than other contenders for political power within their countries. Western critics have not infrequently accused these men of "pro-Communist neutralism." It has largely escaped notice, however, that any fundamental change in the political regimes of most neutralist countries would probably take one of two forms. Either the country would lapse into internecine political warfare and perhaps outright anarchy, or else even *more* militantly anti-Western forces would take over the government. The result in neither case could be counted on to enhance the diplomatic fortunes of the West. For if leaders sympathetic to at least some features of Western political thought and practice cannot hold the allegiance of the masses, their successors could be expected to exploit historically ingrained animosities toward the West to the fullest.

An editorial appearing in a 1957 British publication on

Asian affairs, entitled "Mr. Nehru's Leadership" emphasized the realities we are discussing here:

> It is now generally recognized that had it not been for
> Nehru's leadership, India by this time would have moved
> farther away from Britain and the West. . . . The combina-
> tion of Nehru's policies, Western power-pressures, and the
> general trend of world events made a leftward inclination in
> India almost inevitable. In Indian popular opinion, progress
> in this direction is not even fast enough. Nehru's friends and
> supporters find fault with the administration and the Con-
> gress Party for not being attuned to the people's mood. . . .
> Instead of attacking Nehru, British conservative opinion
> should be thankful for his moderating influence on India.[20]

The third characteristic of the neutralist political milieu
is in some instances the most significant in creating official
and mass support for nonalignment in foreign affairs. This
is that political contests are likely to be waged among
three rival groups seeking control of the state. The first
are the strong nativistic elements, whose approach to external affairs tends to be ultranationalistic, ideologically
atavistic, and sometimes xenophobic and isolationist. Such
groups are exemplified by the powerful Moslem Brotherhood in Egypt (finally suppressed by President Nasser)
and by tribal units and advocates of "ultra-Africanism" on
the African scene. Then there are various left-wing groups
—Communists, neo-Communists, and socialists—whose
anti-Westernism and open admiration for certain features
of the Soviet or Chinese systems orients them toward the
Communist bloc. In the third place, there are the pro-
Western elites and their followers, who provided leadership in the national liberation movements and who usually managed the affairs of state in the postindependence
period. This group has widely appropriated the symbols,
phraseology, concepts, and institutions of "Western de-

mocracy"—if, in some instances, only as ultimate goals toward which their countries profess to be moving.

More than any other conceivable approach to foreign
relations, nonalignment serves to hold these disruptive political forces in check and to make possible that degree of
political unity which is the minimal price for internal stability and national survival. For a policy of nonalignment
is generally acceptable to (or is, at any rate, not actively
opposed by) the principal groups jockeying for power and
affords some basis for compromise among them. Nativistic
and tribal groups can support nonalignment because it
signifies above all else the absence of foreign domination
in policy-making and permits the nation to define the
external role that best accords with its own traditions. As
long as Communist ideology sanctions nonalignment (as
the Soviet Union, at any rate, has done fairly consistently
since the death of Stalin), Communist and other left-wing
elements can support the concept because it is held to promote the Marxist revolutionary struggle, because it con-
templates reasonably amicable relations with Communist
countries, and because it signifies freedom from Western
diplomatic control. Pro-Western groups can also accept
nonalignment, since it enables them to preserve friendly
ties with the West, and to derive assistance from it, while
(1) leaving the nation free to *choose* what it wishes to
take from the West in material assistance and in ideological affairs, and (2) permitting such leaders to reconcile
their affinity for the West with the necessity to prove their
independence from the West in policy-formulation.

There are also internal political advantages to be derived from a position of nonalignment. For example, the
regime of Sir Abubakar Balewa in Nigeria, together with
other former members of the "Monrovia group" of West
African countries, has repeatedly been obliged to prove
that its open friendship with the West entailed no diplo-

matic subordination to foreigners or abandonment of the nation's neutralist position in foreign affairs. To the north, King Hassan II of Morocco has been confronted with much the same challenge. The leftist opposition neo-Istiqlal Party appeals to Morocco's discontented masses and reflects the "ultra-African" viewpoint favored by other political groups on the continent. Only by continually demonstrating Morocco's "independence" in foreign policy can the monarchy successfully compete with a political opposition that in the elections of 1960 showed unexpected and increasing strength. In situations of this kind, vigorous (if largely symbolic) assertions of the nation's independent role—such as Rabat's demand that the United States close its strategic air bases in the country—are sometimes required by the facts of domestic political life.[21]

We have already referred to the postwar political experience of Burma, which perhaps epitomizes the kind of political turbulence and instability that is latent or overtly evident throughout the neutralist community. For many years, Burma's political stability was threatened by separatist movements among its diverse ethnic minorities, by the intrigues of *two* powerful Communist parties, by the remnants of Chiang Kai-shek's Nationalist armies in its northern provinces, and by ominous Red Chinese military build-ups along its northern frontier. The miracle of present-day Burma perhaps is that it has survived at all as a national entity. As early as 1949, Premier U Nu expressed what was perhaps the only formula for national survival when he declared that "our circumstances demand that we follow an independent course and not ally ourselves with any power bloc." Foreign intervention (or even the *appearance* of intervention) in Burma's turbulent political situation might well have provided the ingredient necessary to precipitate open political warfare.

Much the same problem has prevailed for many years

in nearby Indonesia, where separatist movements in the late 1950's challenged the authority of the central government throughout the archipelago. Rebel groups (joined by certain voices in the West) accused President Sukarno's government of gravitating toward the Communist orbit; in turn, Sukarno charged that separatist movements were Western-supported and were aimed ultimately at "aligning" Indonesia with SEATO, the Western alliance against Communism in Asia. Djakarta eventually suppressed the rebellion. An indispensable element in its ability to do so was the fact that the crisis was kept insulated from Cold War antagonisms. "No one can imagine," President Sukarno declared, "how Indonesian freedom, independence, and national aspirations could survive internal dissension and discord which later flared into foreign-inspired rebellion." Without firm adherence to a policy of nonalignment, he was convinced, "Indonesia could have been torn to pieces by interested foreign powers."

It may have been a premonition of such a possibility that prompted Indonesia's Foreign Minister to make a statement in 1957 that would command agreement throughout the entire neutralist zone. For newly independent societies, he said, involvement in great-power controversies could mean

> that every aspect of the activities of their government and peoples . . . can be exploited by the disruptive forces of the Cold War. And the ultimate effect . . . would not be a temporary *status quo* with stability but, at best, an interregnum of chaos, along with the disappearance of the independent nature of the nation . . . at worst, incessant local wars with the unavoidable risk of their expanding into a world-wide conflagration.

The former U.S. Ambassador to Egypt, John S. Badeau, a long-time student of Egyptian affairs, commented upon the domestic political implications of Western efforts to bring Cairo into a Middle Eastern alliance against Communism. Badeau's observation would apply with equal validity to the majority of countries embracing nonalignment:

> To enter into a pro-Western alliance now would provide a focus for all the bitter-end opposition to the Revolution among extremists and old-time party leaders alike. Once more an Egyptian government must walk the tightrope of foreign policy with grave risk of a slip that would end the performance.[22]

Strategic Calculations of Nonaligned States

IV

Burma, according to former Premier U Nu, is "hemmed in like a tender gourd among the cactus." The leader of nearby Cambodia, explained that "our neutralism is not a doctrine. It is a realism, it is an attitude dictated by fact and situation."

The influences supporting nonalignment that are least understood in the West are those relating to the strategic-military factors shaping the foreign-policy orientations of weak, vulnerable countries in the contemporary era. Frequently, neutralism is construed in the West as a doctrine arising from an attitude of defeatism, escapism, or lack of realism on the part of its adherents. In reality, as American officials since the late Eisenhower period have come to appreciate, some extremely persuasive arguments for non-alignment can be made on strategic-military grounds. Far from losing sight of their own security interests, many countries have accepted the concept of nonalignment precisely because a careful weighing of available alternatives indicates that this course most nearly safeguards their security in the face of hostile external threats.

Neutralist countries are well aware that they are mili-

tarily vulnerable vis-à-vis the major contestants in the
Cold War. Lacking great military power, and—without
sacrificing internal development schemes—the means to
acquire it, neutralist nations are fully conscious of the
verdict of Edwin O. Reischauer: "Neutralism is very com-
monly an unconscious reflection of a nation's military
weakness. Those countries which have espoused it most
enthusiastically have often been those least capable of affecting the world balance of power." Or, as an Arab source
has put it, neutralism serves as "a shelter for young nations
against the Cold War and the threats of nuclear and total
war." [23]

At the risk of oversimplification (and, for the moment,
ignoring the many gradations of "nonalignment"), we may
say that basically two diplomatic choices exist for small,
militarily vulnerable nations in a global atmosphere characterized by Cold War antagonisms. One alternative is
unequivocal alignment with either the Communist world
or the West; the other is nonalignment in Cold War disputes. Some relatively defenseless countries (like Iran,
Pakistan, Thailand, South Vietnam, South Korea, and the
Philippines) have chosen the first course by joining Western-sponsored defense pacts such as CENTO or SEATO.
Other states (such as the Communist satellites in Eastern
Europe, North Vietnam, and North Korea) have voluntarily or involuntarily entered the orbit of powerful Communist states. The countries with which our study is concerned have chosen the path of nonalignment, not because
they *fail* to realize their own precarious strategic position,
but for precisely the opposite reason. They have chosen
this course deliberately, because they are convinced that
nonalignment affords the best (some countries might say,
the *only*) way of maintaining their national existence in
the face of intense hostility between the Communist and
Western blocs.

The reasons for this decision naturally are not identical for Morocco and Lebanon, Afghanistan and Burma. Such factors as geographical location, economic and military potential, the imminence and nature of outside threats, and calculations about the ultimate aims of the Communist or Western worlds are always fundamental. Each nation will inevitably reach its own verdict about the importance of such influences, or may even feel that other considerations are, in its particular case, decisive. Another consideration, which we have already noted, is that it is often difficult for neutralist nations to distinguish between the "protection" offered by great powers and a condition of colonialism or dependency. If this is a concomitant of "alignment"—and many neutralist countries do not see how it can altogether be avoided—it is rejected as totally inimical to their newly gained independence.

But in most instances, this is only one among many considerations. In the West, neutralism is widely regarded as a synonym for diplomatic expediency. And in one respect, at least (though not the respect usually intended), the accusation is valid: From the vantage point of their national security, neutralist states consider it highly expedient to remain clear of great-power conflicts in which they might well become the first victims. Proponents of nonalignment emphasize the fact that world-wide military conflagrations have often originated in *small* countries. Restricting the geographical scope of great power conflicts by expanding the zone of nonalignment thus seems justified both from the narrow view of national security and from the wider view of international security as a whole. In a curious inversion of Western phraseology about the Cold War, an Egyptian source in 1961 formulated a goal for neutralist countries by saying: "The big powers must somehow or other be contained"! An Indian official has stated that New Delhi has sought to limit the extent of the Cold

War "by persuading other countries also to remain unaligned." And a Yugoslav observer has commented:

> The disengagement of large numbers of Asian and African
> countries from blocs is of primary importance to the world.
> . . . Any basic change in this region would shake the exist-
> ing balance of power . . . and would threaten, if not directly
> cause, new conflagrations.[24]

Moreover, the past experience of small states that attempted to obtain security by aligning themselves with
great powers has left an indelible impression on neutralist
minds. The small Southeast Asian kingdom of Cambodia
affords a notable example. After suffering repeated inva-
sions throughout its history, Cambodia in the middle of
the nineteenth century sought the protection of far-off
France. Paris responded to the request for protection, and
within a short time had converted the security treaty of
1863 into outright rule over the country. Cambodia's present ruler has said that the country might have accepted
even this step if France had in fact protected Cambodia
against its enemies. But in fact, during World War II, the
Japanese succeeded in ousting the French from the tiny
country. Vivid recollections of such events prompted its
present-day ruler to declare:

> In the event of a world conflict, we might well become one
> of the first victims of harsh occupation. In that case the "free
> world" would have other things to do besides undertaking
> our liberation—or rather the liberation of what little remained
> of us.

Such strategic considerations led Cambodia in 1957 to en-
act its "neutralism" into organic law.[25]

More recent history tends to confirm the Cambodian experience and to raise substantial questions about the strategic advantages of "alignment" with great powers. The
fate of South Korea, for example, has been widely alluded

to by advocates of nonalignment. As early as 1951, the
Foreign Minister of Yugoslavia declared:

> We will not allow anyone to try to make of Yugoslavia an-
> other Korea, that is, to incite this or that satellite against the
> people of Yugoslavia under the guise of preserving the peace.

South Korea's experience not unnaturally made a particularly vivid impression upon the minds of Asians. To
Premier U Nu, the moral to be drawn from South Korea's
conversion into a Cold War battleground was that a small
nation "cannot have the effrontery to quarrel with any
power." Burma, he affirmed, was not only determined to
"be free of commitments to either power bloc, but to be
seen to be free from them" as well. In the West, the Korean War symbolizes the principle of firm "resistance" to
aggression and is cited as an object lesson in successful
"containment" of expansive Communism. Neutralists have
tended to draw other conclusions. An informed student of
Burmese affairs has written:

> the lesson which the Korean War presents to Asian nations
> such as Burma is very different from the conclusions which
> seem so evident to Powers more remote from possible ag-
> gression, such as the United States. The former see only that
> South Korea's freedom has been paid for by the physical de-
> struction of the country's economy, the uprooting and ruin of
> the lives of millions, and the division of one people into two
> warring factions. From Korea Burma drew the lesson that al-
> most any fate is preferable for a small nation to that of be-
> coming a battlefield for the world's great conflict.[26]

To exponents of nonalignment, the strategic advantages
of the doctrine are not merely theoretical. In a number of
key Cold War trouble-spots since World War II, the principle has successfully stood the test of experience. Two
countries—both small, relatively poor, and geographically
vulnerable to Cold War pressures—are often cited by pro-

ponents of neutralism as particularly relevant examples. One is Yugoslavia. Tito's successful effort to preserve his country's territorial integrity, maintain *de facto* independence in policy formulation, and carry forward a program of economic development—all in the face of efforts by East and West alike to "align" his country with their respective diplomatic blocs—has won the open admiration of neutralist societies. Alternatively, Tito's "break" with the Kremlin in the early postwar era, his ensuing cooperation with the West, followed by creation of a new rapport with the Soviet Union and simultaneous maintenance of harmonious relations with powerful Western nations, have notably enhanced Yugoslavia's prestige in the eyes of small countries. An authoritative Western source has labeled Yugoslavia's position as "one of great strength. Sought by all and, immediately at least, threatened by none, she appeared to have achieved the control of her destiny which was the aim of so many countries." It is therefore not surprising that the President of the Sudan should refer to the "high degree of unanimity" prevailing between his and Tito's viewpoints on global issues, or that an influential Burmese journal should commend the "ties of friendship" binding the two nations in the contemporary period. Tito's adroit pursuit of nonalignment accounts in no small measure for his considerable influence in neutralist diplomatic circles, for the selection of Belgrade as the site for the 1961 neutralist summit meeting, and—perhaps most significantly—for the inclusion of Yugoslavia as the only *European* state regarded throughout Asia and Africa as a genuinely "nonaligned" nation.[27]

The other example is Afghanistan, sometimes called the "Switzerland of Asia." If the country is poor, its Prime Minister, Prince Daud, has explained, the explanation is "at least in part because the nation has for two centuries been continuously engaged in the defense of its independence." Throughout modern history, Afghanistan has found that its internal and external policies—at times, even its boundaries—were an outgrowth of great-power conflicts. Following the "Afghan Wars" of the nineteenth century, for example, control over its foreign relations was transferred to the Viceroy of India (which is to say, to Downing Street). This situation did not change appreciably until 1929, when the country won its independence. Thereafter, Kabul studiously followed a "neutral" course in world affairs, successfully maintaining this position in World War II.

After the war, as the East-West conflict came to infuse nearly all international issues, Afghanistan carefully avoided ideological or diplomatic affiliation with either the Communist or Western blocs, although it tried to remain friendly with both. Afghanistan, according to one observer, is "the strictest of all Muslim countries"; as such, its people are stanchly opposed to Communism on religious grounds. Yet possessing a 700-mile border in common with the Soviet Union, the nation is fully conscious of its continuing strategic vulnerability. The inescapable strategic reality, a *New York Times* reporter noted in 1960, is the "fact of life . . . that if the Russians wanted to take over the country tomorrow, they have the military strength to do so with little difficulty." The disparity between the military power of this small country and the U.S.S.R. is so overwhelming that landlocked Afghanistan could not effectively resist a hostile Soviet move; nor is it likely that the West could effectively defend Afghanistan without resorting to nuclear war. For these reasons—and because economic progress requires maximum assistance from outside sources—Afganistan accepts foreign aid from both the East and the West. Western opinion may manifest deep concern about the country's extensive economic reliance upon the Communist bloc. Officials of Afghanistan answer that the longer the nation remains free, and the more rapidly it builds a stable economic and political base, the greater will be its ability to resist future threats to its independence. A policy of nonalignment is thus regarded as affording the only conceivable avenue to long-range security and stability.[28]

Yet it is precisely as a means of safeguarding national security that the doctrine of nonalignment often seems most indefensible to Western critics. It is in this realm, many Western commentators have argued, that the neutralist mentality is most insensitive to *Realpolitik* and most prone to minimize the Communist threat to defenseless societies. By late 1962, an epochal event seemed to confirm the most dire predictions about the consequences of nonalignment. This was Red China's massive military incursion into India's northern provinces.

In one of the most remarkable expressions of official *mea culpa* witnessed in recent history, Prime Minister Nehru confessed that India had experienced a "profound shock" and that Red China's aggression had brought his nation to a "turning point" in its history. In the United States, the Indian Ambassador conceded that India had made "a great error of judgment regarding the Chinese as being motivated in the same way as ourselves. . . . This, as events have proved, was a profound misjudgment." [29] To Western minds long dubious about nonalignment, such confessions were long overdue; more basically, they seemed to presage a needed reorientation in New Delhi's relations with the outside world, which could be expected in turn to trigger re-examinations of the neutralist credo from Morocco to Indonesia. What seemed additional evidence of a forthcoming diplomatic shift came when Nehru finally dismissed Defense Minister Krishna Menon, a tireless champion of neutralism who had displayed a peculiar talent for irritating Western sensibilities.

In the midst of these dramatic events, however, it was possible to overlook still other developments affecting India's global role in the months following the Chinese onslaught. A crucial one for our purposes was the frequency with which Indian officials reiterated that neither Peking's aggression nor India's subsequent acceptance of massive Western military aid involved "abandonment" of its cherished nonaligned diplomatic position. Even while officials in New Delhi lavishly praised Western governments for their prompt and generous response to India's military needs, the President of the Republic declared that the fundamental policies of his government—democracy, socialist planning, and nonalignment—had been tested "and found adequate" by the Sino-Indian conflict. Stressing the conception of nonalignment we emphasized in Chapter 1, he stated:

> The policy of nonalignment meant that India did not wish to give up the opportunity of offering independent judgment on issues which came before her. This policy was now being put to the test and it has not been found wanting.

Another Indian observer equated Western military assistance to India with American aid furnished the Allies under Lend-Lease in World War II:

> This arms aid is . . . without conditions; it does not affect India's policy or interests. She is free to be nonaligned as long as she likes or as long as it suits her. There are no strings and no financial burdens. The basis is lend-lease.[30]

After the Chinese attack on India, the web of India's external relations—with Pakistan, with the Soviet Union, with Red China, with the United States, with the neutralist world—became even more tangled. Our concern here is with the *strategic* aspects of Indian policy as these affected the principle of nonalignment. And the paramount question which the Sino-Indian crisis posed was this: Did

India's military defeat at the hands of Red China vitiate
the strategic arguments previously invoked to justify nonalignment vis-à-vis East and West? The Indian answer—
and ultimately the answer of virtually every other country in the neutralist zone—was negative. Neutralist sources
were not reluctant to confess (in the words of the Arabic
daily *Al Akhbar*) that China's aggression constituted "a
blow to the concept of nonalignment"; the Lebanese pa-
per *Al Kifah* drew the lesson that "the policy of nonalignment and peaceful coexistence . . . is facing bitter trial.
. . . The path will be long and dreary and the pain enormous." But even in the midst of such confessions, Prime
Minister Nehru could still declare at the end of 1962: "I
do not see any reason why we should not continue our
nonalignment policy." [31]

Such a seeming paradox becomes intelligible only when
certain elemental facts concerning the strategic position of
India (and of other neutralist nations) are fully grasped.
These may be highlighted by two inquiries. Would India's
"alignment" with the West have *prevented* the Chinese
military onslaught? And, after the aggression occurred,
would its membership in a Western-sponsored military alliance have contributed significantly to the *liquidation* of
the Chinese threat—a conflict New Delhi believes will last
for many years, perhaps indefinitely? Again, New Delhi
(joined by other potential victims of aggression in the belt
of neutralist states) believed the answer to both questions
must be No. Regarding the ability of formal "alignment"
with the West to *deter* Communist threats, neutralist
countries have observed that Asian states like Laos and
South Vietnam must also contend with Communist-instigated threats to their security, in spite of the fact that regimes in both states were for varying periods tightly
"aligned" with Western powers. By contrast, leading neutralist states like Burma and Cambodia—no less vulner-

able to Chinese incursions—have thus far successfully preserved their security. Similarly, nonaligned Indonesia has also maintained its independence, and in the process has compelled Peking reluctantly to accept Djakarta's demand that the large Chinese minority opt either for Chinese or Indonesian citizenship.

India's present and future adherence to nonalignment is based on a clear appreciation of strategic realities. Foremost among these are the geographical remoteness and logistical inaccessibility of India's northern provinces; the conviction that the dispute with China may prove interminable; the inappropriateness of the Western nuclear and missile arsenal to the particular military challenge facing New Delhi; the strong belief that, left to its own devices, India will in time successfully repulse the Chinese advance. Above all, however, there is the conviction India shares with all other neutralist states that if military conflicts arise, they must not be allowed to "escalate" into world-wide military conflagrations that would convert the country into a nuclear battleground. Overt military "alignment" with the West—especially if it were followed by extensive Western military intervention in northern India—would run this grave risk, while offering few compensating strategic advantages. By remaining nonaligned, India can still receive needed military and economic assistance from the West—even from the Soviet Union! Such aid, coupled with a build-up of its own long-neglected defense establishment, offers the best avenue available for eventually recouping its military fortunes.

Awareness of these considerations—and of the implications for his own country if India did request "alignment" with the West—undoubtedly prompted American Ambassador Galbraith to concur publicly in New Delhi's decision. Galbraith asserted that U.S. military assistance to India was not intended to involve India in a military alliance or otherwise influence its policy of nonalignment, and that the United States did not wish to see the conflict between India and Communist China "either continued or *extended.*" A dispatch to *The New York Times* late in 1962 reported a speech by Nehru as follows:

> While thanking the Western powers for military aid, the Prime Minister again said it had not meant the abandonment of India's nonalignment.
>
> "As a matter of fact," he said, "the head of one Western country now giving us arms has written me saying he had not wanted India to change its traditional policy of nonalignment."
>
> The Indian leader did not name the country or its head, but the audience believed he meant President Kennedy. One could hear the name of President Kennedy passed from one person to another.[32]

If the Chinese attack had "awakened" New Delhi and its like-minded neutralist partners to Red China's aggressive impulses, it might in time no less "awaken" Western opinion to the strategic advantages—for itself, no less than for neutralist countries themselves—implicit in the concept of nonalignment.

III

Neutralist Strategies in the Global Arena

The diplomatic strategies pursued by nonaligned nations on the international scene reflect a consensus upon three basic convictions. These are (1) the belief that the concept of nonalignment is gaining converts, that it is a diplomatically growing force; (2) that nonaligned nations are actuated by a deeper attachment to moral-ethical values in the conduct of international affairs than are the Cold War power blocs; and (3) that nonalignment is (or, at least, ought to be) a constructive force in the resolution of international tensions and in the maintenance of peace.

Evidence that nonalignment is a progressively influential movement—that it is, so to speak, the "wave of the future," diplomatically—can be drawn from several sources. Between one-third and one-half of mankind is presently included in the neutralist zone. Virtually every newly independent state in Africa has joined the parade of countries espousing nonalignment. A tendency toward greater diplomatic "independence" throughout Latin America—a region long prone to follow the lead of the United States on Cold War issues—has become unmistakable. Within the Western alliance itself, the Gaullist quest for *l'indépendance* in foreign affairs closely parallels a major goal of neutralist states. Less dramatic diplomatic restlessness has also become apparent among other "aligned" states (notably Thailand, the Philippines, and Pakistan) with respect to acceptance of policies and viewpoints formulated in Western capitals. And the gulf between Moscow and Peking is indicative of Red China's intention to pursue an increasingly independent diplomatic role. Such developments have fostered the conviction among proponents of nonalignment that their approach has inaugurated a "new era in human relationships" and have prompted them to conclude that nonalignment has become "a fundamental factor in the preservation of international peace and security." [1]

Addressing the Bandung Conference in 1955, President Sukarno sounded the keynote of a second pervasive conviction uniting countries dedicated to nonalignment:

> What can we do? We can do much! We can inject the voice of reason into world affairs. We can mobilize all the spiritual, all the moral, all the political strength of the peoples of Asia and Africa . . . far more than half the human population of the world, we can mobilize what I called the Moral Violence of Nations in favour of peace.

Nasser has said that the neutralist movement represents the "conscience of the world and its moral spirit"; Tito described the neutralist nations assembled at Belgrade in 1961 as "the conscience of mankind." Whatever the phraseology, advocates of nonalignment view their position as the antithesis of a policy based upon insensitivity to moral-ethical questions. Instead, nonalignment is directed at fostering a renaissance of moral principles in an international environment too long characterized by Cold War ideological rigidities, national animosities and suspicions, and the omnipresent specter of nuclear war. [2]

The third and related neutralist conviction is that nonaligned nations are in a position to make a unique contribution in the resolution of global tensions and controversies. Throughout the neutralist zone, a consensus exists (as President Sukarno expressed it) that "the great powers had manifestly demonstrated that they were incapable of securing peace" and that it was "time for the lesser fry to take a hand in things." Problems of human existence had "become too complex for the great powers to solve." A Yugoslav source has concluded that one reason why the world had not been plunged into the "Hell of an active war" was because of the diplomatic activities of neutralist countries.[3] In short, neutralists are convinced that if nonalignment did not exist, it would have to be invented.

Before dismissing such assertions as little more than the pretentious claims of zealous proponents of a new mode of thought, or discounting them as naïve, it behooves us to examine them in greater detail. We may conveniently do so by focusing upon two broad areas of neutralist diplomatic activity: the attitude of nonaligned states toward the problem of war and international crises, and their activities in strengthening and extending the neutralist movement.

The Neutralist States and Global Crises

If it seems superfluous to observe that peace is a paramount concern of neutralist states, the diplomatic implications of this fact may be less apparent. The neutralist states assume that international peace is possible, that it is an attainable goal. This conviction does not mean that they envision an idyllic international order free of conflicts and controversies; nor, as we shall see, does it postulate a global Nirvana in which violence has been eliminated. The objective is rather an international system which accepts, and increasingly reflects, the idea of coexistence, broadly defined as tolerance of differing ideologies, respect for the right of each nation to determine its own internal political and economic system, and reliance upon negotiations to resolve global and regional conflicts. Coexistence in turn is viewed as both stemming from, and required by, the condition of nuclear stalemate, or nuclear parity, which has conditioned East-West relations since the Soviet acquisition of nuclear weapons.[4]

Nuclear parity—entailing the threat of nothing less than global annihilation—has introduced revolutionary changes in the pattern of international political relationships and has provided neutralist countries with a justification for their "positive" and "dynamic" diplomatic role. Nonaligned states must be given, or must acquire, an equal voice in global diplomatic deliberations, officials from Ghana to Indonesia have repeatedly affirmed. The neutralist case was succinctly presented by Iraq in 1962:

> as members of the world community and being subject to the forces governing international relations, it has become incumbent upon the nonaligned countries to play their part in directing these forces and in orienting the policies shaping relationships among nations. The world is no longer governed by the Big Powers, and therefore it is the right and duty of the nonaligned to intervene effectively in world affairs, particularly with regard to those policies of the Big Powers which affect the present and future destiny of the rest of the world.[5]

Peace, in short, is too important to be left to the great powers, which in the neutralist view have demonstrated both an insensitivity to the world-wide desire for peace and an inability to break the diplomatic deadlock that keeps the world teetering on the brink of nuclear war.

"We need peace because we have neither military nor economic powers," President Keita of Mali has declared. Peace, as Prime Minister Nehru once observed, was "an imperative necessity to my country and other countries round about." Or, in the words of another Indian spokesman, India required peace "because it is only peace that can make it possible for us to build up a prosperous and progressive State." [6] Thus, if nonaligned countries base their attachment to peace upon idealistic and ethical principles, they are no less influenced by certain hard realities. Here, as in many other aspects of neutralist thought, nonaligned states are fully as sensitive to factors affecting their own national interests as are countries aligned with the West or the Communist bloc. The nonaligned nations are militarily weak; neither now nor in the foreseeable future are they in a position to challenge the great powers in the acquisition of military and economic strength as decisive instruments of foreign policy. And they are cognizant that if they endeavor to build up their armed forces, they are likely to discover (as India has found since the Himalayan encounter with Red China in 1962) that they are imposing an extremely heavy burden on their national budgets, thereby seriously impairing internal development programs. Neutralist countries have thus been obliged to choose between two evils: an inadequate defense program, permitting intensive diversion of resources to internal development, or a more adequate defense program, severely jeopardizing schemes for economic and social betterment. In the vast majority of cases, they have chosen the former course—not out of ignorance of the risks involved in doing so, but as a calculated policy choice that these consequences were not as serious as those attending the latter course. However much they may regard adequate armed forces as a vital element in safeguarding national stability and security, they are convinced that armed strength alone, even when augmented by vast foreign assistance, cannot create and maintain that degree of internal unity required to preserve independence; this goal can only be achieved as political elites demonstrate to the masses that independence is being translated into tangible economic and social improvements.

Nonalignment, with its emphasis upon peace, must thus be regarded as a kind of "strength through weakness" philosophy espoused by small, militarily vulnerable nations unable to compete with the great powers in the manufacture and acquisition of arms. If such countries are unable to acquire powerful armed forces, then their diplomatic voices will become influential to the degree that armed forces themselves are rendered less decisive in the conduct of international affairs. Accordingly, in pursuing nonalignment, President Nkrumah has said, "the people and government of Ghana put all their weight behind the peaceful settlement of disputes and seek conditions in which disputes do not become embittered to the point of violence." Neutralist countries, an Egyptian source has emphasized, object to the term "noncommitted" to describe their position; all nonaligned nations are "in reality committed in the sense that they must exert their efforts for the preservation of peace and the defense of the intangible principles without which the world would be ruled by the law of the jungle." [7]

How have such general professions of neutralist intent been translated into the specific diplomatic activities designed to achieve the declared goal? First of all, the neutralist countries have avoided involvement in ideological controversies among the great powers. Guinea, its chief delegate to the United Nations declared in 1959, refused "to participate in the quarrels of rival nations." Indonesia proposed to avoid "ideological problems with either of the power blocs." [8]

The nonaligned nations have also promoted world peace by identifying, and calling public attention to, unresolved international and regional problems likely to engender hostilities among powerfully armed contestants. Focusing global attention upon unresolved international issues was a fundamental purpose of neutralist gatherings like the Afro-Asian Conference in Bandung of 1955, the Belgrade Conference of 1961, and the Cairo Conference of 1964. As a corollary of this obligation, neutralist countries were further required, in the words of Nasser, to devise "a plan that can drive the negotiations between the two blocs to the domain of practical application." [9] Attempts to formulate such a plan led the Belgrade Conference to dispatch neutralist envoys to Washington and Moscow to present the neutralist viewpoint on a host of international issues; and it prompted neutralist countries to make repeated suggestions designed to bring about agreement between the East and West on the nuclear-test-ban treaty of 1963.

Neutralist countries have also sought to encourage high-level diplomatic negotiations among the great powers and to alter the character of such negotiations. An operating premise of neutralist diplomacy is that the great powers are reluctant to enter into serious negotiations, that they tend to perpetuate the existing diplomatic impasse and to reiterate outworn Cold War slogans. The deadlock between East and West can be overcome only if constant pressure is put upon the United States, the Soviet Union, and their supporters to resolve their differences. Neutralist voices therefore demand an expanded role for nonaligned nations in summit conferences and other high-level diplomatic deliberations, such as the disarmament talks at Geneva. Referring to a proposed summit meeting in 1958, Marshal Tito stated that invitations ought to be extended to "countries which do not belong to any military bloc or formation," since such countries could then "advance their constructive proposals, their observations, their advice." [10]

Neutralists also emphasize that since small nations have often precipitated world conflicts, small nations should endeavor to prevent them.

Brief mention must also be made of a point to be discussed at length in Chapter 4. This is the neutralist determination to strengthen and expand the influence of the United Nations in world affairs. Thus, as an Arab source expressed the goal, neutralist states were active in "strengthening this organization so as to enable it to play its historical role in promoting international understanding and cooperation and to widen the area of peace and justice."[11]

Another obligation of neutralist states in dealing with great-power conflicts has been repeatedly emphasized by Indian commentators. Since "neutralism" cannot properly be construed as "the sanctimonious attitude of the man who holds himself aloof" from controversial global issues, Indian spokesmen have underscored the necessity for neutralist states to keep in mind the distinction between "nonalignment" and "policy." The former has been defined as "a state or attitude of mind which does not absolve the government of the responsibility of having a policy." Nonalignment is a theory about how states *arrive at* their policies and about their military and diplomatic ties with East and West. Accordingly, dedication to nonalignment per se does not define a government's position on the problems of disarmament, Berlin, or stability in Laos. Genuine attachment to nonalignment demands that its advocates evolve policies on such issues, and that they do their utmost to win acceptance for them.[12]

Yet, among all the contributions made by neutralist states in seeking to promote international peace and security, none is perhaps regarded as more crucial than the role of nonaligned countries in attenuating, limiting, and resolving diplomatic crises involving, or potentially capable of involving, the great powers. Whether in the Congo, along the Arab-Israeli frontier, in the Suez crisis of 1956, or in the Korean War, neutralist nations regard this role as extremely important, if not literally indispensable, for world peace. To discharge it effectively, they have been led to adopt an approach often severely criticized on both sides of the Iron Curtain. It was aptly summarized by Ghana's chief delegate to the U.N. when he said that the proposals emanating from the Belgrade Conference "did not aim at condemning either side" in the Cold War "but at seeking solutions." An Egyptian source likewise declared that at Belgrade, the participants "were at pains not to condemn . . . the individual attitudes of either of the sides in the Cold War." [13]

It is here, as much as in any other aspect of neutralist thought, that the influence of Prime Minister Nehru was decisive. He repeatedly informed both his neutralist colleagues and the great powers that in pursuing nonalignment, India did not propose to be either a self-appointed "mediator or a busybody" on the global scene. If India's role sometimes proved "helpful" in the resolution of crisis, it was only because of its "friendly relations with both the Powers" in the Cold War. Moreover, Nehru carefully eschewed what he called an "agitational approach" in dealing with outstanding Cold War issues. To his fellow neutralists, he declared:

> Now, as a nation grows in maturity, it adopts the mature approach. . . . It may be occasionally satisfying to a country to utter condemnation of other countries, but if it wants to achieve results that is hardly the shortest way. Sometimes, silence is a little bit louder than noise.[14]

While it would be too much to assert that neutralist diplomatic conduct is always governed by Nehru's principle, or that some neutralist states are not still wedded to an "agitational" approach, it is nevertheless clear that Nehru's conception has set the tone for the neutralist movement. By the 1960's, this was amply borne out by the remarkably restrained neutralist reaction to a host of international crises, ranging from the Soviet-American confrontation in Cuba in 1962, to the continuing Berlin dispute, to the accelerating crisis in Southeast Asia.

Advocates of nonalignment could cite many instances in which their peace-making activities attenuated and limited international crises, some of which at least involved the danger of nuclear war. India played a pivotal role in arranging a cease-fire in the Korean War and in resolving the difficult question of prisoner exchange. New Delhi was also instrumental in bringing about the Geneva Conference of 1954 that endeavored to produce a political settlement for Indochina and Southeast Asia as a whole. Neutralist countries were actively involved in the U.N. Congo operations in the early 1960's. The influence of nonaligned countries, symbolized by U.N. Secretary General U Thant, was highly instrumental in finding a formula for resolving the Cuban missile crisis of 1962. In 1964, Morocco and the Ivory Coast produced a plan designed to resolve a long-standing dispute between South Vietnam and the United States, on the one hand, and Cambodia, on the other, concerning infringements of Cambodia's borders.

Yet of all recent international crises, it was the Sino-Indian conflict in the Himalayas, erupting late in 1962, that most strikingly illustrated the neutralist peace-keeping role. Indeed, the Himalayan contest provided a testing ground for nonalignment—not alone in challenging the sincerity of India's devotion to the principle, but also in testing the ability of other neutralist nations to apply their professed principles to a situation involving one of their own leading spokesmen. In this contest, neutralist states were placed in a dilemma between their overwhelming sympathy for India as the victim of aggression and their realization that no other nation, or group of nations, was in a position to extinguish a blaze that might well ignite a world conflagration. The United States quite obviously could not do so, owing to the extreme animosity that had long characterized Sino-American relations. The U.S.S.R. could not do so, because of its defense ties with Red China, its acute embarrassment over Peking's aggressiveness, and its professed friendship with India and other nonaligned states. The United Nations could not do so, because Red China did not belong to the U.N. and showed no discernible willingness to accept its jurisdiction. Besides, U.N. Secretary General U Thant publicly deprecated the U.N.'s usefulness in the Himalayan crisis. This left the neutralist nations. In spite of their support for the Indian position, they accepted the responsibility for seeking a *détente* in the Himalayan imbroglio.

The course of the intricate negotiations leading to a cease-fire in the Himalayas does not concern us. The essential facts are that at the instigation of Ceylon, six neutralist countries (in addition to Ceylon, Egypt, Ghana, Burma, Indonesia, and Cambodia) gained acceptance "in principle" from India and Red China for detailed proposals designed to bring an end to the Himalayan fighting.*

Our interest centers upon certain convictions and premises guiding neutralist mediation activities. In one neutralist capital after another, there was agreement with the

---

* These proposals endeavored to create a twelve-and-one-half-mile wide no man's land between the battle lines in the Himalayas, after which India and China would negotiate their conflicting border claims. While both countries accepted this idea "in principle" and as a "basis for discussion," Peking coupled its acceptance with repeated demands for "clarifications" of particular points, amounting (in the Indian view) to a *de facto* rejection of the proposals. By 1965, neutralist countries still urged Red China to accept the proposals without further equivocation. See *The New York Times*, February 19, 1964.

Egyptian contention that Red China's attack was "a blow to the concept of nonalignment." If the blow was not to become irreparable, said the Cairo daily *Al Akhbar,* neutralist states were required to narrow "the dispute to the smallest possible dimensions." The future of nonalignment itself obliged these countries "to check and settle the Indian-Chinese dispute." The Prime Minister of Ceylon observed that if nonaligned states had endeavored to play "a positive role, for the cause of preserving world peace" with respect to Cold War issues, "what could be our duty, when we face a dispute . . . among ourselves and between friendly nations?" Gradually, the neutralist world came to the conclusion that high on the list of Peking's objectives was the desire to prove that the very concept of nonalignment was (as a Syrian commentator put it) a "political sham," and that a neutralist third force in reality did not exist. This increased the determination of the nonaligned countries to demonstrate the value of neutralism in a strife-torn international environment.

Although more than seventy nations publicly expressed sympathy with India's position in its contest with China, if they were to discharge their mediatory role successfully, the six neutralist nations at Colombo had to be guided by a maxim of Nkrumah. The Colombo neutralists, Nkrumah maintained, could not behave toward Red China as though "they are condemning her unheard." Nor could they endeavor to "impose" an unacceptable solution upon New Delhi and Peking. As Burma's chief of state, General Ne Win, expressed it: "We are seeking to mediate, not arbitrate, and . . . these functions do not go together." The neutralist goal, according to another Burmese source, was "to help create an atmosphere conducive to the opening of negotiations between China and India."

Throughout the course of their mediatory activities, the Colombo neutralists were mindful that success depended upon one paramount consideration: the extent to which they succeeded in evolving a cease-fire formula compatible with the minimum security interests of both belligerents. Despite its initial skepticism about neutralist mediation, New Delhi ultimately accepted the Colombo proposals. The determining factor in India's decision was perhaps the belief that the Colombo neutralists had placed Red China in an awkward diplomatic dilemma. If China *accepted* the proposals, it would thereby acknowledge the existence and contribution of nonaligned states, its territorial gains would be limited, and India would have gained time in which to strengthen its defenses against any new Chinese incursion. If Peking *rejected* the proposals, it would have to accept sole responsibility for blocking the path to peace, the hollowness of its professed attachment to "Bandung principles would be revealed," and it would largely forfeit any remaining goodwill and influence it had among neutralist countries—at a time when the widening rift with the Soviet Union demanded extraordinary Chinese efforts to counteract Soviet influence in the neutralist zone.

Red China eventually cooperated, at least minimally, with neutralist mediation efforts for a variety of reasons, some of which even now are known only to policy-makers in Peking. Two factors, perhaps, were crucial. Peking's unilateral proclamation of a cease-fire on November 20, 1962, indicated that its objectives were perhaps more limited than had been supposed. As a tide of sympathy for India's cause swept through the Afro-Arab-Asian world, and as the six Colombo neutralist nations made it clear that they did not propose to advance suggestions prejudicial to Indian security, Chinese policy-makers contemplated the consequences of risking a total alienation of neutralist opinion. Their drive to establish China as the dominant power in Asia had led them to call for a "second

Bandung" conference (*sans* the Soviet Union)—a plea
that had received some neutralist support, notably in Indonesia. Rejection of the Colombo proposals would almost
certainly induce a majority of the neutralist states to favor
a new conference of nonaligned nations to which neither
the U.S.S.R. nor Red China would be invited. This development would enhance the Kremlin's position in its
dispute with Peking, by excluding Mao's government from
a summit meeting of the Afro-Asian world. Peking's response, therefore, was to accept the Colombo proposals
"in principle," while rejecting them in fact by repeated
and equivocal demands for "clarifications" from New
Delhi and from the Colombo neutralist group.

What then did neutralist mediation efforts accomplish?
In the Himalayan crisis, as in other diplomatic conflicts involving the risk of a Cold War confrontation and perhaps
of a nuclear war, the neutralist states served as catalytic
agents facilitating a *détente*. They showed ample awareness that any acceptable solution had to take into account
clashing national interests and security needs; their proposals grew out of a search for points at which India's and
Red China's diplomatic interests coincided. Thus, if it
demonstrated nothing else, the Colombo mediation attempt proved that the diplomatic activities of nonaligned
states rested upon more durable foundations than naïveté,
lack of diplomatic realism, indifference toward global issues, or other simplistic explanations sometimes advanced
to explain the attachment to the neutralist idea. If India
and other nonaligned nations were not frightened out of
their diplomatic credo by Peking's aggressiveness, this
was in part because the parties to the controversy, the major Cold War belligerents, and the neutralist community
all recognized the congruence of idealism and of diplomatic necessity that engendered and perpetuated support

for nonalignment as a viable philosophy of foreign relations.[15]

Safeguarding and Extending the Neutralist Movement

Earlier, we called attention to the neutralist belief that
nonalignment is a growing and increasingly influential
global force. As the Himalayan crisis indicated, neutralist
countries are determined that it shall remain so, and they
are resolved to win new converts within the family of nations.

Neutralists have long been convinced that their ideology
is opposed by both the West and the Communist bloc. In
their view, both Cold War power blocs have sought to undermine and discredit the neutralist movement. Egyptian
publications have frequently complained about the "pressures" and "intimidations" directed against neutralist
countries by Washington and Moscow. A delegate from
Guinea to the U.N. publicly deplored the existence of a
"whispering campaign" against neutralist countries, in
which their *bona fides* was impugned by allegations that
they were diplomatically "naïve," or that they were motivated merely by "expediency" in their relations with East
and West, or that their "so-called neutralism" could not
conceal their underlying sympathies and affinities. Indian
sources have complained about Western attempts to
"quarantine" India, and about an apparent State Department belief that "a judicious mixture of tact, sympathy,
and stringless aid would achieve what Mr. Dulles' bluster
failed to accomplish—the conversion of the nonaligned
powers into willing and enthusiastic allies." [16]

These threats to the neutralist cause, whether real or
imagined (and we shall examine the validity of such apprehensions in later chapters), are believed in Belgrade,

Accra, Cairo, and New Delhi to be grave and continuing. It is therefore incumbent upon neutralist countries to preserve and strengthen the cohesion and integrity of their movement in the face of hostile moves against it. A Moroccan official has observed: "By simply refusing to be 'easy customers'" in the diplomatic market place, "the new nations will remove some ground from the realm of the Cold War." [17]

But merely remaining steadfast in attachment to nonalignment is not sufficient. A leading goal of neutralist countries, a prominent Indian official has declared, is to persuade "other countries also to remain unaligned." [18] This objective was highlighted by Marshal Tito's visit to Latin America late in 1963. That the prospects for winning converts to nonalignment were not unpromising was indicated by earlier Latin American participation (if only as "observers") at the Belgrade Conference, by mounting evidence of greater "independence" in the foreign policy of key Latin American states like Brazil, and by over-all Latin American unwillingness to follow docilely in the State Department's wake on such major international issues as Castroism. Against this background, said a *New York Times* reporter, Tito had set out to win "new partners for . . . the nonalignment policy." President de Gaulle's visit to the same region in 1964 gave momentum to this movement. One of the major tenets of Gaullist policy— that the world should not be "split up purely and simply by two foreign hegemonies," the United States and the Soviet Union—found an increasingly receptive audience through Latin America. De Gaulle's insistence upon *l'indépendance* in French foreign policy, and his attempt to achieve *la dignité* for a long-subordinated French nation, closely parallels leading tenets in the neutralist credo.[19]

Efforts to widen the compass of the neutralist zone have also led exponents of nonalignment to propose neutralism

(in some cases, "neutralization") as one method of resolving troublesome international issues and of limiting
Cold War conflicts. This strategy has taken several forms.
Neutralist countries have called upon both Cold War
camps to respect the decision of countries (like Cambodia)
to follow a neutralist course; or they have insisted, for
countries that have had "neutralization" imposed upon
them (Austria and Laos), that the great powers abide by
the terms of their own agreements and cease endeavoring
to "align" such countries with their respective Cold War
systems. In still other cases, notably South Korea and
South Vietnam, Afro-Asian neutralists anticipated by several years General de Gaulle's suggestion that such countries be "neutralized" in order to insulate them from Cold
War power contests.*

Neutralist nations have not been content merely to suggest such proposals to the great powers. India, above all,
has assumed the burden of serving on bodies like the International Control Commission, established in 1954 to
safeguard the independence of Laos. In 1961, New Delhi
offered to supply a contingent of military forces to maintain Laotian security.[20] Then, in 1964, India joined other
neutralist countries in calling for a new great-power conference to put a stop to renewed hostilities in this turbulent
Asian country.

Since the Laotian experience, American officials have
become more skeptical than ever about the value of either

---

* Although Cambodia has repeatedly sought to have its neutralist position "guaranteed" by great-power agreement, neutralists are generally
opposed to such guarantees. Neutralist Premier Souvanna Phouma of
Laos expressed this view when he said in 1961 that Laos wanted the
great powers to "recognize her neutrality rather than guarantee it." In
his opinion, great-power "guarantees" invited great-power interventionism
in the affairs of the country involved, which was precisely what Laos
wished to avoid. See *Asian Recorder*, VII (June 18–24, 1961), 4014.
Laotian independence, said the Indian Defense Minister, must be assured
by the Laotians themselves. "Neutrality by military guarantees would be
worse than the disease." (*Times of India*, May 21, 1961.)

"neutralism" or "neutralization" in promoting stability and security in tension-ridden areas like Southeast Asia. By the mid-1960's, events in Laos and in nearby Cambodia—where the position of the West was rapidly deteriorating, as it was declining in neighboring South Vietnam—increased apprehensions about Gaullist or other proposals designed to "neutralize" Southeast Asia against both Communist and Western control. That the International Control Commission (consisting of India, Poland, and Canada) had been conspicuously unsuccessful in preventing political and military instability in Laos was too obvious to be denied, even by the advocates of nonalignment. Neutralist and American assessments about *why* the ICC's efforts proved futile, however, tended to diverge sharply.

Neutralist observers have claimed (with considerable validity) that American, fully as much as Communist, intervention in Laos subverted the Geneva accord of 1954. The members of the ICC could not be expected to "guarantee" the impossible—which appeared to be, in the State Department's view, that the Communist-led Pathet Lao would not win the loyalty and support of the Laotian masses. The Pathet Lao grew up as an offshoot of the nationalist movement against French colonialism in Indochina. It is regarded by nearly all the neutralist states as essentially a nationalist, anticolonialist force, despite its ties with Communist regimes in North Vietnam, Red China, and the Soviet Union. The most that "guaranteed" neutralization could be expected to achieve in Laos was the prevention of overt *external* intervention. It could not ensure internal unity for the country and put an end to internecine political contests; most certainly it could not ensure the emergence of a pro-Western, anti-Communist regime wholly acceptable to the West. Indian officials deplored efforts by both East and West to supply and encourage their partisans in Laos—a course that could have no other result than the total subversion of the Geneva agreement of 1954 and the conversion of Laos into a new Cold War battlefield.

A few weeks before his death, Prime Minister Nehru reiterated his long-standing conviction that the Laotian controversy was "really for the big powers to decide." If the great powers could not formulate and adhere to a workable settlement for Laos, India and the other members of the ICC assuredly could not do so. Even so, Indian spokesmen have gradually acknowledged that in the future nonaligned states will have to couple their support for the principle of neutralism or "neutralization" with more active steps designed to make it, and keep it, a reality. In 1961, Lyndon Johnson, then Vice President, also urged New Delhi to exert more leadership in safeguarding the security of vulnerable nations "in a Communist-threatened region." And in 1964, an Indian Member of Parliament wrote:

> where neighboring Asian governments endorse a certain course of action they assume a special and separate responsibility for it. India and each Asian country that endorses Cambodian neutrality must, at the same time, bear separate and special responsibility to uphold it, so that American or U.N. men and money step in only as auxiliaries.

In his later years, Nehru was openly skeptical of such proposals. In the face of American accusations about Indian "lack of realism" and "innocence" in world affairs, he discounted a suggestion that Southeast Asian countries jointly endeavor to "contain" Chinese expansionism, saying: "I would like to see a list of these countries and the strength they have to find out if they can contain anything, including themselves." In the last analysis, Nehru realized perhaps better than many of his detractors that the responsibility for "guaranteeing" the integrity of neighboring states implied economic and military *resources* that India, along with most other neutralist countries, did not possess.[21]

Finally, let us look briefly at neutralist diplomatic activities with regard to great-power military alliances and spheres of influence. On the eve of his nation's independence, Kenya's Tom Mboya declared that Kenya refused "to be involved in the East-West power controversy and nuclear or other competition" between rival Cold War power blocs. Citing the examples of the British bases at Suez and on Cyprus, and the French base at Bizerte, Mboya rejected any suggestion that the British might be given access to a military base in Kenya after the country received independence.[22]

Translating such general assessments into specific diplomatic goals has led neutralist countries to emphasize three objectives. One has been to reject, and to condemn strongly, policies based upon the Western theory of the military or diplomatic "power vacuum"—a concept Western governments have applied particularly to the Arab world in recent years. Few Western ideas have encountered such uniform and militant neutralist opposition as the concept of the power vacuum. Nasser has said that nonaligned states "have no need for the protection of either the Eastern or Western blocs. We have no need for instructions issued to us by either the East or the West." Even neutralist regimes normally friendly toward the West have agreed with Nasser, as when the governments of Jordan and Saudi Arabia joined with Egypt in 1957 in

> not recognizing the vacuum theory. It was agreed that Arab nationalism was the only principle on which account could be taken in their countries, and that their countries could not become spheres of influence for any foreign Power.

Neutralist objections to the power vacuum theory, however, were perhaps most poignantly expressed by an Indian commentator, who said:

> We are told by the West that there is now a moral as well as a military vacuum in the Middle East. According to the Western notion, any rich areas without some Western Power or other occupying it, or dominating the spot, is a vacuum.[23]

Hand in hand with opposition to the idea of the power vacuum have gone neutralist attempts to prevent the extension of Cold War alliance systems to unwilling countries, and to disengage nonaligned countries from Cold War military commitments which were often made without their consent. The former strategy has been especially pronounced in Asia, in neutralist opposition to SEATO. Neutralists feel that Western nations have tried to impose SEATO's "protection" upon unwilling countries and have endeavored to draw nonaligned countries into active participation in the organization. Even after Red China's attack against India, Prime Minister Nehru reiterated his opposition to Indian membership in SEATO and declared, "We do not expect any ground troops from any other country" on Indian soil. Arab neutralists have taken much the same view of CENTO,* seeing "foreign occupation or the subjecting of Arabs to the exigencies of Western Cold War strategy" as a "negation of Arab freedom." [24]

Such assessments derive fully as much from neutralist doubts about the *effectiveness* of alliance systems like SEATO and CENTO as from objections to them in principle. Thus, after noting SEATO's largely ineffectual efforts to bring about military and political stability in Asia, a resolution passed by the Indian Council on World Affairs

---

* CENTO (the Central Treaty Organization) was the successor to the Baghdad Pact system in the Middle East. It was established in 1959, after Iraq defected from the Baghdad Pact.

concluded: "Its military advantages are dubious; its effects on internal politics unstabilizing; its social repercussions suspect; and its result on national and military morals weakening." [25]

The latter objective—disengaging neutralist countries from military ties with Cold War belligerents—has led to efforts designed to liquidate military bases on neutralist soil. "It is inconceivable," said an official Moroccan publication in 1959, that "Morocco should be bound by political or military agreements which it did not make." Morocco's subsequent demand for the closing down of U.S. air bases in the country thus grew out of belief that the agreement establishing these bases (made between France and the United States while Morocco was still a dependency) infringed the nation's sovereignty and inevitably involved it in Cold War antagonisms.[26] Iraq, Saudi Arabia, Libya, and Tunisia have also demanded the liquidation of foreign military bases on their soil.

Neutralist opposition to the presence of foreign bases in no sense denotes indifference to the problem of national security and defense, lack of understanding of the role of military force in international affairs, or support for the Gandhian principle of nonviolence. Even Indian officials have conceded that renunciation of force is not possible in foreign relations and that it sometimes has to be used as a "last resort," as in Goa or against Red China. Egyptian spokesmen have similarly stated that a policy of military weakness would "result in the neutralists' lowering their guard at the moment they can least afford to do so." Recurrent crises—those between the Arabs and Israel, and in Kuwait, the Congo, and Tunisia—have made it clear that military weakness . . . would court disaster; strength might prevent occupation and invasion." [27]

This precept has been slow to infuse neutralist policy-making, especially in India. But even belated recognition that military force is a vital instrument of foreign policy has not altered opposition to *foreign* military installations, whose presence creates a continual risk of global nuclear war. Nonaligned nations themselves rely upon armed force, as in India's absorption of Goa, Indonesia's "confrontation" with Malaysia, Iraq's attempts to incorporate Kuwait, Algeria's intrigue against Morocco, and Ethiopia's quarrel with Somalia. Nevertheless, with respect to the great powers, the neutralist outlook remains that of Julius Nyerere of Tanganyika, who told the British Foreign Office: "If we fight our own wars we shall fight them with bows and arrows and we shall thank God we are not a civilized people!" [28]

IV

Disarmament and the United Nations

This chapter is devoted to two topics that are at the forefront of neutralist diplomatic concern: the tortuous quest for arms reduction and the evolution of the United Nations. Here, as elsewhere, it is neither possible nor necessary to enter into an evaluation of the problems of disarmament or of international organization per se. Our inquiry centers upon the viewpoints and activities of the neutralist community and upon the impact of the nonaligned nations in these key areas of international concern.

The Neutralists and Arms Control

On the outcome of disarmament negotiations, Prime Minister Abubakar Balewa of Nigeria said in 1961, "hangs the peace of the world and the happiness of mankind." Earlier, President Kwame Nkrumah of Ghana asked:

Yet what do we Africans see when we look abroad? We see wealthy nations pouring out their vast treasury on sterile arms. We see powerful peoples engaged in a futile and destructive armaments race. We see the precious capital that might help raise up Africa and Asia flung away to potential destruction. What has this to do with the Christian charity

100

proclaimed by the West? Or the human brotherhood we hear so much about from the East? Seen from the angle of Africa's needs and hopes, the Great Powers' rivalry looks like one thing only—a senseless fratricidal struggle to destroy the very substance of humanity.

"Power corrupts, atomic power corrupts absolutely," an Indian editorial commented. And an Indonesian source has asserted: "The present arms race is already curtailing to a great extent the economic development of the under-industrialized countries of the world by diverting the needed capital to building up ever vaster arsenals of bombs and missiles." [1]

As with one voice, proponents of nonalignment have echoed the view of Prime Minister Nehru that disarmament is an "urgent and vital problem" and a prerequisite for the creation of an effective world order. [2] Neutralist concern with the problem of arms control has taken several specific forms—none more important perhaps than the demand that serious disarmament negotiations *proceed,* that they not be permitted to stagnate in an atmosphere of Cold War recriminations or of hopelessness engendered by the lack of positive results. The field of disarmament negotiations, said a Yugoslav source in 1962, had become "poisoned and overgrown with weeds of antagonism and distrust for more than a decade." Owing to the diplomatic activities of neutralist countries, however, the "door is . . . being opened" and the "pre-conditions" created for long overdue progress in the reduction of global armaments. As Nehru declared at the Belgrade Conference, if the great powers "refuse to negotiate then they must inevitably go to war. There is no choice. I am amazed and surprised that rigid and proud attitudes are taken up by great countries, all being too high and mighty to negotiate for peace. . . . It is not their pride which is involved, it is the future of the human race." [3]

On the disarmament question, as on a variety of other international issues, neutralist states conceive of their role as what a Ceylonese observer described as a "golden bridge" between East and West. Neutralist countries must not only support the principle of disarmament; they must also, according to King Mohammed V of Morocco, "unite their action so as to play a dominant part in the disarmament discussions on which the future of humanity depends." And in 1961, Marshal Tito argued that with neutralist participation in disarmament proceedings, "the great powers will be able and, in a sense, bound to adjust their views to the objective need for a solution of the problem of disarmament." [4]

Such neutralist demands have not gone unheeded. Following a protracted deadlock in disarmament negotiations, the great powers accepted a proposal (first made by the Soviet Union) that the disarmament proceedings be broadened to eighteen members to include eight nations (Brazil, Burma, Ethiopia, India, Mexico, Nigeria, Sweden, and Egypt) that represented the neutralist point of view. This new forum met for the first time in Geneva on March 14, 1962.

At Belgrade, the assembled neutralists agreed that it was "essential that an agreement on the prohibition of all nuclear and thermonuclear tests should be urgently concluded . . . the moratorium on the testing of all nuclear weapons should be resumed and observed by all countries." Few issues in contemporary international affairs have elicited such widespread and vocal neutralist concern as the matter of nuclear weapons testing. And nothing has engendered more public and official skepticism about the diplomatic implications of nonalignment, particularly among American observers, than neutralist diplomatic attitudes and behavior with respect to this problem. In the American view, the neutralist response to nuclear testing by the United States and the Soviet Union is a distressing example of the "double standard" that apparently governs neutralist attitudes toward East and West. Before further evaluating the question of the so-called double standard, however, it is necessary that we understand neutralist viewpoints on nuclear testing correctly.

Neutralist sentiment from Ghana to Indonesia is overwhelmingly opposed to *any* nuclear tests and favors a great-power agreement prohibiting such experiments. The feeling of the nonaligned countries was summed up by Nehru in 1961: "I am . . . against nuclear tests any time in any place." [5] After prolonged, and at times seemingly futile, negotiations, a permanent ban on nuclear testing in the atmosphere, outer space, and under water, was concluded on August 5, 1963, by the United States, the U.S.S.R., and the United Kingdom. By the end of the year, ninety-nine countries (with the notable exceptions of France and Red China) had subscribed to the test-ban accord.

Neutralists are deeply concerned about nuclear testing for a number of reasons, a major one being the belief that Afro-Asian societies are much more susceptible to the dangers of radioactive fallout than are Western or Communist societies. A combination of geographical location, prevailing winds and climate, and dietary habits, said Nehru, made the neutralist community "more vulnerable to the effects of strontium-90 than the people of the better-fed countries." Neutralist nations are also convinced that the problem of ever-increasing quantities of devastating arms must not be allowed to grow while efforts are being made to evolve a workable disarmament plan. Cessation of nuclear testing would reverse the deadly armaments spiral and offer a first step toward agreement on other issues that must be resolved. [6]

The serious charge that neutralist nations apply a double standard in judging the nuclear-test activities of the West and the Communist bloc followed the failure of the Belgrade Conference in 1961 to condemn Soviet violation of an existing test-ban moratorium. During the conference, the Kremlin announced its intention not only to resume nuclear experiments, but to explode a 55-megaton atmospheric bomb that would produce the greatest fallout hitherto experienced in tests. In a remarkable example of understatement, U.N. Ambassador Stevenson observed that the Kremlin's decision did not produce "the kind of indignation among the nonaligned peoples that one would expect." [7] To the chagrin of Americans, the neutralists assembled at Belgrade seemed to equate the Kremlin's conduct with American underground testing of devices that produced little or no contamination; the neutralist reaction seemed to be that the Soviet decision was no worse than (and perhaps not as heinous as) such manifestations of "Western colonialism" as the American military base at Guantanamo Bay.

In answering such criticism, neutralist spokesmen have called attention to the fact that the neutralist response to the Soviet resumption of nuclear testing was far more outspoken and more sharply critical than Americans were led to believe. Marshal Tito, for example, called the Soviet act "brutal"; Nehru labeled it a "very harmful, disastrous thing that brings about a war psychosis." [*] The Belgrade

---

[*] Archbishop Makarios of Cyprus said he was "shocked to hear that the Soviet Union had declared its intention to resume nuclear tests." A dispatch prominently featured in the *Iraq Times* called attention to "A widespread private feeling among delegates [at Belgrade] . . . that the action gravely increased the dangers of war." The *Times of India* severely criticized the Kremlin because its action "shows the contempt in which it holds not only those who distrust it but those who put their trust in its good faith"; the Soviet Union reflected "open defiance of world opinion" and seemed intent upon "alienating its friends." The *Hindustan Times* likewise found the Soviet move "a threat to committed and uncommitted alike" and an attempt to "create an impression of overwhelming power

Conference (which, as we noted in a previous chapter, accepted Nehru's "moderate" approach to global issues, over Indonesia's and Ghana's "agitational" approach) was also guided by the principle that had been followed in the cases of the Hungarian revolution and the Chinese absorption of Tibet. This was that little was to be gained by totally alienating the Soviet Union or Red China. If a *détente* between East and West on disarmament and other Cold War issues was to be brought about, it was imperative that relations between the neutralist world and the great powers remain free from the recriminations and mutual suspicions that had long impeded progress toward the ultimate goal—an operative test-ban accord prohibiting all nuclear explosions.

If the volume and intensity of neutralist opposition to Soviet testing did not reach the level that Americans thought appropriate, neutralist spokesmen underscored two additional factors that had to be considered in judging the neutralist response. One of these was the fact (either ignored or imperfectly understood by American critics) that France, not the U.S.S.R., initially broke the moratorium on nuclear testing. Paris began nuclear experiments in the Sahara on February 13, 1961, and exploded a second nuclear bomb on April 1. If the Kremlin was contemptuous of global opinion, a leading Western power had been no less contemptuous. Yet American opinion was curiously unmoved by de Gaulle's conduct, and Washington was apparently impotent to control it. Even nonaligned countries normally friendly toward the United States were thus led to deplore what seemed like an Ameri-

---

which is likely to be used without any moral scruples." For these and other reactions to the Kremlin's decision, see: *Times of India,* September 2 and 4, 1961; *Hindustan Times* (overseas edition), November 9, 1961; *Egyptian Gazette,* November 10, 1961; *Iraq Times,* September 4, 6, and 14, 1961; and *The New York Times,* July 29, 1962.

can double standard in dealing with the actions of an ally and with those of the Communist bloc. Washington's failure to protest against French testing in Africa was widely construed by neutralist nations as another indication of American indifference to neutralist sensibilities on a deeply felt issue.*

This brings us to a second consideration that has loomed large in explaining neutralist conduct. On the issue of nuclear-weapons testing, as on a multitude of other international issues, if Soviet policy-makers clearly were not deterred by neutralist objections, at least they endeavored to make their decision as palatable as possible to the neutralist community. Contrary to American belief, Moscow's decision came as no surprise to the Belgrade conclave. Soviet Premier Khrushchev had sent a personal letter to all participating countries, informing them of the decision and of its reasons. Here, as on other occasions, said Cambodia's Prince Sihanouk, Moscow's approach was one of "smiles, consideration, and deference" in dealing with nonaligned countries. In most instances, the leader of Cambodia declared, in its relations with nonaligned nations, "the Soviet Union . . . has . . . taken the greatest care not to threaten them, to get tough with them or even to reproach them." [8] Now, as we shall see in more detail in Chapter 5, this did not mean that proponents of nonalignment were unaware of the Soviet Union's diplomatic goals or that they were ignorant of the Kremlin's skill in disguising its objectives

---

* Thus, Saudi Arabia's delegate to the United Nations found it "highly amazing" that the United States had made little or no protest about France's nuclear-testing in the Sahara. The Council for Nuclear Disarmament in Ghana stated that American indignation about neutralist "failure" to condemn the Soviet Union would be more understandable if there had been comparable American protest about French nuclear tests, in the face of widespread African opposition. See the speeches cited in *Egyptian Gazette*, October 4, 1961, and the *Iraq Times*, September 8, 1961; see also the summary of viewpoints at the Belgrade meeting in *Straits Times* (Singapore), September 4, 1961.

by resorting to tactical shifts designed to ingratiate itself with other countries. It simply meant that, for whatever reason, the Kremlin's solicitude for neutralist opinion often contrasted markedly with the patronizing, suspicious, and hypercritical attitude displayed by American and other Western policy-makers in their dealings with nations in the neutralist zone.

So far as other issues associated with the disarmament question are concerned, we may say that neutralist policy has tended to avoid two extremes. After neutralist countries joined the Geneva deliberations in 1962, their conduct was far less "irresponsible," demagogic, and disruptive than some Western commentators expected. Nor has their participation in the Geneva disarmament talks proved as "revolutionary" in radically altering the course of the proceedings and in removing entrenched roadblocks in the path of agreement as many neutralist countries themselves anticipated. On a wide range of collateral and interrelated questions—the problem of inspection and control, the sequence of "stages" to be established for reducing the level of global armaments, the scope of proposed schemes in terms of weapons, troops, and other military elements to be included, the problem of maintaining an approximate military "equilibrium" between East and West during all phases of implementation—the neutralist nations have in nearly all cases shunned simplistic and totally impractical schemes in favor of serious efforts to discover common ground between the demands of East and West. Nor have they sought to maintain an arbitrary "equidistance" between Western and Communist proposals; diplomatic equidistance, as we have emphasized, is not regarded as a requirement of the neutralist credo. On some issues, therefore, nonaligned countries have supported Communist proposals, on some issues Western proposals, and on still other issues, their own proposals—

which means that they have disagreed with both the East and the West.

What has been the neutralist approach to such concrete (and, in the American view, vital) questions as inspection and control? Almost invariably, neutralist voices have called for "general and complete disarmament . . . guaranteed by an effective system of inspection and control" (to cite the Belgrade Conference declaration). Along with this demand has gone a mounting neutralist insistence that inspection teams should "include members of nonaligned nations." [9] These two themes—the necessity for a workable inspection system and the contribution to be made by nonaligned countries in policing any disarmament agreement—are fully compatible with U.S. insistence that foolproof inspection is the crux of the disarmament problem, especially as it relates to Communist compliance with any agreement reached.

Nor have neutralist attitudes diverged sharply from American in their endorsement of a stage-by-stage approach to arms reduction, during which methods of inspection and control would be "tested" before substantial quantities of arms are destroyed. In whatever degree neutralist and Communist views on the principle of "general and complete disarmament" have coincided, nearly all nonaligned nations have recognized that the goal remains little more than a propaganda device without concrete steps designed to achieve it and to instill confidence that it can be made a reality. Neutralist opinion has tended to regard the nuclear-test-ban treaty of 1963 as a promising first step in this direction.

In other particulars, the neutralist approach has more closely paralleled the Soviet position on disarmament. Although they have supported the principle of effective inspection, for example, neutralist states have agreed with the U.S.S.R. that it was possible to make limited progress in actually *reducing* armaments without awaiting great-power agreement on all the details of (1) an inspection-control system, or (2) the precise requirements and sequences of each "stage" to be followed in implementing an arms-reduction plan. Believing that a breakthrough had to be made somewhere in the deadly cycle of rising armaments levels, and that some kind of dramatic initial step was required to inspire mutual trust among Cold War belligerents, neutralist countries have favored schemes, such as the one advanced by India in 1964, for destruction of a *limited* quantity of missiles on both sides of the Iron Curtain, even though no agreement had been reached on other collateral disarmament questions. Similarly, neutralist observers like U.N. Secretary General U Thant have criticized the great powers (by implication, chiefly the West) for making a fetish of inspection and control and for engaging in "a game of arithmetic" about the number of control posts needed, instead of working out their differences for the good of humanity.

On still other questions, neutralist countries have taken positions that differed from, and sometimes involved open disagreement with, some or all aspects of Western and Communist proposals. They have strongly opposed the "proliferation" of nuclear weapons—a demand that accords with the expressed policies of the United States and the U.S.S.R. They have criticized both great powers for assisting in (or, at a minimum, not actively opposing) the development of nuclear weapons by France and Red China. And, in the face of both adamant American opposition and waning Soviet enthusiasm, they have demanded that Red China be included in disarmament proceedings.[10] The African nations have made a further demand. At a meeting at Addis Ababa on May 22–25, 1963, the Conference of Independent African States unanimously agreed to coordinate efforts "to declare and accept Africa as a denuclearized zone" and to support "the banning of nuclear weapons and thermonuclear tests . . . and the banning of the manufacture of nuclear weapons." [11] Left-wing, pro-Western, and traditional regimes in Africa have thus joined in endeavoring to remove the entire African continent from the arena of nuclear competition. By 1963, this idea had begun to gain converts in Latin America, where five states—Bolivia, Chile, Ecuador, Mexico, and Brazil—proposed a comparable scheme for the "denuclearization" of the Caribbean and Central and South America. Not unexpectedly, the Soviet Union has consistently endorsed such proposals. The United States has either openly opposed them or been lukewarm toward them, on the grounds that they failed to provide for effective enforcement, that they infringed the rights of individual states to provide for their own defense, and that a continent could not be "isolated" from world-wide military tendencies and developments. [12]

Our brief appraisal of the role of nonaligned countries in disarmament negotiations permits certain concluding observations. Unquestionably, neutralist nations have furnished the impetus for limited progress in resolving some of the vexatious issues surrounding the problem of arms control. The pressure from the nonaligned countries upon the great powers was a major influence in producing the nuclear-test-ban accord of 1963, in the U.N. agreement to prohibit military competition in outer space, and in narrowing the differences between American and Soviet proposals on questions like international inspection and control. Moreover, the behavior of the neutralist states at Geneva had been a decisive influence in altering executive department (if not always legislative and public) viewpoints in the United States about the implications of nonalignment as a global force. Thus in 1962, the State Department affirmed that the eighteen-nation Geneva conference was "the best forum for disarmament negotiations which has been utilized since World War II." It found that the nonaligned states participating in the disarmament proceedings were making "a responsible contribution to the deliberations."

Executive policy-makers in the United States had come to see several advantages in the Geneva approach. It "provided the United States with an unusual opportunity to communicate its views to the other nations present and to demonstrate its own sincere desire for meaningful disarmament agreement." At the same time, it revealed (as debates in the U.N. frequently did not) that the Soviet approach was "superficial and propagandistic." The Geneva forum was regarded as "one of the best available methods of prevailing upon the Soviet Union to accept its responsibility to heed the conscience and aspirations of the world community." American policy-makers have also commented on the "increasing realism" shown by neutralist participants in approaching the complexities inherent in the problem of disarmament. The Geneva method, according to an authoritative study of American policy, had fostered "an increased awareness among the neutrals of the real difficulties inherent in East-West negotiations." If the neutralist countries had not produced a panacea for breaking the prolonged disarmament deadlock, neither had they displayed the "irresponsibility" widely feared in the West, nor had they revealed a congenital preference for the proposals advanced by the Communist bloc. Perhaps their principal contribution was that they brought a fresh approach to stale diplomatic proceedings and provided a new stimulus to the great powers to reach agreement on a transcendent international issue.[13]

The Neutralist Community and the U.N.

Discussing the role of Afro-Asian countries in the United Nations, in 1964, an Indian commentator recalled the words of Secretary General Dag Hammarskjöld:

> It is natural for old and well-established countries to see in the U.N. a limitation on their sovereignty. It is just as natural that a young country, a country emerging on the world scene, should find in the U.N. an addition to its sovereignty, an added means of speaking to the world.

By 1964, said an Indian observer, nonaligned nations believed that the U.N. was "least likely to impair their freedom; consequently they approach it with confidence for the solution of their problems, and indeed rely heavily upon it." "We believe," said Prime Minister Balewa of Nigeria in 1961, that "the United Nations Organization is the only one sure guarantee of preserving the sovereignty of all states that are weak." A year later, after a visit to Washington, the Prime Minister declared that problems like Berlin, Angola, disarmament, and other vital issues "should be brought before the United Nations where all member states can genuinely make their contribution to their solution in the interest of mankind generally." And in the same year, the Foreign Minister of Burma commemorated the seventeenth anniversary of the U.N. with these words:

> To realize what this Organization means to us, we of the smaller countries, and particularly those of us who refuse to become associated with any political-military bloc, have only to think for a moment what our situation would be like today if the United Nations ceased to exist. This is why Burma has always been a firm believer in the United Nations, and a loyal adherent of its Charter.[14]

The dominant theme in these remarks is, of course, massive, not to say at times rhapsodic, support for the United Nations, and recognition that there is an inseparable connection between the influence of nonaligned countries in global affairs and the effective functioning of the U.N. The voice of the neutralist world will be heeded, said an Indian source, "only to the extent that it emanates openly from a third force in the United Nations. Military nonalignment with the contending power blocs should be accompanied by a firm commitment to promote the objectives announced at Belgrade through the closest cooperation among the neutralist countries in the United Nations." [15]

It would be difficult to exaggerate the neutralist impact upon the United Nations. At the end of 1964, the U.N. contained 112 members—of which 54, almost a majority, considered themselves "neutralist" or "nonaligned" in the Cold War.* We have already emphasized that the neutralist community is far from being a cohesive, monolithic bloc, either in the U.N. or outside it. Policy differences among neutralist countries sometimes rival those between the United States and the U.S.S.R. At the same time, on certain issues the neutralist nations display a high degree of unity. If nonaligned countries tend to be among the most outspoken supporters of the principle of international organization, and if they recognize fully the U.N.'s value to their own security, they are also reasonably united on other points. One of these is that indispensable as the

* As always, the problem of defining neutralism or nonalignment involves certain arbitrary judgments about its meaning and scope. In our calculation, following criteria set forth in Chapter 1, all except one of these fifty-four countries (Yugoslavia) is in the Afro-Asian-Arab world. If we regard Ireland, Switzerland, Sweden, Finland, and Austria as "neutralist" or "nonaligned" (which they certainly are not in an *ideological* sense, at least), then the General Assembly of the U.N. is controlled by a majority of countries adhering neither to the West nor to the Communist bloc.

one reason?
Veto

U.N. is, it has not yet played the role in global affairs it is capable of assuming. Another is that this fact places a unique responsibility on neutralist nations to increase the U.N.'s effectiveness, sometimes in the face of great-power opposition. Indeed, some neutralist sources are convinced that if it is to survive and prosper, the U.N. needs the neutralist countries fully as much as they need it. If they can keep their efforts from becoming the "target of sabotage from interested power blocs," said a Burmese source in 1960, then "the Afro-Asian group . . . has a great future in this promising international setting." At the same time, widespread neutralist support could be found for President Nkrumah's idea that the neutralist nations faced genuine difficulties in endeavoring to convert the U.N. into "an effective instrument for world peace." [16]

Let us examine three of the issues that reveal significant aspects of the neutralist outlook and diplomatic approach, and that permit an assessment in brief compass of several important implications of the trend toward nonalignment. These are: colonialism, the question of "bloc" voting and attitudes within the U.N., and suggestions for the "reorganization" of the United Nations, including the Soviet troika proposal.

Colonialism

"Yes or no—are you for the liberation of Africa?" Upon the answer to this question, said President Touré, would hinge Guinea's relations with East and West. A Yugoslav commentator called the organization's role as an anticolonial force "the most characteristic and most important element" in the evolution of the U.N., and noted that "the conception of anticolonialism and . . . the nonaligned policy have been identified in a single doctrine." [17] Such statements call attention to a major reason for focusing upon colonialism as an issue illustrating neutralist viewpoints and behavior: Anticolonialism is possibly the strongest bond uniting African, Arab, and Asian countries behind a policy of nonalignment, and fostering their determination to utilize their newly acquired strength in the U.N. for eliminating colonialism wherever it still exists.

Colonialism provides an illuminating case study for examining the nature and implications of neutralism for another reason, reflected in a headline in *The New York Times* in August, 1962: "Colonial Dispute Points Up Accord Between Soviet and Afro-Asians." The accompanying dispatch voiced a long-standing American complaint about the "working alliance between the Soviet Union and certain African-Asian members in exploiting the new United Nations machinery for attacks on the colonial powers." [18] As much as any other contemporary international issue, the colonial question has engendered deep uneasiness in the American mind about the meaning of diplomatic nonalignment, especially as it implies neutralist support for, or cooperation with, the Communist bloc. Conversely, perhaps no issue has elicited greater neutralist skepticism about the principles actuating American foreign policy than the problem of colonialism.

On three subordinate issues implicit in the larger colonial question—the liquidation of existing colonial systems, the steps to be taken in dealing with racist policies in the Rhodesias and South Africa, and the measures designed to deal with postcolonial political turbulence, chiefly in the Congo—the verdict must be that in its relations with the neutralist world, the United States has suffered a series of greater and lesser diplomatic defeats on the first two questions, and that it has achieved a moderate diplomatic victory on the third. On balance, American diplomatic losses have heavily outweighed gains, although by the mid-1960's, neutralist spokesmen acknowledged that new tendencies were discernible in the American approach to colonial issues.

Throughout the greater part of the postwar period, the

colonial question has been in large measure responsible for
the fact that the American dialogue with neutralist countries has been marked by charges and countercharges, mutual suspicion and ill will, disillusionment and emotionalism
—sufficient in some periods to disrupt meaningful communication between neutralist and American spokesmen.
Events revealed that for many years, American and neutralist officials were not, in the popular phrase, on the same
wave length in discussing colonial questions. Why, public
and official sources in the United States were prone to ask,
did champions of nonalignment appear to be ignorant of
the "record of the Western grant of freedom" to nearly
fifty countries, containing nearly one billion people, since
the end of World War II? And why were they so indifferent to expansive "Communist colonialism" that held
millions of people in bondage and still sought to bring
areas like Laos and South Vietnam under its control? One
American U.N. correspondent phrased a question asked
almost daily by American citizens: Why did the neutralists persist in concentrating upon "forms of Western colonial rule which are fast coming to an end," and give "little
or no attention to those much more stubborn and subtle
forms of domination practiced by the Soviet Union . . .
and by Communist China?" Why, this observer asked,
should the neutralists in the U.N. not "be most forceful
and insistent with those who persist most stubbornly in
injustice?" [19]

Confronted in one U.N. session after another with
American accusations of double standards and diplomatic
opportunism, neutralist spokesmen have replied in kind.
For in their view, nothing better illustrates a diplomatic
double standard, or a foreign policy dictated by expediency, or a balancing act, than the American position on
colonialism throughout most of the postwar period. Neutralist policy-makers are fully mindful of America's own

anticolonialist heritage, of its influence during and after World War II in behalf of independence for countries like Indochina, Indonesia, and Syria, and of its consistent endorsement of the Wilsonian principle of self-determination. For these reasons, they thought it all the more inexplicable that the American approach to colonialist questions in the U.N. has consisted of a patchwork of official hesitations, equivocations, qualifications, negative votes, abstentions, and positive votes, adding up to a pattern of diplomatic fence-straddling and tightrope walking. This is the very response that Americans believe "immoral" when practiced by neutralist countries on Cold War issues.*

* The nadir of American relations with neutralist countries on colonialism was perhaps reached in 1960. One observer summarized African reactions by saying: "Those of us who have been friends of the United States are almost ashamed of that fact now. . . . It is detrimental to our position at the U.N. for our representatives to be seen too frequently talking to members of the United States delegation." He continued: "We used to have reservations when the Soviet Union said the U.S. was colonialist. Now we are ready to believe it." And even from African countries friendly to the United States came the judgment that "the United States suffered a disastrous political and ideological defeat" in the 15th General Assembly session. This verdict stemmed from the fact that—in the face of Soviet sponsorship and support for anticolonialist measures—the U.S. delegation either abstained or voted against nearly every significant anticolonialist proposal coming before committees or before the General Assembly itself. Even when neutralist countries took the initiative in watering down certain resolutions to make them palatable to the State Department, the United States still abstained or opposed them. Ironically, on a key resolution on the Algerian controversy, calling merely for U.N. support of the principle of self-determination, France voted for the resolution; the United States abstained. On twenty important votes dealing with colonialism, the U.S.S.R. sided with the anticolonialist majority thirteen times; the United States did so five times—but it sided only once with that majority against its European allies. One issue of apparently vital concern to the United States—keeping Soviet influence out of the Congo—also generated neutralist criticism because of the fact that on this issue, as on others related to colonialism, American concern seemed to be dictated chiefly by anti-Communism, not by interest in the problem per se. The diplomatic "initiative" displayed by the United States on colonial questions contrasted markedly with its initiative in generating U.N. concern for questions like Hungary and Tibet. One extraordinary event testified to this schizophrenic American behavior: After the American dele-

If it was too much to expect America's position on colonialism to be shaped solely by moral and ideological considerations (and neutralist policy-makers were not so naïve as to think that any country's policies can be governed solely by such factors), at least American officials might be expected to recognize certain unalterable realities. One of these was that colonialism was doomed in Asia, the Arab world, and Africa; the only meaningful question was how existing colonial systems could be terminated smoothly and with a maximum residue of goodwill between dependent societies and their former European masters. Another reality was that, in the light of American apathy and equivocation on colonial issues, the Communist bloc was virtually handed a ready-made issue for cementing cordial relations with the neutralist world and for undermining Western influence. And surely one of the most incontestable realities in postwar international affairs has been, as the British experience in India confirmed, that the degree of pro-Westernism in newly independent countries is directly dependent upon the willingness of colonial powers to cooperate in granting freedom to subject peoples. Another reality the United States appeared to ignore was that its position on colonialism had, in neutralist eyes, all but effaced the distinction between the "Free World" and the Communist bloc in dealing with small, defenseless societies.

---

gation, whose members were known to *favor* a resolution calling for the termination of colonialism, was required by State Department direction to vote against it, one U.S. delegate arose after the vote and applauded the majority decision in favor of it! On balance, Afro-Asian countries concluded that the United States was concerned "not primarily with the welfare of Africa," but was determined chiefly "to boost its strategic position in relationship to the Soviet Union." See George M. Houser, "Cause for Concern," *Africa Today*, VIII (January, 1961), 5–6, 10; *New Times of Burma*, July 24, 1960; *The New York Times*, December 18, 1960; C. L. Sulzberger, "To Change Their Image of Us," *The New York Times Magazine*, March 5, 1961, pp. 28, 96–97.

But the paramount reality, to which American policy seemed strangely oblivious, was the fact that anticolonialism is to the neutralist world what anti-Communism is to the United States. Somehow, Americans have never quite understood that the one principle uniting Ghana, Ethiopia, Egypt, Afghanistan, India, Cambodia, and Indonesia is (as an African expressed it) that "we are still at war with colonialism" and that "the face of the enemy is Western." In one nonaligned country after another, the response to the American complaint about neutralist "indifference" to Communism or its tendency to "equate" Communist activities with those of the West has been basically the same. A citizen of Mali said, "we must not forget that it is the NATO powers that we are fighting against." An Algerian remarked: "For six years, we begged the United States to make the French understand. It was no use and now we are turning to the Russians and the Chinese." And a long-time European observer in Africa has commented:

> There's no point screaming "Beware of the Communists." . . . It is not the Communists who are treating Africans like subhumans in South Africa, and it is not the Communists who are shooting Africans in Salisbury. . . . Telling Ghanaians to beware of Communists is like telling a man in a burning house not to go outside because it may start to snow.[20]

The neutralist response to Communist offers of support against colonialism are governed by the old axiom "The enemy of my enemy is my friend"—or, as Winston Churchill said during World War II, if Satan himself opposed Hitler's aggression, then Great Britain would be allied with Satan.

If neutralist states tend to "equate" Western and Communist moves jeopardizing their security, they do so because of an unfortunate but simple truth seldom perceived by the American mind: From Ghana to South Africa and the Rhodesias, to Tunisia, to Egypt and the Suez, to Palestine, to the Arabian Peninsula, to Laos, to Malaysia, the West has sometimes equaled, and more often exceeded, the record of the Communist bloc in threatening the security and freedom of societies in the Afro-Arab-Asian zone. It is therefore no more remarkable that neutralist societies are less concerned about the dangers of Communism than that Americans today are less concerned about the possible revival of Japanese or German militarism than about the present-day threat of Communist intrigue in South Vietnam. American policy-makers naturally are not oblivious to the former threat; but they rank it merely as a *potential* danger. Anyone who suggested to the State Department that the possible revival of Junkerism ought to concern policy-makers as deeply as Communist aggression in Laos would be accused of a total lack of realism. Under the circumstances, the real miracle is that neutralist countries are (or have sometimes become) reasonably pro-Western in their approach to Cold War issues.

By the early 1960's, three developments had begun to reverse the current of alienation between American and neutralist opinion on colonial issues. One of these was the change that became evident in Washington's position on colonial questions—symbolized by the American delegation's support in 1961 for a resolution calling upon Portugal to terminate its "repressive measures" in Angola. This act, at long last, gave unequivocal and tangible expression to President Kennedy's conviction that the United States must ally itself "with the rising tide of nationalism . . . the most powerful force in the modern world." [21] This vote was followed by other positive indications of American support in the neutralist-sponsored campaign against colonialism, such as direct appeals to Portugal to comply with

U.N. demands and an increasingly militant position against apartheid in South Africa.

Second, the American role in dealing with the Congo crisis elicited widespread neutralist admiration. Almost from the beginning of the Congo episode, the United States recognized that a fundamental identity of interests linked it with the neutralist members of the U.N. Both the United States and the neutralists wanted the Congo stabilized, the great powers excluded from the heart of Africa so that a Cold War confrontation could be avoided, and the non-aligned nations to shoulder the burden of "policing" the Congo. If the American treasury subsequently had to pay a substantial part of the cost for the U.N. Congo operation, this was an insignificant price both for avoiding a commitment of American forces and for preventing the intrusion of Soviet "volunteers," whose presence might sooner or later demand new Western "containment" efforts costing millions of dollars more than U.N. peace-keeping entailed.

Third, the very success of the anticolonialist campaign (in winning independence for some fifty new nations) meant that with the passage of time, the colonial question would largely recede as an issue of active international and U.N. concern. By the mid-1960's, only a few large dependencies, notably Angola and Southwest Africa, remained. True, racial discord continued to prevail in South Africa and the Rhodesias; and from all indications, such crises might well become progressively acute. Furthermore, some neutralist states (Guinea, Ghana, Egypt, Iraq, and Indonesia, for example) remained deeply apprehensive about "neocolonialism"; the simmering controversy between Malaysia and Indonesia was merely one dispute that brought such concerns to the fore. Yet with the years, colonialism and neocolonialism were bound to become of less

concern to the neutralists. Gradually, the "colonial mentality" of formerly dependent societies was giving way to
more intimate ties with the West; at the same time, the
West was coming to terms with twentieth-century nationalism and was recognizing neutralist sensitivity on colonial
questions. Serious and largely unnecessary though it may
have been, if the American failure to evoke neutralist admiration for its position on colonialism could not be
erased, it could be overcome. And at least some of the damage could be repaired by new American policies (which we
shall examine more fully in Chapter 6) designed to intro-
duce a new and more constructive dialogue between the
United States and the members of the neutralist community.

Even more than the colonial issue, the threat of a "neu-
talist bloc" capable of controlling the U.N.'s deliberations
and of cooperating with the Communist bloc on a multitude of global issues has caused deep concern in the West.
By the early 1960's, this was extended to the United Nations itself. The activities of the allegedly "irresponsible"
and anti-Western neutralist majority in the U.N. led to demands from congressmen and public commentators that
the United States rely less heavily upon the United Nations
to achieve its foreign-policy goals and that it base its security (in Senator Fulbright's words) primarily upon a
"community of free nations" anchored in the NATO alliance.[22]

At the outset, it must be noted that considerable impre-
cision surrounds discussion of the problem of the so-called
neutralist bloc in the United Nations. Phrases like "neu-
talist bloc," or the broader term "Afro-Asian bloc," tend
to be used loosely—and, in most instances, inaccurately.[*]

Bloc vote

---

[*] The so-called neutralist bloc consists of those countries in the U.N.
that espouse diplomatic nonalignment between East and West; the so-
called Afro-Asian bloc is a larger group, including such countries as Iran,

As we emphasized in Chapter 1, neutralists themselves reject the concept of a separate bloc. Referring to the Belgrade Conference, Prime Minister Nehru declared: "I have consistently opposed the formation of a third bloc. Nobody wanted it there and nobody mentioned it there." During his tour of Latin America in 1963, Tito similarly disclaimed any neutralist intention to form a third bloc in world affairs; like other spokesmen for nonalignment, Tito deprecated the idea of diplomatic blocs per se. In his view, the concept of nonalignment—which assumed the existence of a Western bloc and a Communist bloc with respect to which other countries could remain unaffiliated—was itself becoming outdated, since even the Cold War blocs were rapidly losing their solidarity and cohesion.[23]

Neutralist intentions aside, what has experience in the U.N. revealed about the diplomatic cohesion existing among neutralist countries? Does a neutralist bloc really exist, and if so, does it exhibit a pronounced inclination to join with the Communist bloc to the detriment of Western diplomatic interests? Our inquiry must begin with a question often passed over lightly, or altogether ignored, by those apprehensive about the neutralist role in the U.N.: What is meant by a bloc? All too frequently, as Andrew Boyd has observed, the term is merely an epithet applied

---

Pakistan, Thailand, South Vietnam, North and South Korea, and the Philippines, which maintain formal military and ideological ties with either the West or the Communist bloc. Within these larger groupings, there are also certain geographic and regional "blocs" embracing members of both of the larger groups. One commentator wrote concerning the Belgrade Conference: "The Arabs are pleased over the decision of the Belgrade neutrals not to form a 'third bloc.' The only bloc the Arabs want—and even on this they are not unanimous—is an Arab bloc." (The *New York Herald Tribune*, September 19, 1961, dispatch by H. A. R. Philby.) Among African states, considerable support (along with some opposition) exists for Nkrumah's view: "We are going to see that we create our own African personality and identity; it is the only way in which we can show the world we are masters of our own destiny." (*I Speak of Freedom* [New York: Frederick A. Praeger, 1961], p. 107.)

to any U.N. vote "when it's against you." If the United
States has been defeated in the U.N., it tends to blame the
coalition between the neutralist bloc and the Communist
bloc. Communist policy-makers have long regarded the
U.N. as dominated by the "NATO bloc" or the "aggressive
imperialist camp." In turn, neutralists excoriate both "Cold
War blocs." If our discussion is to rise above the level of
such epithets and simplistic designations, we must define a
"bloc." Boyd had described it as any U.N. group that
acts in "disciplined unison"; Margaret Ball has defined a
bloc as "any group which consistently votes as a unit on
all or particular kinds of issues"; and Furey has added that
"essential to the definition of a bloc is a sense of solidarity
and a definite purpose." [24] Such definitions imply two corollaries: a "bloc" requires a high degree of *unity* in voting
behavior, and a reasonably *predictable* position on closely
related issues before the United Nations.

When "bloc" is so construed, the concept of a "neutralist
bloc" within the U.N. becomes an almost total illusion. In
reality, there are many blocs and voting groups of greater
or lesser cohesiveness; the composition of such groups
changes and overlaps as issues change, and nearly all discernible blocs in the U.N. are held together by regional,
cultural, or other affiliations, rather than by common dedication to a principle such as nonalignment. The outstanding fact about U.N. voting behavior, a British authority
has said, is "the tendency of member states to affiliate differently for different purposes."*

---

* See the views of Sydney Bailey, as cited in Boyd, *op. cit.*, p. 74.
Without entering into the extremely complex statistical computations involved in (1) identifying existing blocs within the U.N., and (2) measur-
ing the degree of cohesiveness among them, we may merely cite some
of the more revealing findings of Arend Lijphart. He believes that "nine
caucusing blocs and groups" within the U.N. can "quite justifiably be
called blocs." Only one—the Soviet Caucusing Bloc—has a consistently
high level of discipline; the others are more properly called "caucusing
groups." Eight of these can be identified: the Afro-Asian, Arab, African,

Let us concede, however, that one limitation inherent in studies of U.N. voting behavior for the purpose of assessing the neutralist role in international affairs is that these studies make no distinction among issues on the basis of their *importance*. They are based on an assumption any intelligent student of foreign relations knows to be untrue —that all U.N. votes are qualitatively comparable, that the consequences for American foreign policy, for example, of an adverse U.N. vote on French Togoland (a vote included in Lijphart's analysis) is as crucial as an adverse U.N. vote on the Soviet troika proposal (which is omitted from his evaluation).* So far as proving or disproving the popular contention that neutralism "consciously or unconsciously favors the Communist cause" is concerned, it is apparent that even if it could be shown that neutralists always vote

---

Benelux, Commonwealth, Latin American, Scandinavian, and Western European Caucusing Groups. A few countries—notably the United States, the Republic of China, Israel, and certain European states—belong to no bloc or group. Relying upon roll-call votes on colonial issues (an arbitrary selection of issues, bound to affect the results obtained), this commentator has found that the Communist bloc has the highest degree of voting cohesion; a group consisting of Iraq, Saudi Arabia, Jordan, and Libya (what we might call a "militant" neutralist, two usually pro-Western neutralists, and a passive neutralist, respectively) showed high cohesion among Arab states. A much less cohesive bloc could be discerned as a coalition between the Communist group and selected Afro-Asian countries, notably Ceylon, Ethiopia, Tunisia, Greece, and Yugoslavia. Again in this latter group, it is interesting to note the presence of a fairly quiescent Asian neutralist, two normally pro-Western neutralists, a West European ally, and a "militant" neutralist that favors the Communist cause ideologically. The study reinforces the views of other authorities that "the Soviet Caucusing Bloc was the only one of these which was also a consistent voting bloc." This study also highlights the difference in the cohesion of regional blocs: the Arab Caucusing Bloc had relatively high cohesion; the African Caucusing Bloc did not. For these and other findings, see Arend Lijphart, "The Analysis of Bloc Voting in the General Assembly," *American Political Science Review*, LVII (December, 1963), pp. 904–17. For other analyses, see the two studies by Thomas Hovet, Jr., *Bloc Politics in the United Nations* (Cambridge, Mass.: Harvard University Press, 1960), and *Africa in the United Nations* (Evanston, Ill.: Northwestern University Press, 1963).

* For a discussion of Lijphart's analysis, see note on p. 124.

with the Communist bloc on questions like French Togo-land, we would still have to decide (1) whether the neutralists were siding with the Communist bloc (or vice versa) and (2) whether five, ten, or twenty such votes could be equated with neutralist support of the American position (or vice versa) on a vital question like the U.N. Congo operation. Another fact that must constantly be kept in mind is that many vital Cold War issues, like Berlin, Laos, and South Vietnam, are not brought before the United Nations—frequently because the United States itself does not want them discussed there.

Faced with deep-seated public and legislative misgivings about the role of neutralist countries in the U.N. and elsewhere, American officials have been prone to emphasize qualitative considerations in evaluating the neutralist impact upon global affairs. Thus, in 1962, Secretary of State Rusk, in replying to perennial American complaints about India's alleged support of the Communist bloc, conceded that India was the "real patriarch of neutralism." He added:

> But I do not believe that applies to commitments on . . . matters of importance to us in terms of the general shape of the international community, and what kind of U.N. we should have and what kind of commitments we should make to law and the processes of law in international relations.[25]

On another occasion, Rusk reminded an audience of President Kennedy's assertion in 1961 that there were really only two groups or blocs in the United Nations. Said Rusk:

> There were those who were trying to build the kind of world laid out in the United Nations Charter, and there were those who were trying to prevent that kind of world from coming into being. And on that underlying issue, there are only two sides . . . in the most fundamental sense our interest, both in allies and in neutrals, is the same—a world community of

independent nations, cooperating voluntarily across national frontiers in the common interest. . . . I think allies and neutrals are together [on this issue]. . . . We have almost instinctive allies wherever we turn in trying to build the kind of world that fits our own traditions. . . .[26]

Ambassador Adlai Stevenson has also underscored the fact that so far as the goal of constructing a viable international organization is concerned, it is in no sense remarkable that the General Assembly majority "supports our view because the spirit and the method of the U.N. are second nature to American Democracy—and basically alien to the habits of dictatorship." Earlier, Stevenson had commented on "one of the great untold stories of the United Nations"—the failure of Communist strategy to pit the neutralist world against the United States and its allies. Noting that none of the accomplishments of the U.N. "would have been possible without some measure of support—often very solid support—from the countries of Africa and Asia," Stevenson continued:

There is an illusion in some quarters that the so-called "Afro-Asian bloc" always votes with the Soviet Union against the so-called "Western bloc." That is three mistakes in one, since, in the first place, neither the Afro-Asians nor, in the second place, the Western nations vote mechanically as blocs in the United Nations—and as long as each member is free to think for itself they never will.

Furthermore, the record abundantly proves that the members from Africa and Asia have not been afraid to find themselves voting on the same side as the United States; indeed, on great issues they have been doing so very often.[27]

Executive policy-makers in the United States had thus become increasingly convinced that, in most vital respects, only one bloc division within the United Nations really mattered: the separation between those countries endeavoring to strengthen the U.N. and to build up a

sense of international community and those opposing such
steps. The significance of this division becomes more meaningful when we consider one final aspect of neutralist diplomacy in the U.N.: the Soviet troika proposal and other
attempts to reorganize the machinery and structure of the
United Nations.

Reorganize

In the course of a dramatic speech before the U.N. General Assembly on September 23, 1960, Khrushchev
launched what Herter, then U.S. Secretary of State, described as "an all-out attack, a real declaration of war"
against the Office of Secretary General and, by implication, against the U.N. itself. For many months, Communist countries had regarded Secretary General Hammarskjöld as *persona non grata;* Hammarskjöld, lamented
Khrushchev, "upheld the interests of the United States
and other countries of monopoly capital." Climaxing the
Communist bloc's long war of nerves against Hammarskjöld, Khrushchev proposed *de facto* abolition of the Office of Secretary General and its replacement by a "collective" executive; that is, one official each from the Western, the Communist, and the neutralist camps. Each of
these officials would possess a veto over the actions of the
collective executive. In practice, the Office of Secretary
General would be rendered as ineffectual as the Security
Council in dealing vigorously and promptly with threats
to international peace and security.

The Soviet troika proposal derived from the Kremlin's
recognition of five basic realities: (1) increasingly, the
United Nations was reflecting the newly found strength
and the interests of the neutralist community; (2) one of
the cardinal goals of neutralist diplomacy in the U.N. was
to maximize the organization's effectiveness on the international scene; (3) another neutralist goal was to bring
about what nonaligned states regarded as long overdue
modifications in the U.N.'s administrative machinery that

would take account of changes in the size, geographic distribution, and diplomatic orientation of the present and future membership; (4) despite the coincidence of neutralist and Communist objectives on issues like colonialism, the advocates of nonalignment did not hesitate to *oppose* the Communist bloc on critical issues, like the Congo crisis, in which the U.S.S.R. endeavored to discredit both the West and the United Nations itself; and (5) all in all, the trend toward a larger neutralist voice in U.N. affairs—repeatedly and loudly applauded by the Communist propaganda apparatus—had taken a turn that surprised and disconcerted Communist officials fully as much as it did the West.

Khrushchev's troika scheme thus indicated a deep ambivalence in the official Communist mind about the consequences of a neutralist-controlled U.N. On the one hand, an important prong of Khrushchev's strategy of peaceful coexistence was aimed at winning and holding the friendship of nonaligned countries, regarded by the Kremlin ideologists as "fraternal partners" and as members of the "peace zone." Moscow's increasingly bitter dispute with Peking put a greater premium than ever upon maintaining cordial relations with nations throughout the Afro-Arab-Asian world. On the other hand, Communist policymakers may have been even more surprised than Western officials to discover that their neutralist protégés were unwilling to serve as diplomatic sycophants. In the Congo and elsewhere, the diplomatic independence espoused by the neutralist world applied to Communist, as much as to Western, efforts to control and direct the destiny of newly independent nations and to reduce them to unwilling participants in disputes that were of secondary concern to them. The troika idea seemed an ingenious way both of flattering the neutralist countries (by offering them more formal participation in U.N. decision-making) and of negating their influence (by subjecting their role to a Communist veto) in the organization which they had come to rely upon heavily for achieving their diplomatic objectives.

That neutralist policy-makers have never been as naïve about Communism's underlying goals as Westerners imagine was demonstrated by the well-nigh unanimous neutralist opposition to the troika idea. A prominent Indian journal declared that adoption of the troika system would "soon grind the U.N. to a halt." Instead of a troika, this source continued, the newly independent countries in the U.N. desired a "strong, independent, and completely impartial Secretary General at the head of the Secretariat." Premier U Nu of Burma stated unequivocally that the troika would "seriously impair" the value of the United Nations in world affairs. From Egypt came the verdict that there was "no substitute for a Secretary General invested with proper powers and authority by the Security Council and the General Assembly and responsible only to these groups as a whole. Anything less will bring chaos, and even disintegration to the United Nations." Reporting from the neutralist Belgrade Conference, another observer found virtually no disagreement with the idea that the troika system was merely "a device to neutralize the United Nations as a potential force." A Malayan source was convinced that Communist officials believed that the U.N. "has grown too strong for them and they have discovered in the Congo that they can no longer impose their mischief on small nations. They are therefore attacking the Secretariat and its Charter functions." And from the U.N. came a report that summarized neutralist opposition to the troika: "The more active a part a nation is playing in U.N. affairs, the more unpalatable the troika apparently becomes." [28]

Neutralist opposition to the troika principle did not mean that nonaligned countries favored the *status quo* in the

U.N., or that they were unsympathetic to one idea implicit in the Soviet scheme: a more "impartial" Secretary General, whose views were independent of both Cold War antagonists. If they rejected any proposal seeking to immobilize the U.N., they rejected no less a conception of the Office of Secretary General that the West had long been accustomed to accept as a natural right. This was the expectation (based upon the attitudes displayed by Secretary General Trygve Lie, and, to a lesser extent, by Dag Hammarskjöld) that the chief officer of the U.N. should be overtly or normally *pro-Western* and that he take few pains to disguise his antipathy toward the Communist bloc. What the neutralist countries wanted was a top U.N. official who stood outside the Cold War arena and who could, by virtue of his position, seek to mitigate Cold War tensions. Neutralist countries discovered such a person in Hammarskjöld's successor, U Thant of Burma.

U Thant's accession to the Office of Secretary General might be interpreted as great-power acknowledgement that nonalignment was the dominant diplomatic philosophy represented in the U.N. That his appointment occasioned no great initial enthusiasm in the West was indicated by the following statement of one American commentator who traced the evolution of the office: "From Lie to Hammarskjöld to U Thant there has been a drift to the political East—ally to neutral to neutralist. Now the time approaches when Moscow again prepares a squeeze." [29] Such judgments indicated that stereotypes do not die easily. In the United States, neutralism had long been regarded as a kind of halfway house between pro-Westernism and pro-Communism; for some reason (never clearly explained) the assumption was that neutralism was a "step toward" Communism. Yet within a few months after U Thant's appointment, he had not only succeeded in becoming "tolerated" by both East and West, he had won wide respect in Western circles, and the Soviet Union's willingness late in 1962 to support his reappointment to a full term indicated that, at least for the time being, it had shelved its troika proposal.[30]

Significantly, if U Thant proved more personally acceptable to the Communist bloc, his policies (although not always his approach and manner of *presenting* his policies) differed in few respects from those of Hammarskjöld. Like his predecessor, U Thant championed an activist role for the U.N. in global affairs. This led him to support a continued and effective U.N. "presence" in the Congo, in the face of continuing Communist opposition. It also led him to insist that financially delinquent nations pay their assessments. And, once more in spite of obvious Communist efforts to keep the controversy inflamed, U Thant was highly instrumental in resolving the bitter dispute between the Netherlands and Indonesia over West Irian. Although his solution was openly criticized in the West as an "appeasement" of Indonesia, it at least had the virtue of damping a fire that threatened to flare into another Cold War confrontation, where the odds would likely favor Communist intrigue, and of preserving at least a minimum of goodwill between the West and the key Asian state of Indonesia. U Thant's conciliatory role in the Cuban missile crisis of 1962 was also regarded by East and West alike as extremely constructive, not to say imperative, in helping to prevent what all parties to the conflict wished to avoid—a nuclear confrontation imperiling the future of humanity.

In such instances, U Thant's conception of the U.N. reflects the dominant conviction of all nonaligned countries, whatever their other policy differences. Neither through the United Nations nor outside it did neutralist countries seek to "impose" solutions on the great powers. In company with other neutralist spokesmen, U Thant believes that the U.N. is "not a big power with armed forces, nor is it a mere moral force"; it is something in between. It provides a mechanism whereby countries pursuing non-alignment "can play an important role by bringing pressure to bear on the two powers to reach some kind of compromise on the problems dividing the world." Among Western statesmen, perhaps only General de Gaulle would take issue with this conception or with U Thant's conviction that the U.N. "should develop into an organic thing; the United Nations should get stronger and stronger, so that ultimately it will assume the attributes of a sovereign state." [31]

If Western and Communist misgivings about an avowedly "neutralist" and "activist" Secretary General gradually receded, one reason at least was that U Thant was uniquely equipped for his role in global affairs. He succeeded in discovering overlapping zones of common interest between Cold War factions—starting with their mutual interest in survival in the nuclear age—and in convincing each side that, whatever the merits of its own views, diplomatic rigidity and reiteration of Cold War slogans offered no prospect for avoiding an ultimate military encounter. It is not necessary to idealize neutralism, or to accept all its ethical-moral claims, to recognize that U Thant's effectiveness was made possible to an appreciable extent by increasing great-power acceptance of this neutralist conviction.

V

The Communist Bloc and the Neutralist Zone

In the first thoroughgoing revision of Marxist doctrine since Lenin's time, Nikita Khrushchev in 1961 presented a new manifesto of Communist belief. Referring to Communist relations with nonaligned countries, this new ideological testament warmly approved "pursuit of an independent [i.e., neutralist] foreign policy of peace" by newly emergent countries. It further declared that

> A vast peace zone has taken shape on earth. . . . There is a growing number of countries that adhere to a policy of neutrality and strive to safeguard themselves against the hazards of participation in military blocs. . . . It is possible to avert a world war by the combined efforts of the mighty Socialist camp, the peace-loving non-Socialist countries [i.e., the neutralist countries], the international working class and all the forces championing peace.[1]

A newsworthy—and, to the Western mind, disquieting —example of Communist efforts to cement more cordial relations with countries in the "vast peace zone" occurred in 1964, when the Kremlin awarded the Lenin Peace Prize to President Ben Bella of Algeria. Ben Bella was lauded as an "ardent champion of peaceful coexistence," the "voice of Africa," and the leader of a nation that sought "peace for the realization of its ambitions." That the honor bestowed on Ben Bella would be translated into tangible Soviet assistance for his country was indicated within a week, when Moscow announced the extension of a new $128 million credit to Algeria, whose "socialist" program was hailed by the Kremlin as equivalent to the "socialism of the Communist bloc." [2]

This episode clearly paralleled others since the mid-1950's, in which Communist policy-makers have endeavored to identify closely with neutralist countries.* Let us

* It is necessary to distinguish between the positions of the Soviet Union and its satellites and the viewpoints of Peking and its followers toward the neutralist movement. Throughout this chapter, the emphasis is on the Soviet conception, since this remains the dominant point of view in the Communist camp. Increasingly, as part of the broader ideological divergence between Moscow and Peking, fundamental differences have appeared in the Soviet and the Chinese appraisals of, and approach to, the neutralist community. At a later stage, we shall see that the concept of the "national bourgeoisie" (i.e., the nationalist leaders who led the struggle against Western imperialism) plays a key role in the Kremlin's ideological justification for harmonious relations with neutralist states. Moscow has (with some equivocation) contended that this group was capable of gradually leading such states into the next stage of Communism, in conformity with Khrushchev's emphasis upon "peaceful coexistence." Friendly relations between the Soviet Union and Algeria, Ghana, Egypt, or India could therefore be justified on this basis. Officials of Red China—clinging to their conviction that only "revolution" internally and globally can usher in Communism—naturally evaluate the "national bourgeoisie" quite differently, as illustrated by Peking's description of Prime Minister Nehru as a "running dog of imperialism" and a member of the "Tito clique." The Sino-Indian conflict in the Himalayas brought differing Soviet and Chinese assessments of nonalignment into sharp focus. Although there was some initial hesitation in the Kremlin, in time the Soviet Union unequivocally supported India. Its spokesmen condemned China for an "adventuristic position which has nothing to do with Marxism"; Mao Tse-tung's regime was strongly criticized for engaging in conduct which, though "camouflaged with pseudo-revolutionary phrases," was "particularly harmful and dangerous." The U.S.S.R., said Khrushchev, in mid-1963, stood "side by side" with India on many global issues, especially on "the problem of securing peace." By contrast, the *Peking Daily* complained bitterly about the Kremlin's position: "Here is the first instance in history in which a socialist country, instead of condemning the armed provocations of the reactionaries of a capitalist country [i.e., India], condemned another fraternal socialist country." For

evaluate the relationship between neutralism and Communism by examining three broad aspects of the problem in some detail. These are: the neutralist view of Marxist ideology; Communist support for Afro-Asian nationalism; and Communist endorsement of the principle of neutralism, along with economic and military assistance programs ostensibly designed to meet the needs of nonaligned countries.

Neutralist Assessments of Communist Ideology

Confronted with repeated Western charges that the political coloration of his supposedly "neutralist" regime was red, President Sukarno of Indonesia freely accepted the label. Red, he asserted, "is the color of the rising sun, which will bring about bright weather in the morning." And when the Soviet Union forged decisively ahead of the West

---

many years, Chinese propagandists had sought to discredit Nehru's regime by bracketing it with the "Tito clique" that favored ideological "revisionism." Yugoslavia, and inferentially its admirers in the neutralist zone, said *Red Flag*, sought to "present [themselves] as being 'above the blocs'" and have "opposed the socialist camp and the international Communist movement and carried out activities detrimental to the unity of all peaceloving forces and countries, in an effort to serve United States imperialism." And when six neutralist countries at Colombo attempted to mediate the Himalayan conflict, an official Chinese source stated: "That the Tito group [i.e., the neutralist nations] is so shameless as to try to participate in mediation over the Sino-Indian dispute is something at which one can only laugh with scorn." This group "has always acted as an eager pawn" of American imperialism and "has always lived up to the needs of U.S. imperialism by backing full tilt the Indian reactionaries in their frantic anti-China drive." As the Sino-Soviet dispute became more openly heated, Mao Tse-tung's government hardened its attitude toward the ideological "revisionism" that permitted the Soviet Union to arrive at a *modus vivendi* with neutralism. Said the Chinese journal *Jenmin Jih Pao*: "Marxism-Leninism must not be contaminated! Modern revisionism is doomed to utter failure! Marxism-Leninism will certainly triumph throughout the world!" See: *The New York Times*, September 18, and December 4, 1962, and July 21, 1963; *Indian Express*, March 6, 1963; *Asian Recorder*, Vol. VII (October 22–28, 1961), 4224; and *Hindustan Times*, December 4, 1962.

in space technology by launching its first Sputnik, the *Manila Times* declared editorially: "The people sandwiched between the two great powers might well wonder whether they have not been misinformed about the nature of the Soviet state." [3]

That widespread admiration and respect for the Communist bloc exists throughout the neutralist zone is a point too well known to require lengthy elaboration here. Affinities between the bloc and the neutralist community take many forms. There are obvious similarities between the one-party political systems widely found throughout Africa, the Arab world, and parts of Asia, and the governments behind the Iron Curtain. Common elements are the existence of a highly disciplined centralized party structure effectively controlling the state; the absence of an effective opposition party and the tendency of ruling political elites to equate political opposition movements with treason; rigid censorship of all forms of communication; a secret police whose activities are unhampered by legal restraints; and the prevalence of "charismatic" leaders exalting personalities over laws.

Economic affairs offer comparable parallels. Officials in the United States Information Agency, for example, have long been aware of the obstacles that concepts like "capitalism" and "free enterprise" pose for the West in its contest with the Communist bloc for the minds of men. Outside the West, "capitalism" tends to be synonymous with "little concern for the poor, unfair distribution of wealth, and undue influence of the rich." Conversely, "socialism" is just as widely regarded as a "system favoring the welfare of common people." To the leader of Senegal, socialism "is a sense of community which is a return to Africanism"; the leader of Tanganyika has said that "no underdeveloped country can afford to be anything but 'socialist'"; Bourguiba of Tunisia has declared that Mohammed's followers "were socialists before the invention of the word"; and Cambodia's Prince Sihanouk has conceived of socialism as "first and foremost an application of Buddhism." [4]

If these and other ties that bind Communist and neutralist regimes are often painfully obvious to Western observers, the same cannot be said for the opposite side of the coin of neutralist-Communist relations. Prone to regard diplomatic nonalignment as "the next thing to Communism," most Americans remain strangely unaware of the extent to which neutralists have been sharply critical of Marxist ideology, or of the degree to which profound differences exist between the "socialism" professed in Ghana, Egypt, or India and the version prevailing behind the Iron Curtain. Space is not available for a point-by-point comparison of these ideologies, nor is such a task necessary for our purpose. Moreover, this is a matter in which the richness and heterogeneity of the neutralist movement produces significant differences in the outlook of an official in Guinea, an editor in Tanganyika, a political leader in Iraq, or an army officer in Burma. Nevertheless, there are certain common themes in the neutralist response, irrespective of whether it comes from Africa, the Arab world, or Asia.

Léopold Senghor of Senegal has been at the forefront of those African leaders who differentiate carefully between African socialism and Marxism. Like other prominent Africans, Senghor regards Marxism as highly vulnerable on a number of points. He has attacked Marxism's "scientific" pretensions; its preoccupation with, and incorrect understanding of, the class struggle; its neglect of the peasantry and of agricultural problems generally (which rank perhaps as Africa's foremost economic concerns); its simplistic and doctrinaire conceptions of "capitalism," including the assumption that capitalism is incapable of re-

good criticism

forming itself; its belief in the inevitability of depressions and other cataclysmic economic developments; its fixation on economic trends in Western Europe, to the neglect of those in the underdeveloped world; its stereotyped assessments of movements like colonialism and trade unionism; and its one-sided, equivocal, and mechanistic conception of man.

Other African spokesmen have been particularly outspoken in rejecting the Marxist conception of the class struggle as both irrelevant for conditions in Africa and as incompatible with the idea of class cooperation, a central precept of African socialism. Moreover, despite African apprehensions about capitalism, it is noteworthy that even in African states that ostensibly have borrowed heavily from Marxist ideology, like Nkrumah's regime in Ghana, the trend is toward a "mixed" economy, in which private ownership and foreign corporations are assigned a significant role in national development.[5]

Nor do neutralist appraisals of Marxism ignore or gloss over what the Westerner is likely to regard as the most serious deficiency of Marxism as a philosophy of life: its incompatibility with moral-ethical precepts central to Christianity, Judaism, and the world's other great religious systems. Arab critics, for example, emphasize the conflict between atheistic Communism and Islam. For devout Moslems, the Koranic traditions constitute an even more authoritative and comprehensive scheme for the organization and regulation of human society than do the *Communist Manifesto* and other Communist writings. Because it makes no distinction between secular and religious spheres of life, Islam perhaps collides more violently and fundamentally with Marxism than do Christianity and Judaism.[6]

Hindus and disciples of Gandhi have been no less vocal in indicting Marxism for its messianic compulsions, its urge to proselytize, its tendency to regard itself as the definitive philosophical system for all societies and all times, and its philosophic "exclusivism." Thus Nehru condemned Communism for its doctrinal rigidity, its fanaticism, and its conspicuous lack of toleration for competing systems of thought. Indian spokesmen have been equally repelled by Communism's emphasis upon, and use of, violence to achieve Marxist ends. Thus Indian elder statesman C. Rajagopalachari found Marxism's reliance upon violence "abhorrent to the Indian way of life." Communist espousal of "democracy" "should not lull democratically minded Indians into believing that the Communists will shed their violence any more than the leopard can change its spots." And the President of the Congress Party of India indicted the Communist movement for a variety of sins of omission and commission: for fomenting internal dissensions and factions; for seeking to infiltrate and control the government; for placing the interests of the Communist Party ahead of those of the nation; for endeavoring to capitalize upon their identification with Indian nationalism, when in fact the Communists had done nothing whatever to help India gain its independence; for encouraging and supporting separatist movements throughout India instead of assisting the government in overcoming centrifugal forces. For these and other reasons, Prime Minister Nehru observed that Soviet Russia's "methods were different" from India's, and that the Soviet path was not India's path, and, he hoped, never would be. In 1955, Nehru had commented candidly:

> Russia does not have a democratic system of Government. People there had to pay a heavy price and undergo great suffering in order to achieve what they have done. Many of the freedoms which the people enjoyed in India are lacking there. We are trying to achieve our goal by democratic methods.[7]

Criticisms of the moral-ethical deficiencies of Communism have also figured prominently in assessments by Buddhist commentators. A Burmese spokesman contrasted Communism with "Burmese socialism" by condemning the former for its assumption that man is "a mere element of the material forces of production, serving the impersonal economic interests of the State." An acceptable system of socialism should rest upon a conception of "the individual in society" and upon the idea that "his spiritual lot is as important as his material lot." Marxism collided with this principle, since "when man is treated as a mere element of the material powers of production, he loses his personality and his human dignity. And thereby the aim of socialism is defeated." A Burmese article had this to say with regard to censorship behind the Iron Curtain: "The noncommitted, the neutral, the nonaligned cannot exist without free access to all available information and differing points of view." [8]

The common theme in these neutralist appraisals of Marxism is suggested by the Burmese critic who found Marxism guilty of "treading the feet according to the shoe." Advertising themselves as realists and pragmatists, Communists in reality were just the opposite; they were completely incapable of understanding "the historical and social conditions of Burma" and hence of adapting "their institutions and program to the culture and needs of Burma." Consequently, Burma remained dedicated to a brand of socialism that "was best suited and applicable to the material conditions of Burma and its spiritual and cultural heritage." [9] This same motif pervaded a letter sent by Egyptian legislators to Premier Khrushchev, in which the Soviet Premier was bluntly informed:

[The Arabs reject Western ideological concepts, like capitalism] not because we hate it but because we believe it does not suit the nature, conditions, hopes, needs and requirements of our people. . . . This does not mean that Communism, which proved successful in conditions prevailing in other countries, is suitable for successful application in our country. Our people refuse to be limited to this choice [between capitalism and Communism] and believe that the ideological scope in the world is bigger than this closed circle. They also believe our people are capable, without becoming isolated from the world's wealth of ideologies, of participating creatively in adding to this wealth.

Or, in the words of another Arab spokesman, Communism is regarded

as an alien ideology born in the West as a result of clashing nationalities and conducive socio-economic conditions. For the Arabs to choose between their own way of life, their heritage, their spiritual, metaphysical, religious values and their mission on the one hand and Communism on the other hand is not difficult. The Arabs, no doubt, will choose their own way of life.[10]

From Ghana to Indonesia, then, neutralists view Marxism, no less than American-style democracy, as an *alien* philosophy, totally unsuited to the traditions and needs of neutralist societies. This conviction has both a negative and a positive aspect. Negatively, it means that neutralist countries in principle oppose the importation or imposition of *any* foreign political credo, since this creates the same kind of ideological "dependency" most of them experienced under colonialism. Although neutralist societies may and do borrow freely from existing political creeds, they are convinced that the ideological synthesis must be their own and must be consonant with certain deeply held traditions and beliefs. Positively, as we emphasized in Chapter 2, a basic premise of the neutralist movement is the conviction that nonaligned nations are capable of enriching the global ideological environment by evolving their own unique philosophical systems, thereby proving that the range of philosophical possibilities extends beyond Western-style democracy or Communism.

Communism and Afro-Asian Nationalism

A curious coincidence occurring on the island of Zanzibar after a successful African revolt against its traditional Arab masters highlights another significant dimension of neutralist-Communist relations. Following the revolution, the Soviet Embassy moved into an ancient building bearing the Koranic inscription: "Surely we have given you a great victory." [11] If Communist policy-makers might appropriately extend this message to Zanzibar's new rulers, they could no less apply it to many other neutralist countries attaining independence from the West since World War II.

Neutralist spokesmen have made no effort to conceal their gratitude to the Communist bloc for moral and material assistance furnished to nationalist movements against Western colonialism. Likening Communist support for nationalist causes to the mutual assistance among the Allies during World War II, a high Indonesian official observed: "The Communists are . . . fighting genuinely for colonial freedom. It is their doctrine . . . when they support colonial peoples, they are genuine, and that's why their help is being accepted." Referring to Algeria, the Foreign Minister of Iraq commended Moscow for the "great part played by the Soviet Union and other socialist countries" in winning Algeria's independence. This indicated that "Russia and other Communist countries defended freedom and liberty." And the Prime Minister of the Sudan declared during a visit behind the Iron Curtain:

We highly appreciate the good intentions of the Soviet Union with regard to the liberation and industrialization of African countries. We know that the Soviet Union is not a State which exploits other peoples. Therefore, we believe in its friendship and cooperate with it.[12]

Such neutralist tributes to the Communist bloc cause Americans to ask to what extent neutralist governments are aware of the real motives of the Marxists in supporting nationalist causes throughout the Afro-Arab-Asian world. Are the leaders and masses in Zanzibar, Indonesia, Iraq, and other neutralist societies mindful that Moscow and Peking seek to displace Western "imperialism" with a new and more ruthless form of Communist domination? In accepting Communist assistance, are nationalist leaders ignorant of the fate of those who try to "ride the tiger's back"?

Advocates of nonalignment answer such reservations in various ways. Before examining some of them, however, we must note that the American fixation on neutralist "awareness" of the "true aims" of Communism itself frequently poses a serious psychological barrier to better understanding between Western and neutralist societies. On this point, Americans are prone to reveal both a curious naïveté of their own about neutralist governments and an insensitivity to the feelings of societies only recently emerging from a prolonged period of Western political and diplomatic tutelage. Anxiety about neutralist understanding of Communism's true objectives suggests that Americans believe that the leaders of neutralist countries are politically illiterate and unsophisticated, that they require "guidance" in order to comprehend their own national interests "realistically." To officials in neutralist societies, such thinking is distressingly reminiscent of the colonial ethos; it suggests that Western states have not yet abandoned the habit of thinking for other peoples politically. Western anxieties further imply that nonalignment has its origins essentially in ignorance and naïveté about

international issues and ideological currents, rather than
in carefully considered policy choices by neutralist governments. Neutralist leaders are often affronted by the
insinuations implicit in such questions, interpreting them
as tantamount to a vote of no confidence in their own political astuteness.

An official of Tanganyika observed in reference to Communist infiltration efforts at an Afro-Asian People's Solidarity Conference early in 1963:

> I think it is high time now those overseas should take recog-
> nition that the Africans have also a brain. . . . We in Tan-
> ganyika agreed to play host to the Conference because we
> have confidence in ourselves. . . . We believe in our brain,
> we do not think that any other race has a more superior brain
> than ourselves. . . . I do not accept the argument put by
> our friends overseas that the Africans are the people to be
> won either by the West or by the East. They cannot be played
> [with] as if they are little boys to be won by whoever is
> clever.

The President of Tanganyika, Julius Nyerere, has similarly
remarked: "The people who anxiously watch to see whether
we will become 'Communist' or 'Western democrats' will
both be disconcerted. We do not have to be either." And
the late President Olympio of Togo expressed a prevalent
neutralist conviction when he declared: "At last we are
beginning to think of ourselves as Africans and not simply
as *extensions* of European Powers." [13]

There is perhaps no greater illusion in the Western, particularly in the American, mind than the idea that neutralist governments are insensitive to, or ignorant of, the
ultimate goals of the Communist movement. President
Kwame Nkrumah has stated bluntly: "I and my party are
well aware of the realities of our time. As we would not
have British masters, so we would not have Russian masters, or any masters for that matter. It is not our intention

to substitute one imperialism for another." [14] An Arab spokesman has commented that "Arab nationalism does not need Western instigation or Western bases to take a stand against the spread of Communism in the Middle East." Another Arab has said that, after Stalin's death, Soviet strategy in global affairs "was undergoing, and in fact rediscovering, Lenin's tactics of supporting nationalism in the false belief that it is the first step toward the ultimate goal of Communism." This spokesman continued:

> No one knows better than those same countries of Asia and Africa which passed through bitter experiences from Western colonialism and are very jealous of their newly won independence than to accept in any manner the substitute [sic] of one form of [foreign] influence by another.[15]

Political elites in neutralist governments are cognizant of two facts that make the Communist bloc's support of nationalist movements highly suspect. Neutralist policymakers know (probably better than most Westerners) that a deep ideological ambivalence characterizes Marxist viewpoints toward the "national bourgeoisie"—the political elites in newly independent countries that led the struggle for freedom from Western domination. If this group was manifestly anti-Western (in the sense that it wished to terminate Western colonialism), time revealed that it was no less militantly anti-Communist. Nkrumah's dictum —"As we would not have British masters, so we would not have Russian masters"—succinctly defines the attitude of nationalist leaders toward Moscow and Peking. This fact has placed Communist officials in an exceedingly uncomfortable dilemma. Obviously, it was in the Communist interest to support any and all anti-Western movements. Yet, in almost all cases, these movements were led and controlled, not by Communists, but by groups who continually demonstrated their opposition to Communist, no less than to Western, domination. It was the intent of the so-called national bourgeoisie to liquidate and prevent *all* alien control over the affairs of their societies.

Until the early 1950's, Communist propagandists referred to the "national bourgeoisie" in language normally reserved exclusively for "Wall Street warmongers" and the "imperialist NATO clique." One Soviet African specialist wrote in 1950, for example, that the national bourgeoisie supported anticolonialist movements "only with a view to taking advantage of the fruits of revolution and seizing political power for the suppression and enslavement of the masses of the people of its own country." Even so, he counseled that Communism could use this group during the "special strategic stage" when the national bourgeoisie "still supports the revolutionary movement." Not content with ideological generalization, Communist spokesmen actually named prominent African, Arab, and Asian nationalists—calling them variously "feudal or semi-feudal lords," supporters of "petty bourgeois national reformism" (i.e., heretics, who rejected revolution for evolution and gradual reform), and (in reference to a then still obscure Arab leader, Gamal Abdel Nasser) members of a "reactionary group of officers connected with the United States"![16]

Then, in 1955 (coincidental with the Afro-Asian Conference at Bandung, when neutralism first gained global prominence), the Kremlin's line shifted abruptly. The Czech-Egyptian arms agreement of 1955 provided a graphic indication of Moscow's new assessment of the national bourgeoisie. Instead of condemning nationalist leaders like Nasser, and of pursuing a policy of overt hostility toward them, the Kremlin began to supply their demands for arms and economic assistance. In Egypt's case, this meant that the Soviet Union had successfully hurdled the Baghdad Pact defense wall and was now actively engaged in cementing more cordial relations with Arab nationalists. Such episodes afforded tangible evidence that Moscow had earlier made "serious mistakes" in dealing with the national bourgeoisie. Now it began to refer rhapsodically to nationalist leaders "of ability and energy" who were rightfully claiming their "place in the sun." Other Soviet measures and programs—vigorous support for anticolonialism in the U.N., increased military and economic aid for selected neutralist countries, intensified propaganda and cultural activities (for example, the establishment of Lumumba University in Moscow)—provided additional proof of the esteem in which Communist policy-makers held the national bourgeoisie.

By the early 1960's, however, the Kremlin's evaluation of the political elites governing newly independent countries shifted again; its line now fell somewhere between the indiscriminate castigations of the Stalin era and the equally unqualified endorsements of the national bourgeoisie of the early Khrushchev period. Thus the 1961 Party Program referred favorably to "national liberation revolutions," to the emerging nations "as active participants in world politics" and as a "revolutionary force destroying imperialism." At the same time, Communist oracles cautioned that the revolution in such countries had not yet been "completed," and nationalist leaders were denounced for belonging to "the reactionary circles of the local exploiting classes" and for serving as "the allies of imperialism." It remained for Communists to carry the revolution forward in order to achieve a truly "anti-imperialist, antifeudal, democratic revolution" that would finally usher in a "national democracy." Concurrently, Communist spokesmen opened a new propaganda barrage against those members of the national bourgeoisie (including nearly all leaders of neutralist countries) who contended that Soviet-style Marxism did not "fit" the conditions prevailing within their societies.[17] In 1963, an Indian commentator described the dilemma of Soviet officials who sought to push nationalist leaders "onto the path of what is called Marxist-Leninist development":

> [Communist strategy] instigates a Nasser to intransigence only to find the protégé turning on itself; it encourages a Kassem [in Iraq] in his madness only to discover the madness to be omniverous; it seeks to take a Sékou Touré under its wings only to be told off impudently. . . .[18]

Nasser, Kassem, and Touré—along with nearly every other political leader throughout the neutralist zone—understood thoroughly that Communist strategies toward nationalist movements had been governed by four cardinal considerations: (1) the nationalist movements were anti-Western; (2) they were inordinately successful in achieving their goals; (3) although nationalist leaders accepted Communist assistance in their struggle for independence, not a single newly independent government showed a serious inclination to "go Communist" after independence, but more often than not moved quickly to suppress Communist activities within the country; and (4) unless the Communists were prepared to alienate nationalist regimes throughout the Afro-Asian-Arab world, they had no alternative except to reach an ideological *modus vivendi* with neutralist regimes.

Neutralist policy-makers realized perhaps better than many of their Western detractors that Communist endorsement and support of nationalism had been purely *expediential and instrumental*. To officials in Moscow and Peking, the nationalism sweeping the colonial world was essentially a *means* for achieving ends defined behind the Iron Curtain. In Communist jargon, the "national democracies" created by the political elites in neutralist countries were merely halfway houses toward establishment of still

unattained "people's democracies"; once they had fulfilled
their historically ordained "mission" of destroying Western colonialism, the national bourgeoisie would be rele-
gated to the refuse heap of history, along with the "capitalist exploiters" and other groups standing in the way of
the new Communist order. Thus, in 1959, Nasser stated:

> While the Communists have been attacking me, I have been
> attacking them. In Egypt, of course, Communism has been
> under attack steadily for the seven years of the revolution.
> . . . We had to expose the tactics of the Syrian Communists,
> who had formed a strange alliance with the feudalist land-
> owners. . . . I attacked the Iraqi Communists, who were
> making a concentrated assault against Arab nationalism, the
> [United Arab Republic] and Nasser. . . . We wanted to in-
> noculate our people . . . against Communist infection, to
> put them on guard against the penetration planned by the
> combined plotting of all the Communists in the Middle East.
> . . . We are still watching the Communists because we know
> they can never relent in their opposition to Arab nationalism.

And in the same period, Nasser declared that trouble between Cairo and Moscow

> really started when I attacked the Syrian Communists. . . .
> I was shocked when the answer came from Khrushchev in
> such a manner as to suggest that he had assumed responsibil-
> ity for the protection of Arab Communists. . . . I cautioned
> him against supporting the Communist party in our country.
> I reminded him of the fact that the friendly attitude of our
> people to Russia did not exist because of the Communist
> party but in spite of them.

He continued:

> I had no alternative but to tell the Russians that we do not
> want this new type of colonialism. . . . The result was that
> the enormous goodwill built over three years of friendship
> was lost in less than three weeks.[19]

Nasser's statement suggests a second fact about Communist support of nationalist movements that has made neutralist policy-makers apprehensive about Communism's ultimate goals. The neutralist community is well aware that Moscow and Peking have already inaugurated campaigns to subvert governments headed by the "national bourgeoisie." From West Africa to the Pacific, from Iraq to the Congo, Communist elements have intrigued against established authorities, fostered separatist tendencies in what are often internally divided societies, and openly opposed movements like Pan-Africanism and Arab unity that seek to foster supranational cooperation among poor, militarily weak states. This pattern of intrigue has engendered deep animosity toward the Communist bloc among peoples who had been (and probably still are) genuinely appreciative of its assistance during the struggle for independence. As an example, in the early 1960's, Communist sources referred to President Touré's regime as a "Guinean experiment" and to his party as merely a "proletarian kernel." After Marxist groups had openly connived against his government's authority, Touré informed the Soviet Union that Guinea "refuses to be drawn into choosing sides in a power struggle between two blocs" and that "revolutions cannot be imported or exported, but . . . are the fruits of the people's will." Late in 1961, Touré was forced to expel the Soviet Ambassador from Conakry because of complicity in Communist-instigated plots against his regime. And when the President of the Republic of the Sudan declared that "foreign intervention, overt or covert, from which the Congolese people have suffered so grievously during the past year, should not be repeated," he was addressing his remarks fully as much toward Moscow as toward capitals in the West. Of the African scene generally, one authority has observed: "Indeed, the stronger and more neutralist the party in power in Africa, the more effective have been the barriers to the formation of Communist parties because the doctrine of African neutralism has shown itself essentially hostile to subordination to a European ideology." [20] In no less unequivocal language, Arab sources have denounced continuing Communist intrigue against such Arab unity movements as the merger between Syria and Egypt in 1958. Ever since the Czech-Egyptian arms agreement of 1955, commented an Egyptian critic, "the Western press has persisted in claiming that we were fast on our way to becoming a satellite"—a prediction that found "attentive and happy ears" behind the Iron Curtain. Communists were "looking with great expectation to the budding flower of the Nile shores, the new Arab convert which London, Paris, and New York had ceded to Communism." The "disappointment of the Communists," who had imagined "they could gather us into the fold," was therefore fully understandable. Yet, Arab nationalism "did not shake off the yoke of imperialism to choose another form of foreign interference, nor did it abolish the system of foreign influence which for centuries plagued the whole region to open the way to Marxism." Another Egyptian commentator observed that Arab nationalism "was not meant to open the doors of the Middle East to Soviet Communism." It had unfortunately become apparent that Communism's support for Arab nationalist causes "was dictated by the dual aim of weakening and breaking Western influence in the region in order to install itself there and assure freedom of action for the local Communist parties." Severely castigating attempts by Marxist forces to infiltrate and control political movements throughout the Arab world, this critic asserted that the "Middle East and the Afro-Asian world will be closed to all alien principles, be they Communist or otherwise." And it accounted for the Soviet Union's continuing hostility toward Tito's regime in Yugoslavia by saying that Tito's adherence to nonalignment "is liable to encourage other countries within the Soviet sphere to join this new grouping whose policy imposed itself on international events. . . . These are the basic and real reasons behind the red campaign which was launched by Communism against the U.A.R. . . . It is a question of spite provoked by disillusion." [21]

Several months later, the new revolutionary regime of Colonel Aref in Iraq was required to address Moscow in the same tones. Communists inside and outside Iraq had carried on a campaign of subversion against the regime of General Kassem, and had supported rebellions by the large Kurdish minority living in the north. Ironically, Kassem had endeavored (with very limited success) to suppress the Kurdish revolts with arms supplied by the Communist bloc. Kassem's regime showed itself increasingly ineffectual in dealing with Communist intrigues. The new government of Colonel Aref, however, moved vigorously against Communist elements. A high Iraqi official declared: "Gone is the time when foreigners could plan and shape our life." In a clear reference to Soviet-instigated machinations in Iraq, Baghdad charged: "Certain states are carrying out a reckless campaign against the government's measures against Communists." Aref's regime denounced the "strange hostile campaign" being undertaken by the Soviet Union and its supporters against the ruling authorities.

The confrontation throughout the Afro-Arab-Asian world between nationalism and Communism was dramatically illustrated by events in Zanzibar in mid-1964. The revolutionary junta that overthrew the island's traditional Arab rulers was massively assisted by Communists, and Western observers began to describe Zanzibar as the "Cuba of Africa." Yet, as the Communists entrenched their position, African nationalists—led by Julius Nyerere—moved to counter Communist influence, if necessary by calling upon troops from other independent African countries. Zanzibar's merger with Tanganyika succeeded in thwarting Communist designs. In the words of one report, it presented the Communists "most of whom are Arabs, with the choice of giving in to African nationalism or fighting it, thus showing themselves up for what they are —Marxists, not nationalists." [22]

Communist Support of Neutralism

We do not seek to get any advantages. We do not need profits, privileges, controlling interests, concessions, or raw-material sources. We do not ask you to participate in any blocs, reshuffle your governments, or change your domestic or foreign policy. We are ready to help you, as brother helps brother, without any interest whatever, for we know from our own experience how difficult it is to get rid of need. Tell us what you need and we will help you. . . . We do not ask you to join any blocs . . . our only condition is that there will be no strings attached.[23]

This official statement of the Soviet Union's aims at the 1957 Afro-Asian People's Solidarity Conference emphasizes another aspect of the Communist bloc's approach to newly independent governments. Communist verbal endorsement of diplomatic nonalignment has been coupled with offers of military and economic aid to enable neutralist governments to solve their pressing national problems.

Ecstatic and unqualified support for the principle of nonalignment has been a major tactic in the Communist bloc's relations with the neutralist "peace zone" since the mid-1950's. "We know that Afghanistan is unswervingly adhering to its policy of neutrality and has always worked for world peace and security," Marshal Bulganin remarked in 1955. And when Bulganin visited Burma, the communiqué issued at the end of his trip called attention to the agreement between Moscow and Rangoon that "the policy of nonparticipation in blocs guarantees security for the peoples and plays a positive part in establishing world peace." Five years later, in Indonesia, Khruschev told his hosts: "We support the independent [i.e., nonaligned] and active policy carried out by the Indonesian Government. . . ." And when Soviet First Deputy Premier Mikoyan went to the new African state of Mali, he joined with his African hosts in expressing the conviction that

> the positive neutralism exercised by some African and Asian countries is a way which is acceptable to them and which conforms to the specific conditions in these countries. . . . The uncommitted African and Asian countries are making a positive contribution to the peoples' struggle against colonialism, neocolonialism and all imperialist forms of oppression, thus strengthening the camp of peace. . . . The positive neutralism of these countries is an expression of the will of their peoples for strengthening their individuality and countering any foreign hegemony. . . .[24]

By mid-1963, Khrushchev was prepared to go one step further. Referring to Yugoslavia's policy of nonalignment —and observing that Tito's dedication to this credo "does not interfere with anything . . . [and] is not an obstacle" to better Soviet-Yugoslav relations—the Soviet leader said that "the expression 'blocs' is superficial and evanescent." (Hence by implication, even the "Communist bloc," in Khrushchev's view, was merely a temporary phenomenon.) Moscow thus not only conceded the right of nations to remain diplomatically nonaligned; it also accepted another key idea of neutralist thought by agreeing that the division of the world into ideologically antagonistic power blocs was coming to an end.[25]

Repeated and unambiguous endorsement of the princi-

ple of diplomatic nonalignment has unquestionably created
goodwill for the Communist cause throughout the neutralist zone. Not infrequently, neutralist spokesmen have
contrasted such behavior with the widely prevalent American viewpoint that neutralism is "immoral," or with Secretary Dulles' revocation of aid to Egypt for constructing the
Aswan High Dam (a move plainly intended as a rebuke
to Nasser for "playing both sides of the street"), or with
America's official and public skepticism about neutralism
as a diplomatic philosophy. As the *Egyptian Gazette* complained in 1961: "The barren Western reaction to the apparent identity of views on so many questions between the
neutrals and the Eastern [Communist] States has been to
accuse the neutrals of Communist bias. Nowhere have they
shown any really firm desire to impress and work with the
neutral countries as has the Soviet Union." Or, as an Indian source observed: "India finds itself in a peculiar difficulty. So far as political ideology goes, she is anti-Communist, but so far as international relationship goes she has
been shown greater consideration by the Communist
camp. This is apparent to anyone who studies the moves
which Mr. Dulles, for instance, has made over the years.
. . . The U.S. Secretary of State has often tried to cause
embarrassment to Mr. Nehru with a view to making it
known that he resents India's 'neutralism.'" [26]

Hand in hand with its verbal endorsement of the principle of nonalignment has gone tangible Soviet assistance
to leading neutralist countries. Indonesia, India, Nepal,
Ceylon, Afghanistan, Iraq, Syria, Egypt, Yemen, Sudan,
Algeria, Ethiopia, Somalia, Guinea, Ghana, Mali have all
been recipients of substantial Communist military and
economic aid. As if to demonstrate conclusively that the
Communist world attached no strings to its assistance, limited aid has also been extended to such countries as Argen-
tina, Brazil, Pakistan, Tunisia, and Turkey, which main-

tain either formal or *de facto* military ties with the West
and which usually side with the West on international
issues. Communist policy-makers have taken pains to assure neutralist countries that their ties with the West raise
no barrier to participation in Communist aid programs.
Thus, when Chinese Foreign Minister Chou En-lai visited
Afghanistan, he "gave unstinted approval to his hosts' acceptance of American aid. At the very moment he was
approaching Kabul it was being said in Washington that
United States aid to Afghanistan was 'countering Moscow'" in that area.[27] That such Communist tactics have
been effective is indicated by the judgment of a Syrian
official, following his visit behind the Iron Curtain in 1957:

> The U.S.S.R. does not want to interfere in our affairs nor does
> it want to interfere with our political or social systems. It
> wants Syria to have a strong economy to support Syria's po-
> litical independence. The Russians have no ambitions in our
> country. . . . The U.S.S.R. has given us political support
> and supplied us with arms, which we were completely un-
> able to obtain from countries other than the U.S.S.R.[28]

In relying upon economic and military assistance programs to win friends in the neutralist world, the Communist bloc has several advantages over the West. Neutralists themselves have pointed out a number of the positive
features of Communist aid: Communist officials can extend
offers of assistance quickly and directly, without the necessity of having their offers laboriously "studied" by legis-
latures, where they are often revised, pared down, or
sometimes eliminated outright; similarly, prolonged negotiations in aid agreements are not required, in contrast to
the interminable negotiations surrounding efforts by the
Western "consortium" extending assistance for India's development programs; in general, Communist officials have
not sent their *surplus* commodities to neutralist countries,

but (as an Indian commentator put it) have endeavored "to cut their own cloth in order to meet our needs"; nor have Communist officials hesitated (even at the expense of the needs of their own citizens) to send *heavy industry*, rather than light industry or consumer goods, to neutralist societies; whatever their real purposes in making such assistance available, Communist policy-makers have in the main studiously avoided any suggestion that their aid is tied to neutralist support of Communist causes or systems of government; the Communist world has *not* (despite widespread American misconceptions on this point) confined its aid chiefly to selected showplace projects, but has sought over the years to broaden its assistance programs to an ever widening circle of countries; Communist aid is fully competitive with American aid as regards prices, interest rates, the duration of loans, and other features.[29]

It should also be noted that Western policies themselves have sometimes greatly facilitated the growth of Communist aid activities throughout the neutralist zone. During the late 1950's and the early 1960's, American foreign-aid programs often appeared to be governed by a patent desire to express American misgivings about neutralism, or by other considerations indicating a lack of interest or concern in Washington about the economic and military needs of neutralist governments. In some instances, foreign aid was plainly used as a method of discipline, if not outright coercion, in dealing with neutralist states. Nonaligned nations gained the impression, rightly or wrongly, that Washington relied upon foreign aid to express its disapproval of neutralism as a diplomatic philosophy—an objective that seemed unmistakable in Secretary Dulles' decision to withdraw assistance for the Aswan High Dam. In 1959—after requesting American assistance and being denied it—Sékou Touré stated that Guinea had faced a Western "attempt to isolate us politically," and when that occurred, several nations had "come to offer us their help: East Germany, Czechoslovakia, Poland, and the Soviet Union." [30]

In other instances, the United States has engaged in end-less negotiations offering little ultimate promise that a firm American commitment was forthcoming; in still others, it has insisted upon measures (like a total trade embargo with Red China) that would seriously impair the econ-omies of certain neutralist governments, without offering to buy embargoed goods from these countries. Arab sources thus attributed growing aid-and-trade ties be-tween Egypt and the Communist bloc to American refusal to purchase Egyptian cotton during the late 1950's; con-fronted with Western unwillingness to buy its chief export, Egypt "had no other alternative but to accept these [Communist] offers and to trade with these countries. A new horizon thus was opened and, with it, a re-examina-tion of Egypt's foreign policies was thus in the making." In the case of Afghanistan, British and American neglect of that country's economic and military requirements in the 1940's and early 1950's, coupled with growing Western economic and military assistance to Pakistan at a time when the two countries were quarreling over their bor-ders, induced Kabul to turn to Moscow for military and economic aid. One British observer noted that the British and U.S. refusal to help Afghanistan defend itself against Pakistan's growing military power opened the door to Rus-sian infiltration, and Russia was ready to seize the oppor-tunity offered to assist Afghanistan technically as well as militarily. Arab governments repeatedly complained about the State Department's reluctance to supply arms to their countries for fear of offending Israel. According to an Arab source, Syria, when it approached the United States for assistance, was given conditions and terms that under no circumstances could be accepted by a sovereign people. Again, during its crisis with France over the future of the Bizerte naval base, in 1961, Tunisia also requested moral and material support from Washington. Denied such assistance—even though Tunisia had long been regarded as a leading "pro-Western" neutralist government—Bourguiba's regime turned to Moscow for diplomatic and military support. And in 1964, after prolonged study, Congress rejected the White House's request for funds to construct a new steel mill at Bokaro, India. A majority of legislators was convinced that American support for this project would inhibit "free enterprise" and promote "socialism" in India. This legislative intransigence opened the way for a dramatic gesture of Soviet support, which was forthcoming in the Kremlin's announcement that it would finance the new Indian steel mill. Indian officials had warned that a negative decision by the United States would impair much of the goodwill that America had accumulated by its earlier assistance programs in India; confronted with unalterable legislative opposition to the project, New Delhi finally "withdrew" its formal request for American funds—at the same time, it requested the State Department to cancel plans for constructing a new Voice of America radio transmitter on Indian soil.[31]

To say that American officials have been apprehensive about the implications of Communist economic and military aid programs in the neutralist world would be to understate the matter. The official American mentality on this point was illustrated by the remarks of a State Department officer who was asked in 1960 to comment about Communist assistance programs to countries like Egypt, Guinea, Ethiopia, among others. This official declared candidly:

> [Communists] move into soft spots where the government is soft, either because it is intrinsically soft . . . or where through a revolutionary, emotional process the government

has been softened up. So I think it is a little like being susceptible to a disease. When a country is susceptible, they [Communists] strike, as it were.

Two years later, an official from the Agency for International Development commented that while some neutralist countries were aware "that bloc aid is based on the strictly political motives of the moment," other neutralist notions

still have much to learn, of the serious risks of political subversion when they deal with the bloc, of dangerous dependence on bloc sources and markets which can be cut off at will, of critical spare parts difficulties, of pricing, cost, and repayment problems.[32]

And in 1964, with regard to one of the largest recipients of Communist aid—Ben Bella's regime in Algeria—an American observer wrote that the West could expect Algeria "increasingly to represent Soviet interests in Africa, supplying men, money, arms and ideas to revolutionaries with much more skill and purpose than Cuba has shown in similar activity in Latin America." [33]

To what extent have such American apprehensions been justified? Has the Communist bloc been successful in relying upon economic- and military-aid programs to infiltrate neutralist governments and to control their policies in accordance with Moscow's or Peking's purposes? Have neutralist regimes, in accepting Communist assistance, become consciously or unconsciously "dependent" upon the Communist world, to a degree that jeopardizes their newly gained independence? The answer must be that experience thus far has shown Western apprehensions to be largely groundless. Admittedly, in a handful of cases, Communist military assistance has been used for purposes obviously detrimental to Western diplomatic interests. The outstanding example probably is Indonesia's reliance upon massive Communist arms in its "confrontation" with Malaysia. On a more limited scale, Algeria has no doubt used such arms to intrigue against King Hassan's government in neighboring Morocco. And Ethiopia and Somalia have both relied upon Communist-supplied weapons in their conflict with each other—a contest that keeps a key region of East Africa in a state of political turmoil. Yet in these and other instances, it would be difficult to prove that Communist arms or other assistance *created* international incidents and crises like Indonesia's hostility toward Malaysia. In fact, there is every reason to suppose that Sukarno would have acquired arms elsewhere (perhaps from illicit sources in the West) to pursue his anti-Western policies in the Pacific. At worst, Communist arms aid has proved an aggravating element in, and not a primary cause of, neutralist behavior inimical to Western diplomatic interests. Furthermore, Communist-supplied arms have perhaps been used just as frequently *against* Communist interests as against those of the West. Outstanding examples are India's use of Communist arms in the Himalayan crisis, Burma's suppression of its two internal Communist movements, and Iraq's use of Communist weapons against Soviet-backed Kurdish rebels and against the Communist Party.

Concerning the deeper question—the extent to which policy-makers in neutralist countries are cognizant of Moscow's and Peking's ultimate objectives in supplying military and economic aid—Western fears have always been highly exaggerated. As with Communist support of anticolonial movements, neutralist leaders are aware that military and economic assistance from behind the Iron Curtain is extended primarily to achieve goals formulated by Communist hierarchies in Moscow and Peking. If the Aswan Dam episode provided a warning to American officials about how *not* to deal with neutralist governments, the Kremlin was furnished with an equally dramatic, and perhaps even more far-reaching, example in its relations with Yugoslavia. Intermittent Soviet harassment of Tito's government has made a profound impression upon many neutralist countries. Thus in 1958, an Indian journal devoted considerable attention to Moscow's apparent unwillingness to deliver promised assistance to Belgrade because of Soviet uneasiness about Tito's growing "independence" in world affairs. This journal lamented that the U.S.S.R. "now seems bent on pulling the invisible strings of economic aid to realize her political ambitions in Yugoslavia." It cautioned: "That a country like Yugoslavia has thus been thwarted is bound to have its repercussions in other countries similarly placed. It is a warning to them that Soviet aid carries political strings." And it concluded that "no country could confidently accept economic aid having an element of uncertainty about its fulfillment conditioned by political considerations." Five years later, in the midst of the Himalayan conflict, another Indian journal called attention to several other techniques used by the Kremlin to "toughen" its position toward certain countries. It noted that oil deliveries had been cut to France, in the hope of precipitating political unrest there; that "demonstrations" had been ordered against the Iraqi Embassy in Moscow because of Baghdad's treatment of the Iraqi Communist Party; and that the Soviet Communist Party had sent a confidential memorandum throughout Eastern Europe suggesting that the satellite governments take a tougher line with primary recipients of Communist assistance like Syria, Iraq, Yemen, and Egypt. While this journal did not anticipate comparable Soviet pressures upon India, it did note that New Delhi's reliance upon Soviet oil and other strategic imports increased Indian vulnerability.[34] Earlier, a dispatch by the Afro-Asian News Service alerted neutralist governments to Communist strategies

in seeking to penetrate Africa, particularly by utilizing
lavish Soviet and Chinese aid programs:

> Under the impact of this munificence, irregularities and cor-
> ruption are relied on to develop before long, leading to labor
> and other unrest. Direct interference in the business of gov-
> ernment is scheduled to follow, with the concomitant strikes,
> insurrections and intimidation, leading to a complete Com-
> munist takeover.[35]

Even when Communist policy-makers have made no
direct effort to subvert or infiltrate neutralist governments, beneficiaries of Communist assistance learned
fairly quickly that Communist aid had decided disadvantages as well as advantages. An American authority
on the Middle East declared in 1963 that "the Algerian
Government may be in for a shock in the field of Soviet
bloc aid, if past experience of other Arab lands provides
a criterion." He noted that

> Egypt, Syria, and Iraq, the three Arab lands which had ac-
> cepted major Soviet assistance, all had important exports
> with which to pay for . . . Communist help. . . . By de-
> grees, the Egyptian, Syrian, and Iraqi Governments have
> become disillusioned with the quality of Soviet products, to
> the extent that all three, wherever foreign exchange has per-
> mitted, have turned back to the West for industrial ma-
> chinery.[36]

From Burma came a highly adverse verdict about Chinese
foreign aid activities in nearby Cambodia. Severely criticizing Chinese aid programs, the source concluded a detailed recital of Communist failures in Cambodia:

> In effect, the Chinese aid projects in Cambodia appear to be
> designed to promote the impression of progress but actually
> have turned out to be inefficient, costly and a drain on the
> nation's resources. Prince Sihanouk [the leader of Cambodia]
> has himself pointed out, on more than one occasion . . .

that the creation of any more state enterprises modelled after the Chinese Communist aid factories would not be in the interest of the Cambodian economy.

Citing the unhappy Cambodian experience, this Burmese source called for Chinese aid programs to "display greater skill in planning, a higher level of technology, and less emphasis on politics." [37]

By 1964, dire admonitions about the consequences of accepting Soviet aid came from a new quarter—Mao Tse-tung's regime in Red China. According to Chinese policy-makers, needy countries ought to hesitate before accepting the Kremlin's largess, since "in their [the Soviet bloc's] economic exchanges with Asian and African countries, there are often cases in which they have no respect for their independence and sovereignty and flagrantly interfere in their internal affairs." According to China, the Kremlin asked for raw materials in exchange for aid, and Soviet offi-cials, it was charged, did not trade fairly; they cut import prices while raising those of exports. Similarly, in providing equipment, the Russians withhold technical advice, so as to make Asian and African countries economically de-pendent. Peking's indictment was authoritative—based on its own experience with the abrupt termination of Soviet aid and the withdrawal of technicians in 1960. And by the mid-1960's, even American officials conceded that many of their earlier fears had been groundless. In taking stock of intensive Communist military- and economic-aid pro-grams in Africa, State Department officials in 1964 found that the Communist bloc was in many cases unable to maintain scheduled deliveries of goods or to keep up a steady flow of certain commodities (like oil) required by African countries; in other cases, the goods supplied were totally unsuited to African needs—for example, heavy equipment not designed for use in the tropics; Commu-

nist technicians often became involved in "racial" problems, so that they "failed to develop popular acceptance
among Africans, even the degree of acceptance enjoyed
by Americans or Western Europeans." [38]

These were merely a few indications that neutralist recipients of Communist assistance were as perceptive and
as critical in judging the Communist bloc's foreign-aid
activities as they were in assessing Western programs.
Whether in Africa, the Arab world, or Asia, recipient
governments were fully mindful that officials in Moscow
and Peking viewed them as *instruments* for the attainment of Communist objectives. They also knew that,
despite the Communist bloc's propaganda and perhaps
an initial neutralist tendency to believe it, there were as
many disadvantages as advantages to Communist aid.
Ample realization of these facts largely explained the
growing tendency of neutralist countries to secure "balanced" aid commitments from East and West, and (even
in cases like Algeria) to preserve their historic ties with
the West.

Referring to the Czech-Egyptian arms agreement, an
official in Nasser's government declared in 1955:

> The greatest thing the arms deal has done is to give our peo-
> ple a feeling of pride. That pride is the best stimulation for
> patriotism and it is the best protection against domination,
> including Communism. I do not think that by buying Com-
> munist arms we made it possible for the Soviet to establish
> a favored position in Egypt. We are importing arms and not
> importing ideologies.

An Iraqi spokesman stated in 1957: "We believe that the
purchase of arms from the Soviet bloc for legitimate defense purposes is one thing and international Communism exploiting Arab nationalism another." Prince Naim
of Afghanistan replied to American apprehensions about

his country's "flirtations" with the Communist bloc by saying: "You can be sure that we accepted no conditions in our [aid] agreements with Russia. We are not the satellite of anyone. We are free and independent—and we intend to remain so." But it was perhaps the influential African newspaper *Drum* that most succinctly and forthrightly expressed the neutralist viewpoint about Communist aid programs. Far from being converted into "pawns of Communism" by accepting assistance from behind the Iron Curtain, said this publication, the "truth is the other way around":

> [African countries were] prepared to milk the Communist cow as long as it makes no demands on them. A cow's job is to yield food quietly. If it does not, it can be done away with.[39]

VI

The United States and the Neutralist Movement

In 1955, a high-ranking American official appraised the results of the Bandung Conference of Afro-Asian States as follows: "The Bandung Conference, as we had hoped, seems to have exerted a restraint on the Chinese Communists. I had always felt that it would be salutary if the Chinese Communists were confronted with the opinion of the free nations of Asia. That opinion was powerfully expressed in favor of peace and against direct and indirect aggression." Not long afterwards, this spokesman asserted: "The United States does not believe in practicing neutrality [i.e., neutralism]. Barring exceptional cases, neutrality today is an obsolete conception." Yet on another occasion, in replying to a question by a legislator, this official had observed: "I think we cannot adopt a policy of not extending a certain amount of assistance to countries which also deal with the Soviet Union. For example, that would in effect, involve writing off India. . . . As a matter of fact we all have some dealings with the Soviet Union, including the United States. Each case must be dealt with on its own facts." Again, when certain legislators were alarmed about growing ties between neutralist countries and the Communist bloc, he declared:

"We need not become panicky because Soviet Communism now disports itself in this new garb. We need not assume, as some seem to assume, that the leaders in the Asian countries are unaware of danger and easily duped by false promises." And when he faced a wave of legislative apprehension about the Czech-Egyptian arms agreement, this official stated that "the Arab countries were independent governments and free to do whatever they wished in the matter." He added philosophically: "It is difficult to be critical of countries which, feeling themselves in danger, seek the arms which they sincerely believe they need for defense." [1] In each instance, the official was Secretary of State John Foster Dulles. → of course

America and the Neutralists in the Dulles-Eisenhower Period

The ambiguity evident in Dulles' statements on the principle of nonalignment and on the behavior of individual neutralist countries has been the outstanding characteristic of the American response to neutralism from the mid-1950's to the present day. That response has been woven of many strands. But the dominant impression it produces upon the student of American foreign relations, and upon observers in neutralist countries, is *uncertainty and ambivalence* about the nature of the neutralist movement and about its implications for the attainment of American foreign-policy goals. The American response to the phenomenon of neutralism has consisted of two primary themes and a multitude of secondary ones, variously combining and often creating a policy dissonance that irritates the sensitivities of neutralist governments. The primary themes have consisted of two extreme and antithetical attitudes alternately displayed by official and public commentators within the United States: active or passive *opposition to* neutralism, and direct or indirect *support for* neutralism. The first was (or was widely thought to be) the leading motif in American foreign policy during the Dulles-Eisenhower period; the second has been dominant during the Kennedy-Johnson period.

Yet it must not be thought that American policy toward neutralism has evolved smoothly and without periodic retrogressions. It is well known that Secretary Dulles criticized neutralism in remarkably unequivocal language; what is less well known is that he found many "exceptions" to his dictum that neutralism was "immoral"—so many as to leave a substantial question as to what particular versions or manifestations of neutralist thought and conduct he found unacceptable. And if Dulles dramatically revoked the offer of aid for Egypt's Aswan High Dam, he no less ardently favored continued American assistance for countries like India and Yugoslavia. In general, he did not countenance movements on Capitol Hill seeking to withdraw American assistance from countries adhering to a neutralist position in world affairs. Similarly, if neutralism gained a new respectability in Washington during the Kennedy-Johnson era, this did not prevent American officials from expressing serious doubts about the Belgrade Conference in 1961, nor did it deter Congress from withdrawing certain trade concessions to Tito's regime in Yugoslavia, a move patently dictated by legislative annoyance with Tito's diplomatic fence-straddling and his seemingly successful exploitation of both the United States and the Soviet Union.

Two other general tendencies have been evident in the American response to neutralism. One of these received detailed attention in Chapter 1; here, we shall recapitulate it briefly. American attitudes and policies toward neutralism have been highly *episodic and pragmatic*. In dealing with extremely diverse manifestations of neutralism

—like Egypt's acceptance of Communist arms aid, Yugoslavia's acquisition of economic assistance from both Moscow and Washington, an officially supported anti-American campaign in Ghana, India's military encounter with Red China, Burma's attempt to "balance" aid from East and West, or Indonesia's militant confrontation with Malaysia—policy-makers in Washington have usually adhered to the characteristically American principle of "one problem at a time," or "each case on its own merits." The chief difficulty with such an approach has been that, in the absence of some reasonably clear principles or theoretical assessments of neutralism as an ideology, the "merits" of each case have often been far from clear. Lacking a typology of neutralism—which would demand a systematic attempt to examine and classify often dissimilar manifestations of the credo—American policy-makers have reacted in a series of isolated responses which fall into no logical or consistent pattern. The missing ingredient in the American response has been a set of criteria enabling official and unofficial observers to decide whether Algerian acceptance of Communist aid strengthens or weakens the ability of the free world to resist Communist expansionism, whether Afghanistan's attempt to "balance" aid from East and West is or is not compatible with American objectives, and whether the results of the Belgrade Conference in 1961 were more favorable to the diplomatic position of the West or of the Communist bloc. If public commentators have often been confused about such questions, the reason is in part that officials in Washington seemed no less confused; they have afforded little guidance in trying to cut through the shell of clichés and stereotypes surrounding discussion of neutralist viewpoints and policies.

A second general tendency in the American response to neutralism has been the increasingly wide divergence between *executive* department attitudes, on the one hand, and *legislative* and *public* attitudes, on the other. In the pages that follow, we shall call attention to the evolution in executive department assessments of neutralism. In its simplest terms, from the 1940's to the 1960's, State Department thinking changed from the belief that neutralism was "immoral" or otherwise unacceptable, to the idea that at worst it was inevitable, and that at best it was often fully compatible with American foreign-policy objectives. The same cannot be said for legislative and public viewpoints about neutralism. Attitudes toward neutralism on Capitol Hill, in the press, and among the people as a whole were in many respects as antagonistic in the mid-1960's as in the mid-1950's. However impolitic his language, Mr. Dulles' assertion that neutralism was "immoral" unquestionably described the dominant conviction of the American people and the prevailing sentiment in Congress. Consequently, for many years, there has existed a hiatus in the official American approach to neutralism, owing to fundamentally different conceptions in the executive and the legislative branches. The official "reassessment" of neutralism after the death of Mr. Dulles took place almost entirely among officials in the executive branch. To date, they have not succeeded (in part because they have not really tried) in altering legislative and public skepticism about the meaning and implications of neutralism for the United States.

That deep and pervasive skepticism about diplomatic neutralism has characterized public and official attitudes in the United States is a fact too obvious to require extensive documentation. Uneasiness and apprehension with regard to neutralism has expressed itself in a variety of ways—ranging from pointed references by State Department officials to "so-called neutralism" and in some cases to condemnations of "pro-Communist neutralism"; to blunt warnings to the Government of Morocco concerning Rabat's proposed purchase of Soviet aircraft; to prolonged hesitation in Washington before offering American assistance for Ghana's "Volta River Project"; to unmistakable chagrin among officials in the Kennedy Administration about the neutralist Belgrade Conference; to a tendency to regard newly independent countries like Algeria, Guinea, and Zanzibar as "Communist bridgeheads" in Africa; to legislative insistence upon revocation of economic concessions to Yugoslavia.[2]

American opposition to neutralism can be traced to five sources. The first—the factor that often pervades the other four—has been a widespread failure to understand the concept of diplomatic nonalignment *correctly.* In its crudest manifestations, American opposition to nonalignment has often stemmed from a distorted conception of what the doctrine involves and has rested upon expected patterns of neutralist behavior that proponents of the ideology have never accepted. Since we have dealt with many of these misconceptions elsewhere, we shall not discuss them again here.*

A second source of American skepticism about neutralism was illustrated by Dulles' widely quoted verdict that neutralism is "except under very exceptional circumstances . . . an immoral and shortsighted conception." Vice President Nixon similarly deplored what he called "moral neutralism" and said categorically that the American people were "getting a bellyful of so-called 'neutralism'" of this kind.[3] In this view, neutralism springs primarily from a lack of sensitivity about moral-ethical issues and distinctions in international affairs on the part of nonaligned nations. Neutralism is thus tantamount to

---

* The leading tenets of the concept of nonalignment—together with prevailing misconceptions about the doctrine—are examined at length in Chapter 1.

moral obtuseness or opaqueness, particularly in judging the global conduct of the Communist bloc, as illustrated by the neutralist tendency to "equate" the conduct of the West with the conduct of the Communist bloc on the global scene.

A third source of American skepticism has been the belief that neutralism is a *transitory phenomenon,* that it derives from the inability or unwillingness of policy-makers in Accra, Cairo, Belgrade, and New Delhi to make up their minds about where they belong with respect to Cold War power groupings. As Vice President Nixon declared in 1956:

> The struggle for the world will be finally determined by what happens to the millions of people *now* neutral who are *trying to decide whether they will align themselves* with the Communist nations or with the free nations.[4]

Believing that neutralist countries were merely sitting on the fence diplomatically, Americans logically expected that in time (and perhaps as a result of some traumatic experience, like Red China's attack upon India), neutralist states would be "converted" to one camp or the other. A logical corollary of this idea was the belief that —by methods ranging from generous foreign assistance (or the threat to *withdraw* foreign assistance), by propaganda and persuasion, or by expressions of official displeasure in Washington—the United States must seek to convert neutralist countries into outright or *de facto* allies.[5]

A fourth source of American opposition to neutralism is the conviction that nonalignment is a policy of sheer expediency and opportunism. This attitude was exemplified by the views of subordinate American officials in New Delhi, whose thinking on the subject of Indian efforts to obtain assistance from both East and West was summarized by a former American official in India:

We ought not to allow ourselves to be jockeyed in a position of being elbowed by these Soviets coming in here or by the Indians allowing them to come in here. Why don't we tell the Indian Government that if it wants to continue to have economic aid from the United States, it must tell these Russians here and now that the United States won't have any truck with them. As long as the Russians are in here bidding against the United States, we are going to be caught in a grindstone or be played off one against the other. We ought not to let the United States get into that position. . . . India must play with us solely or not at all.[6]

For reasons that we shall discuss later, this view was seldom accepted as a basis for U.S. policy.

Yet among all the factors inducing grave concern about neutralism in the United States, perhaps none was as crucial as the fear that "neutralism" was closely linked with Communism and that, deliberately or otherwise, nonaligned countries were "playing the Communist game." This idea had several refinements and variations. Neutralists, it was widely believed, were naïve about the true nature of the Communist "global conspiracy"; they did not "understand" the Communist menace "realistically." Thus, as one official explained in 1954, many advocates of neutralism in Asia are not as aware as they should be of the dangers of Communism and are too neutralist in their approach to it. In 1957, Secretary Dulles informed the neutralist community that "there is no safe middle ground." The United States, he declared, very much wanted "the new independence of others to be something more than a brief twilight preceding the black-out of Communist despotism." And on another occasion, Dulles approvingly cited an earlier remark by Stalin that "neutrality" meant in effect "conniving at aggression."[7]

Others regarded neutralism as little more than an ideological way station on the road to Communism. Thus, a

1956 report to the House Affairs Committee labeled neutralism "the first step toward the eventual expansion of
Communist power." A "neutral Asia" would "allow free
play for Soviet diplomacy, propaganda, infiltration, and
eventually subversion." Again, as a State Department official asserted concerning Communist strategy in Asia:
"The purpose of this campaign is clear. It is aimed at inducing neutralism, weakening our alliances, and lowering
the guard of those opposing Communist expansion." Another State Department official in 1960 described a major
goal of Communist policy-makers as endeavoring "to try
to create neutral areas in Latin America." And another
official held that Communism supported "the concept of
neutrality as a means of weakening or disrupting the col-
lective-security measures of the free world." [8]

Still another variant on the idea that neutralism and
Communism were inextricably linked was the belief that
countries embracing nonalignment either were, or were
in the process of becoming, overtly or covertly, Commu-
nist-controlled. Phrases like "ungrateful Communist
dupes" and the "Kremlin's stooge" have been applied to
various neutralist governments. President Eisenhower
said in reference to Syria in 1957 that the Kremlin was
seeking to offer "economic and military aid, and through
doing so, to penetrate the receiving country with their
agents, for these to get into power, to find stooges that
will do their will, and finally, to take over the country."
A year later, Secretary Dulles said that Sukarno's "guided
democracy" in neutralist Indonesia was merely "a nice-
sounding name for what I fear would end up to be Communist despotism." And in 1960, Secretary Christian A.
Herter asserted that Ghana had passed into "the Communist camp." [9]

The American Reassessment of Neutralism

On April 21, 1956, President Eisenhower declared that most new nations in the world

> have many of the sensitivities that mark our own early years as a free Nation. They are proud of their independence and quick to resent any slight to their sovereignty. Some of them are concerned to avoid involvement with other nations, as we were for many years. Certainly we Americans should understand and respect these points of view. We must accept the right of each nation to choose its own path to the future.

The previous year, a State Department official said that under Prime Minister Nehru, "India will be allied to us in the fundamentals of our objectives—namely, independence of countries from outside interference and individual dignity and personal freedoms. However, India will not join in military alliances and is not impressed by those statements that have been made that 'they are either for us or against us.'" And when John F. Kennedy campaigned for the Presidency in 1960, he declared that in the global contest with Communism, the greatest force favoring the free world "is the desire of people to be free. . . . And my judgment is that they don't want to give their freedom up to become Communists. They want to stay free, independent, perhaps of us, but certainly independent of the Communists. And I believe that if we identify ourselves with that force . . . we can strengthen freedom. We can make it move. We can put the Communists on the defensive." Vice President Nixon similarly declared that "we must remember that the people of Africa and Asia and Latin America don't want to be pawns simply in a struggle between two great powers. . . ." [10]

If bewilderment, skepticism, and sometimes outright

hostility were prominent themes in the American response to neutralism throughout most of the 1950's, by the end of that decade even neutralist sources themselves conceded that new themes usually characterized American relations with neutralist countries. At worst, American officials reserved their strictures for certain *varieties* of neutralist thought and conduct deemed injurious to Western diplomatic interests. At best, policy-makers in the United States increasingly came to terms with the neutralist ideology, endorsed the principle of diplomatic nonalignment (if they did not always endorse specific applications of the principle), and endeavored to establish a new rapport with leading neutralist countries. Washington, in the words of an Asian publication, had entertained "more sober thoughts" about the nature and significance of the neutralist movement.*

Before examining some of the considerations fostering these "more sober thoughts," it is worthwhile to recall two facts about this policy reassessment. First, executive policy-makers were becoming more *discriminating* in their evaluation of the attitudes and conduct of neutralist states. If neutralist conduct could still occasionally evoke apprehension and indignation among State Department officials, these attitudes were nearly always directed at *individual* nonaligned countries (like Yugoslavia or Indonesia) or, more rarely, at selected groups of countries (for example, the radical "Casablanca" powers in Africa).

*David C. Williams, "New Friendship for India," *Eastern World*, XIV (March, 1960), 28. For other neutralist appraisals of the change in American policy, see *Times of India*, June 20, 1961, and the views of Prince Sihanouk of Cambodia in *Asian Recorder*, VII (October 29–November 4, 1961), 4240. Here, as elsewhere in the neutralist world, the opinion was frequently expressed that after the death of Secretary of State Dulles, the true sentiments of President Eisenhower emerged. Eisenhower was always believed to be more tolerant and understanding of neutralism than was his Secretary of State. In the neutralist view, in these and other matters, Mr. Dulles largely dominated the foreign-policy process during his tenure.

By and large, executive officials avoided blanket indictments and stereotypes; their approach reflected growing awareness of the richness and diversity in the neutralist movement. At the same time, this was seldom accompanied by official statements showing *why or how* policymakers differentiated between the neutralism of Guinea, Nigeria, Tunisia, Egypt, Ceylon, or Cambodia; nor was it usually clear *why* the neutralism of some countries was more deleterious to Western diplomatic interests than was the neutralism of other countries. The essentially *ad hoc* character of the American response to neutralism thus left unresolved the question how executive policymakers classified varieties of neutralism and how they evaluated existing varieties.

A number of considerations and influences coalesced to induce an official re-examination of the neutralist ideology. In the first place, this reappraisal was an inevitable by-product of the waning of the more militant anti-Westernism that accompanied nationalist movements in Asia, the Arab world, and Africa in the postwar period. We have underscored the fact that nonalignment and anti-colonialism were companion movements. By the end of the 1950's, much of the tension previously present in American relations with neutralist governments because of colonial questions was rapidly disappearing. One by one, Western powers had liquidated, or were in the process of liquidating, their colonial empires. By the late 1950's, the United States had begun to speak out openly against remaining colonialist and racist regimes in Portuguese Angola and South Africa.

As Western empires were liquidated, American policymakers gradually became aware of a highly significant fact about the attitude of nonaligned governments. This was that there existed in these countries *remarkably little permanent, intractable anti-Westernism*—far less than might have been anticipated in the late 1940's or early 1950's. When he visited the United States in 1956, President Sukarno said: "We may, in fact we do, sometimes oppose what is called the West. But that is not dictated by a feeling of being anti-West." Several months later, another Indonesian official declared that "the natural sympathy which we of Asia and Africa feel for the West is too precious for the West to dissipate. That is one major reason why I regret the tone of much of the comments made about Indonesia recently." By 1961, an Egyptian source similarly commented: "The amazing thing is that no real African resentment against Westerners as such appears to exist. With independence the African has shown himself willing to cooperate with the European at all levels and in all spheres," providing such cooperation was based upon "complete respect for mutual independence and sovereignty." And by 1963, a State Department official found that "new currents of thought in South Asia are sharpening an awareness of values shared with the West and are promoting practical moves designed to protect and promote those values." [11]

Far sooner than many Westerners expected, newly independent countries sought Western assistance and support in meeting their economic needs, in providing military advice and training, in strengthening their educational systems, in broadening their trade relations, and generally in creating a more constructive relationship with the industrialized nations that went far toward erasing the virulent anti-Westernism witnessed during the pre-independence period.

A second force engendering a reassessment of neutralism in the United States was identified by Secretary of State Dean Rusk in 1963, when he referred to the "profound partnership" existing between the United States and

India in international affairs. In a statement prominently featured in the Indian press, Rusk declared:

> We have known in our constant association . . . how much there is of common commitment and common purpose between our two countries. We also know that you have been called upon to serve the United Nations in ways which we ourselves could not.

In New Delhi's mediatorial role in crises like the Korean War, the colonial conflict in Indochina, political instability in Laos, and the vexatious Congo question, Rusk found evidence of India's deeply ingrained respect for "that decent world order represented in the Charter of the United Nations which we all cherish." [12]

Increasingly, American officials had become conscious of the contributions made by neutralist states, most conspicuously India, in resolving issues that could lead to Cold War conflicts. The crisis in the Congo perhaps focused global attention most dramatically upon this aspect of neutralism. For in that crisis India, along with a large number of other nonaligned states (including Ghana, Guinea, Morocco, Egypt, Ethiopia, Tunisia, Iraq, and Indonesia), assumed the burden of maintaining at least minimal political stability in this strife-torn country, thereby averting what could have been, and assuredly in time would have become, a new Cold War confrontation in the heart of Africa. For their part, neutralist sources commented enthusiastically about American "recognition" of the neutralist role in global affairs and spoke of the "common purpose" uniting the United States and neutralist countries in dealing with the Congo issue.[13]

Policy-makers in the United States were no less conscious of the contributions made by neutralist states in other areas. In the United Nations, for example, despite superficial evidence of some kind of neutralist-Communist diplomatic entente, one State Department official declared in 1963 that "there is no indication that Guinea or any of the other countries in that group are following the lead of the Soviet Union." So far as India was concerned, another official declared, it was necessary to look at the "over-all picture"; it was clear that on many issues, Indian officials were obviously "acting in a way that advances not only their interests but very much our own interests."[14] Among the smaller and less influential neutralist states, Ethiopia was commended for its "strong support of collective security" in the Congo and elsewhere; Lebanon was cited as a country deserving American economic support because it served as "an example for other countries of the Near East of the benefits to be obtained from cooperation with the free world"; cordial relations with Libya were justified as a "valuable political asset in United States relations with the Arab world"; Morocco served a useful role as a "bridge between the Arab world and the Western Powers"; Saudi Arabia was viewed as a "major bulwark against Communist encroachment in the Arab world"; neutralist Somalia was "currently oriented toward the West"; Tunisia had been "outspoken in public support of United States policies"; and the example of Yugoslavia was "widely acknowledged to have been a major factor contributing to increasing tendencies towards national independence in Eastern Europe." [15]

In brief, American officials had discovered many areas in which the national interests of the United States and of neutralist countries coincided, particularly in crisis situations in which nations openly identified with the West or the Communist bloc would have had great difficulty discharging the role assumed by the neutralist states.

A third, and extremely important, consideration leading policy-makers in the United States to reassess the neutralist ideology was their realization of an earlier theme in official American appraisals of neutralism—usually submerged by Dullesian condemnations of the movement—that the ability of neutralist countries to *preserve* their independence, and to meet the social and economic needs of their societies, was itself a substantial diplomatic gain for the West, far outweighing any minor (and usually temporary) damage done by Ghana's denunciation of Western "neo-colonialism" or India's support of the Communist bloc's position in disarmament proceedings.

This argument was repeatedly invoked to justify American economic assistance to India, in the face of legislative and public opposition to many aspects of New Delhi's foreign policy. As early as 1953, one high-ranking executive department spokesman alluded to the "spectacular" competition between India and Red China—a competition that "is going to have a very vital effect in my opinion upon the welfare of us all." Accordingly, it was imperative that the United States "make some contribution to help see to it that the free methods of India produced better results than the police state, collectivist, totalitarian methods of Communist China." Essentially the same idea was invoked by this spokesman to justify American assistance to Tito's regime in Yugoslavia. In its own interests the United States was obliged "to assist Yugoslavia in maintaining its independence from the Soviet Union—independence which has been vigorously asserted and which holds out a hope to other countries of Eastern Europe now satellites . . . that they may try to follow the example of Tito in asserting their independence." The official who advocated American understanding and generosity in dealing with neutralist India and Yugoslavia, as well as with a number of less influential nonaligned countries, was Secretary of State Dulles.[16]

By the late 1950's, Dulles' view was reflected in official

American appraisals of neutralist viewpoints and policies. "Diplomatically," said one official in 1958, the United States should "put a greater premium on the posture of governments toward the modernization of their own societies than on their day-to-day position in the politics of the Cold War." Another official declared in 1960: "The African nations prize their independence; they have a vested interest in freedom, and they are unlikely at the decisive moments to mistake the enemies for the friends of freedom." Still another one described what he called a "reverse domino effect" favoring the West: By providing assistance to neutralist countries like India and Israel, the United States enabled these countries in turn to assist other developing nations. This spokesman was convinced that "free peoples everywhere will prefer to continue free . . . economic progress to the state of self-sustaining growth." Another official observed that American assistance to Cambodia, Burma, and Indonesia, and other "freedom-loving countries is based on the belief that by helping those who seek to remain free we are helping our own security and our own efforts to preserve freedom." Any time a nation within the free world makes "economic, social, and political progress" this "expands the frontier of freedom." Even in the case of Indonesia—whose unique version of nonalignment is perhaps viewed more apprehensively in Washington than is any other variety—the controlling fact was that President Sukarno "doesn't want to come under the domination of anybody." [17]

Executive officials in the United States, in other words, had concluded that even in countries like Indonesia—where nonalignment in practice often meant overt identification with policies favored by the Communist bloc or undisguised opposition to Western-sponsored proposals like the Federation of Malaysia—the decisive fact about Sukarno's government was its unswerving commitment to national independence. So long as officials in Djakarta and other neutralist capitals were devoted to this goal and capable of maintaining it, this fact served the diplomatic interests of the West.

A fourth consideration prompting a re-examination of neutralism was an outgrowth and refinement of the previous one. Neutralist dedication to the principle of national independence logically implied opposition to, and measures to counteract, Communist-instigated threats to the independence of neutralist societies. Despite neutralist and Communist agreement on a variety of international issues, by the late 1950's it had become fully apparent to perceptive observers that political leaders in neutralist countries not only recognized the dangers posed by Communist global intrigues; they were actively taking steps—in the vast majority of cases, extraordinarily *successful* steps—to resist subordination to the Communist bloc. A Senator expressed the prevailing attitude among executive policy-makers in this period, when he said with respect to Egypt:

> The Soviet Union has supplied a lot of arms to the United Arab Republic. We have for a long time been terribly concerned about the United Arab Republic being a satellite of the Communist bloc by virtue of this arms supply. . . . We are beginning to wake up to the fact that the United Arab Republic may not be a satellite at all, despite the extent of Soviet involvement there. It is one African country where all the Communists are in jail.

The U.A.R. was by no means the only neutralist country where Communists were in jail because the Communist movement had been declared illegal. Ironically, in nearly all African and Arab countries (and, to a lesser extent, in Asia), Communist groups face more stringent legal restraints on their activities than they do in the United States and in Western Europe. As early as 1957, after his tour of

Africa, Vice President Nixon found that although Africa was an area of high Communist priority, "Communist domination in the states of the area is not a present danger. All of the African leaders to whom I talked are determined to maintain their independence against Communism or any other form of foreign domination." In 1964 a State Department study concluded that "the leaders in most African countries are extremely wary of unquestioning acceptance of Communist aid or influence." A major finding of this study was that Communist-bloc aid activities in Africa were "dwarfed by contributions from the United States, France, and other Western powers." That this phenomenon was not confined to Africa was indicated by another official who, a few months earlier, had pointed to the example of Iraq: "The Soviets have been putting a lot of money . . . and the recent revolution in Iraq [led by Colonel Aref] was plainly directed against the increasing dependence on the Soviet Union. The Government now in control in Iraq is strongly and definitely anti-Communist." [18]

Events had revealed that in practice a foreign policy of nonalignment meant precisely what Nkrumah, Touré, Nasser, and Nehru had always contended it meant: the determination to preserve independence in policy-making from *all* alien forces, including those supported by the Communist bloc.

A fifth consideration leading American officials to reappraise the concept of neutralism was identified by Secretary Rusk, when he told a congressional committee in 1963:

> there is nothing that the Communists want more than for us to withdraw our support from other independent countries. . . . The number one objective of Communist policy in regard to Europe, Asia, the Far East, Africa, and Latin America can be summed up in three words: "Yanks, go home." [19]

Four basic alternatives were open to the United States in its relations with neutralist countries: Officials in Washington could actively oppose the principle of neutralism; they could ignore, or be indifferent to, the efforts of countries to remain diplomatically nonaligned; they could come to terms with the neutralist ideology; or they could endeavor to cooperate with neutralist governments to achieve common diplomatic purposes.[20] The first two alternatives involved active or passive opposition to neutralism; the last two involved active or passive acceptance of neutralism.

Executive policy-makers concluded that the last two alternatives offered far more possibilities for achieving Western diplomatic goals than the first two. As with most foreign-policy decisions, this did not mean that the State Department was unaware of certain drawbacks in this course of action; nor did it signify that, after 1960, policy-makers were as uncritical in endorsing neutralism as they had been in condemning it earlier. This new appraisal meant simply that on balance the advantages of coming to terms with neutralism and of seeking to maintain a *modus vivendi* with neutralist governments outweighed the disadvantages of doing so.

Experience with neutralism during the late 1940's and 1950's had tended to confirm (1) that all attempts by the United States to intimidate neutralist states, to coerce them, to isolate them, to discipline them, or otherwise seek to "convert" them into unwilling allies were doomed to failure; (2) that such attempts more often than not produced the opposite results from those intended by the State Department, by creating new opportunities for Communist ties with neutralist countries; and (3) that whatever Americans might think of nonalignment as a diplomatic philosophy, the ideology was firmly established and was gaining adherents.

To illustrate the likely consequences of a policy of active
or passive opposition to neutralism, let us focus upon the
specific problem of American economic and military aid to
countries in the neutralist communist. When it encountered
requests for economic and military assistance from these
nations, the United States had basically two choices: it
could either extend limited aid to these countries, or it
could withhold such aid on the ground that it was not in
the interests of the United States to assist countries that
sat on the fence diplomatically or worked both sides of the
street in economic and military affairs. What would be the
likely consequences of following this latter course?

Judging from past experience, policy-makers could anticipate a number of reactions—nearly all of them injurious
to the Western diplomatic position. A significant one was
alluded to in our earlier quotation by Secretary Rusk and
was reiterated by another official, who stated in connection
with American aid to Asian countries: "The principal alternative to American aid in the Far East today is Communist aid and we can be certain that wherever and when-
ever we step out, the Communists stand eager and ready to
step in." Or, as another official said with reference to Yugoslavia, without American assistance "the Yugoslav people
would have suffered severe economic distress. The country's resistance to Soviet domination would have weakened,
with consequent dangers to the West." By contrast, continued American assistance "provided the internal strength
on which the Yugoslavs can base their independence, and
on which they can maintain it, unmoved either by Soviet
enticements or threats." But it was perhaps in connection
with Tunisia that the idea we are discussing here was most
poignantly expressed. Tunisia, along with all other developing nations, "will continue to need very large amounts of
assistance for foreign sources for some time to come." This
being true, said one official, the United States "cannot

afford to place the Tunisian Government in a position where it would be faced with the alternative of turning toward the Eastern bloc or seeing its economy disintegrate." [21]

Aside from the obvious danger of permitting, if not in some instances compelling, exclusive neutralist reliance upon the Communist bloc in economic and military affairs, Western assistance to neutralist countries had another advantage that events had shown to be of primary importance. This was the opportunity it afforded neutralist countries to compare Communist and Western aid programs. Although State Department officials were not so naïve as to suppose that this comparison would always redound to the credit of the West, in a significant number of cases it had already done so. At a minimum, it would permit neutralist governments to achieve the kind of balance among foreign sources of aid that most of them sought to maintain and which would afford some assurance that one country or great-power bloc did not become economically or militarily dominant within the country.

If it is obvious that policy-makers in the United States were apprehensive about complete or preponderant neutralist reliance upon Communist-bloc assistance, it is less thoroughly appreciated that American officials were only slightly less concerned about neutralist reliance solely upon the West in meeting their economic and military needs. For, with opposition to foreign-aid programs steadily growing on Capitol Hill, few developments would have created greater consternation among State Department officials than a diplomatic note from a neutralist country, reading substantially as follows:

> For many years, the United States has expressed its concern about our acceptance of Communist economic and military assistance, despite the fact that we are determined to preserve our independence fully as much from Communist as

from Western domination. Experience has confirmed that we are prepared to act upon this conviction. Nevertheless, we might be prepared to scale down economic and military aid from the Communist world, provided the United States is willing to extend assistance on the same scale as we currently receive it from the U.S.S.R. and Red China. If you are prepared to assume this obligation, we shall be glad to discuss the problem with your government.

Almost certainly, American officials would have to reply in effect: "Sorry, but we are not only unprepared to assume new foreign aid commitments; we are under mounting congressional pressure to pare down existing programs." Perhaps nothing would be better calculated to foster neutralist disillusionment with the West, and to open the door for expanded Communist bloc activities throughout the neutralist zone, than this dog-in-the-manger attitude. American officials would be saying in essence: We are neither prepared to meet your economic and military requirements ourselves nor do we favor your relying upon the Communist bloc to meet them. And this would be tantamount to saying that the United States was totally indifferent to the efforts of neutralist governments to promote economic development and to preserve their security from hostile internal and external forces.

Heretical as it may sound, there had been a perceptible tendency for the State Department to regard neutralist acquisition of Communist aid as a *beneficial* development, insofar as it stiffens the fiber of the free world to resist internal and external Communist pressures. Officials in the United States have tended to reason that there is an intimate connection between the ability of a country to resist Communism, or other forms of political extremism, and its success in solving formidable economic problems and in preserving its own internal security. To the extent that foreign assistance from Communist sources—or from *any* sources—contributes to this long-range political and economic stability, it strengthens the ability of individual neutralist countries, and all of them collectively, to preserve their national independence.[22]

A long-time goal of American foreign policy, said a State Department spokesman in 1963, was "to maintain moderate pro-Western regimes in power." To achieve this, the United States was obliged to maintain constructive relations with political leaders in neutralist countries, who "find it politically imperative to diversify their sources of assistance in order to counter charges of submitting to neocolonial dependence."[23] The extent to which the principle can be carried was illustrated by the case of Ethiopia, which during the 1950's had outside foreign-aid technicians and advisers from no less than seven different countries. While other nonaligned countries perhaps do not go as far in "balancing" their foreign aid, the Ethiopian experience is not an isolated phenomenon. In the neutralist view, both psychologically and actually, a proper balance among outside aid sources is widely regarded as a vital step in maintaining national independence and in guaranteeing that no foreign country or power bloc exerts a disproportionate influence upon the affairs of the host country.

A sixth major influence persuading American officials to re-examine the neutralist ideology involved certain significant *strategic and military* realities. Many of the strategic advantages to the West of nonalignment came to the fore as a result of Red China's attack on India late in 1962. Since we discussed the implications of this crisis earlier,* we shall merely summarize here the principal strategic considerations at stake in India's decision to remain nonaligned after the Chinese attack. In New Delhi and Washington alike, the verdict was that little would be gained and much would be lost by India's renunciation of nonalign-

* See Chapter 2.

ment and its entry into a Western military pact. India's adherence to nonalignment permitted New Delhi to utilize both Western and Soviet aid for its defense and for its economic-development programs (some of which at least were jeopardized because of the new defense outlays now required); it prevented Red China from demanding Soviet support for its Himalayan venture, as would surely have occurred if India entered a Western military alliance; it encouraged a national response to the Chinese threat that both New Delhi and Washington favored—a maximum effort to repel the Chinese invader by national self-reliance instead of by reliance on outside assistance; and it avoided (at a time when the United States was deeply involved in the Cuban missile crisis, Southeast Asia, and the Formosa Straits) a new and perhaps massive American military commitment which Washington neither desired nor was prepared to carry out.

The Sino-Indian crisis, in other words, underscored a fact that is often overlooked in the United States. This is that the possession of new allies inescapably entails the assumption of new military obligations. An alliance with a weak and vulnerable country, American policy-makers were reminded by the Sino-Indian conflict, may prove a decidedly mixed blessing, particularly if it means (and, to signify anything, it could hardly mean otherwise) that the United States and its NATO partners must assume the burden of protecting the Indian subcontinent from further Chinese incursions. Or, if India's accession to the Western camp did *not* mean this—if this climactic event were *not* accompanied by a vast expansion in Western economic and military assistance to India and a military commitment sufficient to assure eventual liquidation of the Chinese threat—what then did India's formal alignment with the West really signify? And what would be the likely consequences if the United States permitted its newly gained ally to suffer a series of defeats at the hands of the Chinese aggressor? Could it really be contended, from the vantage point of military strategy or any other relevant consideration, that this would constitute a "victory" for the West, or that it would predispose other neutralist governments to move closer to Washington?

The Himalayan crisis demonstrated the truth of a contention by a State Department official in 1958 that "even if [neutralist states] made military alliances [with the West], their contribution to the military effectiveness of the alliance would be negligible." Or, as another official declared with reference to African states in 1961: "We do not expect that the small, lightly armed forces of African nations receiving our military aid will make any military contribution to the free world defense in the event of global war." [24] *meaning: American defense* Such countries could best strengthen the defense of the free world by following the example set by India in its contest with Red China. This was to rely first and foremost upon its own resources to repel a foreign threat; to utilize foreign assistance as effectively as possible in expanding its defense effort; to continue its economic development programs, on which the political stability and defense capacity of the country ultimately depend; to maintain a high degree of political unity and social cohesiveness; and to prepare for any eventuality in dealing with Communist-instigated expansionism. Neither these nor any other steps could of course "guarantee" future Indian security; but they were clearly prerequisite to its achievement. And, ironically, it was nonaligned India that realized these facts better than such "aligned" countries as South Korea and South Vietnam.

The seventh and last factor fostering a re-examination of nonalignment in Washington was in many respects the most influential of all, since it was implicit in and infused the others. This was the growing recognition among American policy-makers that overt or passive opposition to neutralism introduced and perpetuated a basic *ideological ambivalence* in American foreign policy. This ambivalence, injurious in its own right, served as a needless irritant in American relations with neutralist governments on a great variety of global issues.

In the American view, the Cold War involves a clash between the forces of tyranny and liberty, between enforced political compliance and freedom of choice, between monolithic political systems and pluralistic political orders, between imposed philosophical unity and broad ideological diversity—this, at any rate, is the argument the United States has used throughout Africa, the Arab region, and Asia.

Yet efforts by the United States to win acceptance of this conception have been seriously impaired by its own hostility to the idea that ideological freedom of choice entails the freedom of countries to "choose" a diplomatic position different from that identified with Washington, Moscow, or Peking. If the Western conception of freedom does not mean the freedom of neutralist countries to work out their own political and diplomatic salvation—including the freedom to make their own mistakes—then what does it mean? To advocates of nonalignment, it sometimes seems little more than a thinly disguised and sophisticated demand that other countries do what the Communist bloc also demands—follow dutifully in the diplomatic wake of one of the great powers.

When American officials appraised the ideological dimensions of the problem of neutralism, it became clear that among all the ways a particular country might be considered "aligned" or "nonaligned," the ideological sphere was the most fundamental. This does not imply either that neutralist governments, any more than Western or Communist governments, are motivated in their foreign relations solely by ideological considerations; or that great ideological divergencies cannot be found within the neutralist community. It simply means that the most meaningful and crucial fact about any nation's diplomatic alignment or nonalignment is its dedication to national independence and its determination to preserve this in the face of internal and external threats. By the late 1950's, American foreign policy toward neutralist countries tended to be governed more and more by the realization that if neutralist countries *desired* to safeguard their freedom and if they were *capable* of doing so, they were already in effect "aligned" philosophically and ideologically with the West against the Communist bloc.

Self-justification

Actually, this idea was far from new. As early as 1952, in his message to Congress asking for favorable action on foreign aid, President Truman said that recipients of American aid

> are our friends, and not our satellites. As friends, they contribute to the shared wisdom and faith of the free world—a wisdom and faith on which no single nation can claim a monopoly. We must accordingly take care to treat them as friends. We must not act as though we wished to degrade them to the rank of satellites by exacting a rigid and humiliating subservience which no free nation could with dignity accept. We will never be defeated as long as we truly stand for a free partnership of free peoples. The unconquerable power of the free world lies in the fact that loyalties are not coerced.[25]

A few years later, the American Ambassador to India said that the United States would be fully content if India "pursues her own course and her own policy in the direction of world peace." Secretary Dulles himself told a congressional committee in 1958:

> The free world seems dominated more by differences than by harmony. . . . But we need constantly to remember that the

hallmark of freedom is diversity. The United States does not seek the kind of unity that has to be bought and paid for, or that would flow from our using our power to coerce other free nations and to impose our will. The United States associates itself with those who, as a matter of conviction, want to share in a common effort on behalf of independence and freedom.[26]

Such judgments about implications of neutralism were made even more explicit after 1960. Thus, in 1961, Secretary Rusk declared that the United States and its allies sought "a world of free choice in which a great diversity of nations, each faithful to its own traditions and genius, will respect the ground rules for human survival and orderly international life." Regarding differences between neutralist countries and those formally "aligned" with the West, Rusk observed that "if we see the underlying issue of our time as that between a world of coercion and a world of choice, the differences between ally and neutral becomes somewhat less important." The real philosophical conflict centered around "the world of coercion against the rest, between those who would build a United Nations and those who would tear it down," between those who would join in promoting respect for world law "and those who would be a law unto themselves." Rusk emphasized that "there are no differences of substance between those who call themselves neutrals and those committed by alliances; this is an issue in which it is the Communist bloc against the rest of the world." [27]

President Johnson was no less explicit. In 1964, he was asked: "Is a more and more diverse world, with the diminishing of the importance of great alliances, a trend toward a safer world?" The President replied: "Yes, I think so." He acknowledged that, consciously or unconsciously, many Americans "feel that all we need to do is mash a button and determine everybody's foreign policy. But we are not living in that kind of a world any more. They [other countries] are going to determine it for themselves, and that is the way it should be. And we are going to have to come and reason with them and try to lead them instead of force them." [28] But it was President Kennedy who most forcefully articulated the new assessment in Washington of neutralism as an ideology. The United States, he declared, sought to create a "peaceful world community of free and independent states, free to choose their own future and their own system as long as it does not threaten the freedom of others." The vital distinction between Western and Communist goals in this matter, the President emphasized, was this:

> Some may choose forms and ways that we would not choose ourselves, but it is not for us that they are choosing. We can welcome diversity—the Communists cannot. For we offer a world of choice—they offer the world of coercion and the way of the past shows clearly that freedom, not coercion, is the way of the future.[29]

However much the fact may have been obscured by irritation with individual neutralist states, executive policymakers had come to realize that a common dedication to freedom, independence, self-determination, justice, and other shared ideological and ethical principles provided the strongest bond linking the West with societies throughout the neutralist zone. So long as these links held—so long as peoples in this region *retained* their dedication to these principles and their determination to defend them—the distinction between "neutralist" governments and "allies" was of minor importance.

VII

The Future of Nonalignment

The doctrine of diplomatic nonalignment arose in response to a particular set of historical circumstances and causations. In common with all credos and political principles, it both affected its environment and was affected by it. And like other doctrines that continue to elicit support, to remain viable, it was forced to take into account significant trends in the context within which it was articulated and applied.

At the time neutralism, or nonalignment, as it came to be called later, first appeared—and it was initially identified with India, after that country became independent in 1947 —the political environment was dominated by the struggle between the West and the Communist world. Even before the end of World War II, tensions had developed among the major Allies. In the early postwar period, the Cold War contest between the United States and its supporters and the Soviet Union and its supporters dominated the international scene. From Western Europe to the South China Sea, there was scarcely an international problem that was unrelated to this contest. The struggle affected nearly all aspects of the international political life: political developments in Europe, colonial issues in the Arab world, disarmament questions, the structure of the United Nations, questions of trade and commerce.

Furthermore, it evoked on both sides a depth of feeling and commitment that has seldom been equaled in history. Stemming from totally antithetical ideological and value systems, and from seemingly irreconcilable national demands, this contest affected the very language of international discourse, so much so that it often proved impossible for the two sides to communicate and to define precisely the issues dividing them. In the Marxist lexicon, phrases like "peace," "self-determination," and "democracy" were given connotations that, in the Western view, denoted the opposite of what they had traditionally meant. Evincing an almost pathological suspicion and insecurity in their relations with the West, Marxists simply could not accept the idea that Western nations wanted, or were capable of achieving, a *modus vivendi* with the Communist world. During the Stalinist era of ideological rigidity, capitalism was held to be "collapsing" and the victory of the "revolutionary struggle" was deemed to be "inevitable."

For its part, American society exhibited a dogmatism of its own in indiscriminately attributing all threats to world peace and security to "international Communism." Whether confronted with an outright Communist military thrust in Korea, or a Soviet-instigated takeover in Czechoslovakia, a nationalist movement in Indochina, a *coup d'état* in Iraq, or an anti-American demonstration in Latin America, the explanation in all cases was likely to be the machination of "international Communism." And as with all oversimplified explanations of extremely complex phenomena, the developments raised serious questions about the adequacy of such an explanation and about its usefulness as a basis for responding to crisis situations. Among other defects, it left unanswered the question of which manifestations and activities of international Communism the United

States could tolerate and coexist with, and which were totally inimical to the well-being and security of the West.

Against this background of seemingly irreconcilable conflict, East and West continued to expand their arsenals, particularly their nuclear weapons and missile-delivery systems. Phrases like "inevitable victory," "massive retaliation," and "brink of war" illustrated the degree to which both sides believed that the conflict would sooner or later end in a global Armageddon.

This was the international environment which the nascent nations of Asia, the Arab world, and Africa entered and which they were expected to survive. They were not only supposed to survive—they were expected to tackle age-old problems of poverty, disease, illiteracy, and human misery. Prodded by the public and political opposition groups, the new governments were required to translate political independence into improved living standards and to produce evidence of the emergence of a better social and economic order. Throughout the Afro-Arab-Asian world, the "revolution of rising expectations" conditioned the attitudes and policies of governments toward internal and external developments.

It is therefore not surprising that newly independent governments tended to adopt the following foreign-policy objectives: (1) to give priority to domestic, rather than foreign, affairs; (2) to avoid participation in the Cold War —a struggle whose outcome they were not likely to affect appreciably and from involvement in which they could expect only injury; (3) to conduct relations with the great powers on an *ad hoc* basis, to avoid either permanent diplomatic alignment or permanent alienation, and to contract ties on the basis of reciprocated friendship and concern; (4) to apply constant pressure on the great powers to resolve outstanding Cold War issues; and (5) to seek help and support from all available sources.

The most remarkable fact about this approach to foreign relations is that it worked extraordinarily well—much better, in all likelihood, than early advocates of neutralism like Nehru, U Nu of Burma, or Tito could have anticipated. If champions of neutralism could claim some credit for its success, they were also obliged to give credit to certain developments on the international scene that greatly facilitated this result.

The first of these was the passing of Stalinism. After 1953, Khrushchev—subjected to mounting pressure at home for a higher standard of living, confronted with repeated crises in Soviet agriculture, and faced with growing diplomatic restiveness among the European satellites—inaugurated a new era of peaceful coexistence, or (perhaps more accurately) peaceful competition with the West. The "world-wide victory of Communism" was still as "inevitable" as ever; self-appointed Marxist undertakers still proposed to "bury" capitalism. But these were to come about by a process of historical "evolution," in which the masses would "accept" Marxist truths, in part because of the demonstrated "superiority" of the Communist system over competing systems.

In time, the Kremlin actually endeavored to break the protracted Cold War stalemate and to supply the "deeds, not words" that American officials had long demanded as a prerequisite for agreement with the Communist bloc. By a variety of moves—including new programs of educational and cultural exchanges with the West and with neutralist countries, a gradual soft-pedaling of once-intractable Soviet demands in Berlin, a loosening of the Soviet grip on the European satellites, attempts to restrain bellicose tendencies in Peking, obvious efforts to proceed cautiously in episodes like the Cuban missile crisis, and the negotiation of a nuclear-test-ban accord with the West—Khrushchev's government demonstrated its awareness that a steady drift toward a great-power nuclear confrontation would obliterate Communist as thoroughly as Western society. Khrushchev, of course, was still a Marxist; international Communism still existed and still troubled the peace and security of non-Communist societies. But Presidents Eisenhower, Kennedy, and Johnson concluded (as heads of state in Europe and in the neutralist zone had concluded earlier) that Khrushchev's international Communism was a vastly different phenomenon from Stalin's, and that it appeared possible to arrive at some accommodation with it on at least selected international issues.

A second factor favorable to the growth of neutralism was in some measure an outgrowth of the changes inaugrated by the Khrushchev regime in the U.S.S.R.: the Sino-Soviet split. As Mao Tse-tung's Red Chinese government gradually adopted a more independent line at home and abroad, tension mounted in relations between the two power giants of the Communist movement. By the mid-1960's, the schism in the house of Communism had reached the stage at which the Kremlin's apologists referred openly to Mao's "deviationism," his addiction to "Trotskyism," and his "adventurist policies" in international affairs. Chinese propagandists reciprocated by accusing Khrushchev of "great-power chauvinism" in seeking to dominate the affairs of the Communist world and of being openly allied with the "American warmongers"; for good measure, Peking called upon Soviet citizens to overthrow Khrushchev's government.

Khrushchev's ouster late in 1964, many informed commentators believe, was in some measure brought about by the increasingly acrimonious dispute between the Soviet and Chinese Communist elites. Almost as a first order of business, Khrushchev's successors endeavored to arrive at a *modus vivendi* with their Chinese comrades. For their part, Chinese officials were amenable and expressed their willingness to seek common ground by sending Foreign Minister Chou En-lai to Moscow. Ensuing conversations between Russian and Chinese officials were decribed as "frank" and "comradely." Yet by the end of 1964, there was no reason to believe that the fundamental issues responsible for the Sino-Soviet split had disappeared. The Soviet Union, for example, remained committed to peaceful coexistence in its relations with the non-Communist world; Red China did not abandon its insistence upon revolutionary policies abroad or its determination to become the dominant power of Asia, even at Soviet Russia's expense. The damping of the propaganda animosity between Moscow and Peking, therefore, indicated no real resolution of underlying differences between the two Communist giants.

This disruption of the once fairly monolithic Communist bloc opened new opportunities for neutralist governments to evolve a highly intricate network of relations with the U.S.S.R., with Red China, and with their respective satellites. For the increasing competition between the Soviet Union and Communist China meant that when one government was not interested in supplying economic aid or military assistance to a particular neutralist state, the other was. The contest for leadership led to intensive efforts by both Moscow and Peking to "identify" with members of the neutralist community and, if possible, to prevent its rival from obtaining a dominant position in any neutralist country or region.

A third momentous development contributing to successful pursuit of nonaligment has been the steady advance in scientific and military technology, which in turn revolutionized strategic planning and long-standing military concepts. Owing to the particular character of its military strength—resting on massive air and naval power and on a system of interlocking military alliances—this change affected Western policies much more than Communist. During the late 1940's and early 1950's, Western security was believed to rest upon uncontested control of a far-flung network of American and allied military bases, from which nuclear strikes could be carried out against the Communist heartland in the event of aggression. From Western Europe to the Philippines, from Greenland to Saudi Arabia, Western strategic bombers were poised to launch "massive retaliation" against the enemy. Western control over, and access to, these vital military installations were guaranteed by a series of interconnected military pacts, beginning with the NATO system in Europe, and extending to the Baghdad Pact covering the "northern tier" in the Middle East, to SEATO and ANZUS (reinforced by certain bilateral defense agreements) in Asia. The United States also maintained bases in countries not included in these pacts—as for example, Morocco, Libya, and Saudi Arabia.

Two developments made many of these defense pacts and bases—along with the strategic concepts that prompted them—largely obsolete. One was the shift in Communist strategy from Stalinist threats of military aggression to tactics of peaceful coexistence—involving Soviet construction of a steel mill in India, support for General Kassem's *coup d'état* in Iraq, provision of military aircraft to Yugoslavia, and extension of generous scholarships to university students in Ghana. Communist China, meanwhile, was utilizing such techniques on a smaller scale by covertly supporting the Pathet Lao in Laos, by granting credits to Zanzibar, by sending Chou En-lai on a "good-will tour" of the Arab world. Western officials found the Baghdad Pact, SEATO, and strategic air bases of minimum usefulness in countering these often highly successful Communist maneuvers. Indeed, formal military agreements and overseas bases frequently *interfered* with the formulation of an effective Western response, by serving as an irritant to local sensibilities and by providing Communist and other extremist political groups with a ready-made issue that could be exploited effectively against indigenous governments.

But the other development was unquestionably more significant. This was the technological breakthrough that made possible the nuclear submarine and the guided missile. These new weapons largely emancipated Western air and naval units from dependence upon fixed military bases, especially in countries where such installations had become unwelcome. Now it no longer mattered much from a military-strategic point of view that the Baghdad Pact had collapsed with the defection of Iraq to the neutralist camp; the State Department could react with reasonable equanimity to Moroccan demands that strategic air bases in that country be closed; and there was less compulsion to draw India or Egypt into a regional defense agreement. For these losses were largely counterbalanced by the ability of Polaris-type submarines to cruise undetected along the Eurasian coast and by the ability of long-range missiles to reach virtually any target in the Communist world.

In brief, both the changing nature of the Communist threat and the weapons available to the West for meeting it combined to produce the realization that the United States needed allies much less than it had in the early postwar period. Or, we may make the same point somewhat differently by saying that the United States sought a *new kind* of ally—as signified by the different connotations of the terms "the Western alliance" and "the free world." It needed defense pacts and overseas bases less than it needed what we might call "ideological allies"—friendly countries dedicated to the maintenance of their independence and to freedom in policy-formulation, determined to solve grave internal problems that threatened political stability, and to collaborate with the United States and its European friends to achieve these goals.

If these developments nourished and sustained the neutralist movement, another factor powerfully reinforced the decision of a broadening circle of nations to remain nonaligned. This was the demonstrated ability of nonalignment to safeguard the security of its adherents, particularly during periods of crisis, and to achieve other internal and external goals to which neutralist states were committed. The principle that nothing succeeds like success went far toward explaining why most of the new African nations immediately committed themselves to the neutralist credo. For African policy-makers were fully aware that nonalignment had been subjected to a number of crucial test throughout the postwar period and that the principle had survived these tests better than observers inside and outside the neutralist zone might have expected. In the face of alternating inducements and intimidations by Moscow and Washington, for example, Tito's regime in Yugoslavia continued to preserve its independence; in the process, it had been extremely successful in eliciting assistance from both sides of the Iron Curtain. As a result, Yugoslavia had gained enormous prestige among smaller nations. Tito had clearly emerged as one of the most influential voices of the neutralist movement and one of neutralism's most indefatigable champions.

Similarly, Egyptian neutralism had been put to the test in the Suez crisis, when it appeared inevitable that Nasser's regime would be toppled as a result of the Anglo-French-Israeli invasion. To counter this threat, Nasser received assistance from both the United States and the Soviet Union, and moral support from nearly every country in the neutralist zone. Moscow offered Soviet "volunteers" to assist in repelling the invaders and referred openly to Europe's vulnerability to massive Soviet missile power. The United States applied diplomatic pressure on its allies and took the lead in the United Nations to bring about a withdrawal of hostile forces from Egyptian soil. Although he had depended upon great-power support to extricate his regime from what seemed certain disaster, Nasser emerged from the Suez affair with enhanced prestige and still free of permanent diplomatic or military entanglements with East and West.

Then, in 1962, came the supreme test of nonalignment. The government of Nehru—architect of the doctrine and perhaps its most influential expositor—was attacked and humiliated by Communist China. Yet nonalignment was reaffirmed as the cardinal principle of Indian foreign policy and India's decision to remain nonaligned was applauded and its example emulated by virtually every country in the neutralist zone.

Another fact that strengthened and encouraged the growth of neutralism was that by the end of the 1950's, both the United States and the Soviet Union had very largely come to terms with the idea of neutralism. The Kremlin's ideologists regarded the neutralist world as part of a vast "peace zone," whose activities supported Moscow's goal of "peaceful coexistence." Executive (if not always public and congressional) attitudes in the United States had largely lost their tone of Dullesian suspicion and moralizing. Toward the end of the Eisenhower period, policymakers conceded that neutralism was an established doctrine, that little was to be gained by antagonizing neutralist states, and that the primary goal of all neutralist countries—successfully preserving their independence—was fully consonant with the objectives of the United States. Neutralist countries found themselves as never before the objects of concern of both great powers, as Moscow and Washington alike sought to "identify" with them and to prove their

friendship by extending the tangible assistance required
by neutralist regimes.

Yet in underscoring the environmental influences producing an international climate favorable to nonalignment,
we must also emphasize the extent to which the concept
of nonalignment itself has been affected by that environment. Experience in applying the doctrine—particularly
during periods of regional and global crisis—has fostered a
general tendency among exponents of nonalignment to
abandon many of the more romanticized, extraneous, and
irrelevant arguments made in its behalf and to base the
case for a neutralist position on the only foundation strong
enough to withstand the vicissitudes of world affairs. This
is the extent to which nonalignment promotes national
security and other goals of foreign and internal policy.
Once again, the experience of India serves as a case study.

Nonalignment, as we have seen, survived India's Himalayan encounter with Red China. Indeed, New Delhi discovered a number of *new* reasons for remaining nonaligned.
What, then, was the impact of this traumatic experience
upon New Delhi's world view? Was the concept of nonalignment, alone among features of Indian national life,
in no way affected by an encounter which Indian officials
themselves admitted was their most serious foreign-policy
crisis since 1947?

Nonalignment emerged "refined" and "purified" from
the fires of the Himalayan contest. If India's adherence to
the principle remained unaltered, the principle itself was
modified significantly. This was true in at least three respects. First, the Himalayan contest provided graphic evidence of the increasingly *complex* pattern of relationships
that could be accommodated by the idea of nonalignment.
Even Indian officials conceded that nonalignment was no
longer possible in relation to China—a country which had
committed aggression against their territory. Yet India re-

mained nonaligned vis-à-vis Soviet Russia, Communist China's formal military ally; in turn, the U.S.S.R. practiced its own form of "noninvolvement" in this conflict. And India also remained nonaligned with regard to Britain and the United States, despite the fact that India was a member of the Commonwealth and accepted military assistance from the West. It continued to be nonaligned in the sense that it asked for, and desired, no overt military "intervention" on Indian soil; that it entered no Western military alliances; and, that diplomatically (as the ensuing discussion in the United Nations over Communist China's admission made clear) it showed no inclination to follow Western policy dictates.

Parenthetically (although nonalignment refers to a country's position toward Cold War powers), it is interesting to observe that the Sino-Indian crisis also highlighted the complexity of relationships that is possible *among* neutralist countries. Yugoslavia, Egypt, and Malaya were most vocal in supporting India's cause; Ghana at first opposed British military assistance to its Commonwealth partner, but later withdrew this objection and became sympathetic to India; African countries by and large played a passive role in the crisis (although some tended to criticize India as much as they criticized China); Nepal, Ceylon, and Burma were extremely cautious in their attitudes toward both India and China; the Indonesian reaction was perhaps the most openly anti-Indian and brought New Delhi's relations with Sukarno's government to their nadir.

Second, India discovered painfully that the invocation of the concept of nonalignment and "the spirit of Bandung" could not in itself safeguard national security. If there had been a tendency in New Delhi to suppose that nonalignment was some kind of magical incantation that would ward off evil spirits, or that belief in nonalignment was a legitimate substitute for adequate defense measures in the face of threats to national security, this was ended by Mao Tse-tung's aggression. Perhaps because Nehru originated the doctrine, there was a greater disposition in India than elsewhere to romanticize it, to attribute to it all manner of miraculous powers, to eulogize it, and to believe that India had discovered some kind of diplomatic panacea that would guarantee immunity from every external threat. Peking's perfidy, however, had driven home the lesson that despite its many attractions, nonalignment was not a sacrosanct precept that possessed a peculiar efficacy in safeguarding national security.

This leads to the third, and perhaps most important, respect in which the Indian conception of nonalignment was substantially modified as a result of the Himalayan dispute. This lay in belated Indian recognition of a reality that had long been accepted by such neutralist leaders as Tito, Nasser, and Sukarno. With its heritage of Gandhiism—and its extraordinary success in winning independence from Britain by nonviolent methods—Indians had been slow to learn that there was no incompatibility between adherence to nonalignment and a condition of *military preparedness*. Indeed, it was now evident that there was a correlation between dedication to the latter and successful pursuit of the former. This was perhaps the most crucial lesson that Indian policy-makers learned from the Himalayan imbroglio. For a variety of reasons (chiefly because of the necessity to divert Indian resources to internal development schemes), the increasing apprehension felt by Nehru's government over Peking's intentions had not been translated into defense measures adequate for coping with a Chinese military incursion. As a result of its near disastrous encounter with Red China, India had been made aware—and, in turn, had provided an object lesson to less influential neutralist countries—that *any* successful foreign policy requires the means and the determination to preserve national independence. Nonalignment, backed by adequate national power, could be a valid principle of statecraft; nonalignment accompanied by military weakness and the illusion that the doctrine itself would defend the nation's borders was a certain route to national defeat and humiliation.

India of course was not the only country that supplied refinements and new gradations of nonalignment as time went on. An interesting case was furnished by India's neighbor, Pakistan. A charter member of SEATO and CENTO, Pakistan had become increasingly dissatisfied with certain Western policies, particularly the extension of massive arms aid to India during the Himalayan conflict. The Government of Pakistan used this crisis to arrive at a border *détente* with Red China. In succeeding months, there followed cultural agreements, an accord permitting Chinese commercial aircraft to use Pakistani landing fields, a Sino-Pakistani economic-aid program, and an over-all "normalization" in relations between the two countries. Concurrently, vocal anti-American sentiments and demonstrations erupted in Pakistan; its participation in formal SEATO deliberations became perfunctory and reluctant; and during the Bay of Tonkin crises between the United States and North Vietnam in the summer of 1964, Pakistan's attitude was hostile to the United States.

Formally, Pakistan remained "aligned" with the West. In reality, relations between Rawalpindi and Washington were marked by growing estrangement; conversely, relations between Pakistan and China became increasingly cordial. Had Pakistan's formal military ties with the West become meaningless? In a crisis, who would prove the close ally of the West and the most dedicated member of the free world, Pakistan or India? It was a moot question. But if nothing else was clear, it was evident from Pakistan's behavior that terms like alignment and nonalignment mean little in the abstract. They have meaning only when applied to the viewpoints and policies of particular countries whose approach to international affairs occurs within a specific context of global events.

Or take the case of the most influential country in Southeast Asia—Indonesia. Here again, an intricate web of regional and international relationships makes Indonesia's version of nonalignment very different from nearby Malaya's, Cambodia's, and India's, or from far-away Iraq's Egypt's, Algeria's. For entirely too long, Americans have been content to regard Sukarno as the quintessence of a "pro-Communist neutralist" leader, as a head of state who personifies all the more irritating features of a "neutralism" dictated by pure expediency. In fact, such verdicts are likely to be misleading on several counts. For years, Sukarno has successfully prevented a Communist takeover of his government, and he is perhaps the only Indonesian national leader who was able to do so. And in the light of the fact that the Communist Party of Indonesia is the largest Communist party outside the U.S.S.R. and Red China, this is no inconsiderable accomplishment. Although Djakarta has militantly opposed the Federation of Malaysia and has more than once terminated American aid because of alleged American "intervention" in Indonesia's affairs, Sukarno's government has no less steadfastly opposed Peking's intrigue carried out by the large contingent of "overseas Chinese" resident in the archipeligo. One of Indonesia's strongest arguments against Malaysia is that the influential and wealthy Chinese elements in the new federation might expand its influence southward, where it would be supported by Indonesia's own Chinese minority. Again, in the face of Communist pressures at home and abroad, Djakarta has opposed the calling of a new Afro-Asian conference (a "second Bandung") from which Soviet Russia would be excluded. With countries like India, it has supported the idea that the Soviet Union should be regarded as an "Asian power" and should participate in a new Asian regional conference. This policy—deliberately or indeliberately thwarting Red China's open bid for "Asian leadership"—appears fully consonant with Western interests in Asia and with the interest of other neutralist countries in preserving their independence in policy-making. In short, except for Indonesia's avowed opposition to Malaysia, there is no evidence that Sukarno's neutralism is basically inimical to the interests of the free world or is intrinsically different from the neutralism of other countries.*

If the theory and practice of nonalignment have thus far been responsive to environmental changes, we may logically expect this process to continue. It seems a safe enough prediction that the trend toward "polycentricity" in international affairs will proceed apace. Two recent manifestations of the tendency may be noted briefly. By the mid-1960's, Romania showed signs of manifesting greater "independence" than ever in policy-formulation. In language remarkably like that long identified with apologists for neutralism, Romania's Premier declared in 1964 that "the principle concerning the right of people to decide their own destiny alone is an extremely important principle for international life and an essential element

* Although the West supported Malaysia wholeheartedly in its dispute with Indonesia, an experienced British observer in 1964 cautioned London and Washington about the serious consequences involved in totally alienating Indonesia. Sukarno's government was "the one Southeast Asian country potentially strong enough to act eventually as some kind of balance against Communist China." An intractable Western attitude toward Sukarno might "throw Indonesia into the arms of the Chinese Communists." Western disinclination to see any virtue in the Indonesian case against Malaysia might tempt Sukarno either to isolate himself completely from Western aid, thereby risking the economic disintegration of his country, or to throw in his lot with the Communists. Either course could have catastrophic results for the Western position in Asia. (Peregrine Worsthorne, in the London *Daily Telegraph,* May 3, 1964, cited in *Atlas,* VII [June, 1964], 327.)

of peaceful cooperation among all states." Romania, that is to say, had found a connection between peaceful co-existence and a kind of *de facto* nonalignment within the Communist community, and was asserting its policy of "independence" without apparent opposition from Moscow. It was perhaps more than a coincidence that one of Romania's first acts in this new era was to establish closer ties with de Gaulle's France. For, like France, Romania also sought to establish more "normal" relations with Communist China, in the face of obvious misgivings by the leader of the diplomatic bloc in which it had long been a rather quiescent member.[1]

To the south, the United States encountered wide-spread opposition to its Cuban policies by increasingly "independent" Latin American states. Referring to Bolivia —the largest per-capita recipient of American assistance under the Alliance for Progress—one observer noted that a formal break between Bolivia and Cuba would likely precipitate open political warfare and internecine partisan strife in this key South American state, developments hardly conducive to inhibiting Communist influence in this region. Elsewhere in Latin America, events testified to a growing receptivity to the neutralist idea. Thus *Marcha* (an influential independent, non-Marxist publication in Montevideo, Uruguay) observed early in 1964:

> The point is not to choose between the Soviet Union and the United States. It is not to reject the political and economic demands of one in order to accept those of the other. Washington and Moscow may regard the problem this way; we do not. There may be two blocs in the world, but they are not the Soviet bloc versus the Western bloc. They are the advanced industrialized powers on the one hand and the under-developed, "proletarian" powers on the other. The second

group must exploit the rivalries within the first group and
not sell their souls to anybody.

Several months later, the same publication complained
openly that the relationships between the United States
and Latin America had always been those "between supe-
rior and inferior, tutor and pupil. It never occurs to them
[officials in Washington] that we are created their equals."
And when General de Gaulle toured Latin America in the
spring of 1964, a commentator for *Expreso* (Lima, Peru)
declared: "The hand that France extends should be warmly
accepted; we must not lose this opportunity of aligning
ourselves with a new and vigorous Europe." [2]

Evidence of the centrifugal forces greatly weakening the
cohesion of both the Western and the Communist blocs
led Marshal Tito in 1963 to reassert that a "bloc division"
of the world was "neither unavoidable nor permanent."
From this conviction had derived "the vast historical significance of the policy of nonalignment and of the activity
of the nonaligned countries." Tito conceded that "the conditions under which the policy of nonalignment had come
into being are changing." And he went on to make the
rather startling suggestion that possibly "the term nonalignment has in a way been superseded by the new and
positive evolution of international relations." Since nonalignment was a response to the existence of two fairly cohesive, antagonistic Cold War blocs, and since these blocs
appeared now to be a "temporary phase" of international
politics, Tito saw a new pattern of aligned and nonaligned
nations emerging. More important than Cold War bloc
divisions, in Tito's opinion, was the divergence between
the "reconcilables" and the "irreconcilables" in the international community. The former included the United
States, the U.S.S.R., Yugoslavia, and other countries in the

neutralist zone; the latter included Red China and its satellites (Albania, perhaps East Germany), and certain
right-wing forces in the United States, Western Europe,
and elsewhere which apparently desired a military resolution of international differences. A dominant feature of
the global political landscape now was the fact that within
"each so-called bloc, there was an internal division between 'forces for peace' and the forces that are favorable
to the solution of international problems by war." [3]

There were other signs that the time had come for a reappraisal of the concept of nonalignment. Thus, in mid-
1964, a spokesman for the Indonesian Foreign Office
pointed to two significant developments—the conclusion
of the East-West nuclear-test-ban accord and the death of
Prime Minister Nehru—profoundly affecting the concept
of nonalignment and making a new examination of its underlying assumptions necessary. After returning from a
prolonged, and sometimes heated, series of negotiations in
Geneva on world trade questions, an American official declared that the outstanding fact about the conference was
the emergence of "an alignment based on economic interests rather than political ideology." He felt that old Cold
War recriminations had largely been "drowned out by the
insistent economic demands of the seventy-five developing
nations to the south." And he concluded that "on the
world scene a new North-South conflict of interest has appeared. It may well be the trend of the future." [4] But perhaps the most surprising voice in this chorus was supplied
by former Soviet Premier Khrushchev. In mid-1963, during a visit to Yugoslavia, Khrushchev stated that "the expression blocs is superficial and evanescent. Marxism-
Leninism is the teaching that is in fact the foundation of
everything. And we both stand on that foundation." [5]
Khrushchev, in other words, was prepared to concede that
the "Communist bloc" no longer existed or was no longer

required by Marxist ideology. While there was no guarantee that Khrushchev's assessment would guide his successors in the Kremlin, events after his downfall suggested the likelihood of no abrupt changes in Soviet foreign policy and no inclination by once-pliant satellites to revert to a totally docile and subordinate role within the Communist system. Indeed, the public dismay expressed by Communist parties throughout the world about Khrushchev's ouster suggested that the movement toward polycentricity behind the Iron Curtain had gone too far to be reversed.

Finally, the United States made an admission that was long in coming: that the Sino-Soviet quarrel had all but demolished the Communist bloc and had splintered it into at least two factions with highly divergent interests. This became plain during the Bay of Tonkin episode, when American policy was clearly predicated upon the expectation that the Soviet Union neither would, nor effectively could, assist North Vietnam in retaliating against the United States.

Nonalignment, said the Prime Minister of Ceylon in 1964, "must be responsive to changing circumstances." And an editorial in the *Indian Express* after Red China's Himalayan thrust conceded that Peking's aggression had "swept away many accumulated cobwebs and illusions" about nonalignment in the Indian mind.[6] India has not been alone in allowing its thinking about the concept of nonalignment to become beclouded; and it has perhaps been more prepared, at least since the Himalayan crisis, to examine the doctrine realistically and objectively than have many observers in the West. A decade has passed since nonalignment gained world-wide attention at the Bandung Conference in 1955. During that period, "accumulated cobwebs and illusions" have no less seriously impaired Western appraisals of nonalignment. Our evaluation of the concept has endeavored to dispel them and to emphasize that, in the last analysis, nations embrace non-alignment for essentially the same reason that the United States remains dedicated to "containment" or the Soviet Union advocates "peaceful coexistence." Careful and continuing evaluation of existing policy alternatives has convinced policy-makers in neutralist countries that the principle of nonalignment best achieves foreign and domestic policy objectives. When that condition no longer exists, we may expect nonalignment to be abandoned, just as Great Britain gave up the "balance of power" as its maxim in relations with Europe, or as the United States finally discarded isolationism. To date, however, nothing has happened in international affairs to convince neutralist countries that their approach is unsound or prejudicial to their security. Indeed, experience has afforded new reasons why nations should hold fast to nonalignment. And on this basis, we may expect neutralist countries to adhere to their credo—however modified by circumstances it may become —in a multipolar fully as much as in a bipolar world.

Notes

Chapter 1. NONALIGNMENT: THEME AND VARIATIONS
(pp. 3–38)

1. *The New York Times,* June 2, 1964.
2. Kwame Nkrumah, *I Speak of Freedom* (New York: Frederick A. Praeger, 1961), pp. 97–98.
3. For extensive treatments of the distinction between neutrality and neutralism (nonalignment), see: Khalid I. Babaa, *Arab Positive Neutralism* (Ottawa: The Arab Information Center, n.d. [mimeographed]), *passim;* and Ahmed S. El-Emari, "Positive Neutralism with Non-Interference and Neutrality," *The Scribe* (Cairo), II, June 1, 1960, 42–44.
4. *India News* (Washington, D.C.: Indian Embassy), VI, January 1, 1961, 1, and *Egyptian Gazette,* November 17, 1961.
5. *Africa Digest,* VII, February, 1960, 132.
6. *News of Morocco* (Washington, D.C.: Moroccan Embassy), IV, January, 1961, 7.
7. Shabgai Rosenne, "Basic Elements of Israel's Foreign Policy," *India Quarterly,* XVII, October–December, 1961, 345.
8. *Report on Indonesia,* VII, June–July, 1956, 3.
9. "Cambodia's Foreign Policy: Independent Neutrality and Non-Alignment," Address by Mr. Nong Kimny, Cambodian Ambassador to the United States, on December 7, 1960 (Washington, D.C.: Cambodian Embassy), p. 12.
10. Quoted in the *Times of Indonesia,* October 6, 1960.
11. "Abdel-Nasser's Visit to Tito," *Mideast Mirror* (publication of the Arab News Agency), XII (June 18, 1960), 6; *The New York Times,* December 17, 1961.
12. "Can Neutrals Help?" *The Economist,* CC, August 12, 1961, 298.
13. "Belgrade Diary," *New Statesman,* LXXII, September 8, 1961, 298.
14. El-Emari, *op. cit.,* p. 44.
15. See Alex Bebler, "Role of the Non-Bloc Countries," *Review of International Affairs* (Belgrade), IX, January 1, 1958, 1–2; and "Non-Alignment and the Theory of Equidistance," *ibid.,* XII, November 5, 1961, 1–2.
16. See "Abdel-Nasser says 'Russia Took our Hand,'" *Mideast Mirror,* XII, July 16, 1960, 2; *Documents on International Affairs: 1958* (London and New York: Oxford University Press, 1962), p. 259, citing a speech by Crown Prince Faisal; Babaa, *op. cit.,* p. 34; *Africa Digest,* VI, September–October, 1958, 116, citing Nkrumah's speech to the Ghanaian Parliament; *Asian Recorder,* III, July 6–12, 1957, 1531; "Abdel-Nasser's Visit to

Tito," *op. cit.*, p. 6; *The New York Times*, February 20, 1957, April 28, 1964, and May 2, 1964.

17. *Arab World*, III, November, 1957, 12; *Documents on International Affairs: 1958*, p. 259.

18. *Times of India*, September 17, 1961, dispatch by H. R. Vohra; quoted in *Egyptian Gazette*, March 22, 1961. For comparable comments by the *Egyptian Gazette* on President Kennedy's Seattle speech, see the issue of November 18, 1961.

19. See Dulles' testimony in *The President's Proposal on the Middle East*, U.S. Senate Committees on Foreign Relations and Armed Services, 85th Cong., 1st sess. (Washington, D. C.: Government Printing Office, 1957), Part I, p. 113.

20. *Documents on American Foreign Relations: 1956* (New York: Harper & Bros., 1957), p. 394; and "Moral Neutralism? Bunk!" in *The New York Herald Tribune*, November 16, 1961.

21. Testimony of Seymour J. Janow, in *Hearings, Foreign Assistance Act of 1962*, U.S.H.R. Committee on Foreign Affairs, 87th Cong., 2d sess. (Washington, D.C.: Government Printing Office, 1962), p. 768; testimony of the same official in *Hearings, Foreign Assistance Act of 1963*, U.S.H.R. Committee on Foreign Affairs, 88th Cong., 1st sess. (Washington, D.C.: Government Printing Office, 1963), p. 752; testimony of Roger Hilsman, in *ibid.*, p. 778; testimony of Frank M. Coffin, in *ibid.*, pp. 607–8; cited in *The New York Times*, April 3, 1964, dispatch by Peter Braestrap.

22. See the editorial in *Indian Express*, March 7, 1963.

23. *Foreign Policy and Mutual Security*, Draft Report submitted to the U.S.H.R. Committee on Foreign Affairs, 84th Cong., 2d sess. (Committee print, 1956), p. 56; the text of Secretary Rusk's news conference in *The New York Times*, November 18, 1961.

24. Hans J. Morgenthau, "Critical Look at the New Neutralism," *The New York Times Magazine*, August 27, 1961, pp. 25, 76–77. For another article reflecting not untypical Western value judgments about nonalignment, see Oscar Handlin, "The Gullibility of the Neutrals," *Atlantic Monthly*, CCXI, March, 1963, pp. 41–47. (As the title indicates, Handlin's treatment rests upon pervasive misconceptions about the nature of the neutralist ideology.)

25. For the sequence of events in Guinea, see David Hapgood, "Guinea's First Five Years," *Current History*, XLV, December, 1963, pp. 355–61; David Halberstam, "Touré's Country—'Africa Incarnate.' " *The New York Times Magazine*, July 8, 1962, pp. 10, 17–20; Peter Judd, *African Independence* (New York: Dell Books, 1963), pp. 254–328 *passim*.

26. *The New York Herald Tribune*, October 27, 1961; quoted in *Indian Press Digest*, II (November, 1954), p. 76; testimony of Secretary Dulles in *Hearings, Review of Foreign Policy*, U.S. Senate Committee on Foreign Relations, 85th Cong., 2d sess. (Washington, D.C.: Government Printing Office, 1958), p. 802; and in *Hearings, Mutual Security Appropriations for 1954*, U.S. Senate Committee on Appropriations, 83d Cong., 1st sess. (Washington, D.C.: Government Printing Office, 1953), p. 84.

27. "No Black Pawns," *The Economist*, CXCIX, June 3, 1961, p. 575.

28. *The New York Times*, September 22, 1963.

Chapter 2. THE WELLSPRINGS OF NONALIGNMENT
(pp. 39–76)

1. Gamal Abdel Nasser, "Where I Stand and Why" (Washington, D.C.: Embassy of the United Arab Republic, July 20, 1959), p. 2.

2. Nasser, "The Egyptian Revolution," *Foreign Affairs*, XXXIII, January, 1955, 200.

3. See: "Iraq's Foreign Policy," *New Iraq* (Baghdad: Ministry of Guidance), No. 1, January, 1962, p. 3; Emmet V. Mittlebeeler, "Africa and the Defense of America," *World Affairs*, CXXI, Fall, 1958, 82.

4. See: "Iraq's Foreign Policy," *loc. cit.; Egyptian Gazette*, September 27, 1961.

5. *Egyptian Mail*, September 2, 1961.

6. See: *Report on Indonesia*, VI, June, 1955, 22–23; *Documents on International Affairs: 1958*, p. 235.

7. *The Iraqi Revolution in Its Second Year* (Baghdad: Government of Iraq, 1960), pp. 194, 196.

8. Carlos P. Romulo, "Nationalism, Non-Alignment and World Order," *Indian and Foreign Review*, I, April 15, 1964, 10–11.

9. See: *Morning News* (Khartoum), January 31, 1961; *Asian Recorder*, VIII, August 6–12, 1962, 4726; *The New York Times*, April 17, 1960; *Straits Times* (Singapore), October 7, 1961; and *Times of Indonesia*, August 1, 1960.

10. See *Indonesian Spectator*, January 15, 1958; *Egyptian Mail*, November 18, 1961; and *Times of India*, November 7, 1961.

11. See: *Report on Indonesia*, VI, June, 1955, 20; *ibid.*, pp. 12–13; *Times of Indonesia*, January 27, 1960; *Documents on International Affairs: 1955* (London and New York: Oxford University Press, 1958), p. 405; *Straits Times*, August 29, 1961; "The Belgrade Conference," *The Scribe*, III, August–September, 1961, 13; José Smole, "Preparations for 'The World Without the Bomb' Conference," *Review of International Affairs*, XIII, March 20, 1962, 8.

12. *Report on Indonesia*, VI, June, 1955, 17, and *ibid.*, p. 13.

13. See, for example, various editorials from Iraqi papers, cited in the *Iraq Times*, September 19 and 20, 1961; José Smole, "The Conference of the Uncommitted," *Review of International Affairs*, XII, August 5–20, 1961, 2.

14. "Nehru Visits U.S.A." (Washington, D.C.: Information Service of India, n.d.), p. 53; *India News*, VI, August 1, 1961, 1.

15. "Morocco's National Character and Policy Outlined," *News of Morocco*, III, May, 1960, 1–3.

16. See Khalid I. Babaa, *Arab Positive Neutralism, passim*; Nkrumah, *op. cit.*, pp. 97–98, 196–202.

17. See: *India News*, III, March 15, 1958, 2; Taya Zinkin, "Hinduism and Communism: Are They Compatible?" *Eastern World*, IX, January, 1955, 16–17; "The Buddhist Doctrine of Peace," *New Times of Burma*, May 9, 1960; H. C. Taussig, "Neutral Cambodia," *Eastern World*, XI, September, 1957, 32–35.

18. N. P. Nayar, "Non-Alignment in World Affairs," *India Quarterly*,

XVIII, January–March, 1962, 51. Burma's postwar political experience is analyzed in detail in Russell H. Fifield, *The Diplomacy of Southeast Asia: 1945–1958* (New York: Harper & Bros., 1958), pp. 167–230.

19. Immanuel Wallerstein, *Africa: The Politics of Independence* (New York: Random House, 1961), p. 88.

20. "Mr. Nehru's Leadership," *Eastern World*, XI, July, 1957, 9.

21. See: Ronald Segal, *African Profiles* (Baltimore: Penguin Books, 1962), pp. 209–11; George W. Shepherd, Jr., *The Politics of African Nationalism* (New York: Frederick A. Praeger, 1962), pp. 22–23.

22. See: Hugh Tinker, *The Union of Burma* (3d ed.; London and New York: Oxford University Press, 1961), pp. 342–43; *Report on Indonesia*, IX, August–September–October, 1957, 37; John S. Badeau, "A Role in Search of a Hero: A Brief Study of the Egyptian Revolution," *Middle East Journal*, IX, Autumn, 1955, 381.

23. Edwin O. Reischauer, *Wanted: An Asian Policy* (New York: Alfred A. Knopf, 1955), p. 270; Ahmed S. El-Emari, "Positive Neutralism with Non-Interference and Neutrality," *The Scribe*, II, June 1, 1960, 43.

24. *Egyptian Gazette*, September 4, 1961; *India News*, V, February 15, 1960, 2; Bogdan Crnobrnja, "A Friendly Visit," *Review of International Affairs*, IX, December 16, 1958, 2.

25. V. M. Reddi, "A Study of Cambodia's Neutralism," *International Studies*, II, July, 1960, 190–94.

26. See: *Documents on International Affairs: 1951* (London and New York: Oxford University Press, 1954), p. 382; Tinker, *op. cit.*, pp. 343–45.

27. See: *Documents on International Affairs: 1955;* "Sudanese President's Talks with Tito," *Mideast Mirror*, XII, July 23, 1960, 11; *New Times of Burma*, March 4, 1960.

28. See: *The New York Times*, June 27, 1958; Sir Giles Squire, "The Outlook for Afghanistan," *Eastern World*, IV, February, 1950, 8–9; Lt. Col. H. E. Crocker, "Afghanistan and Russia," *ibid.*, X, January, 1956, 17–19; *The New York Times*, March 11, 1960.

29. *India News*, November 16, 1962, p. 1; *ibid.*, November 23, 1962, p. 8.

30. *Ibid.*, December 28, 1962, p. 1; *ibid.*, January 4, 1963, p. 8.

31. Quoted in *ibid.*, December 28, 1962, p. 2; and *ibid.*, November 23, 1962, p. 2.

32. *Ibid.*, November 16, 1962, p. 1 (italics added); *The New York Times*, November 12, 1962.

Chapter 3. NEUTRALIST STRATEGIES IN THE GLOBAL ARENA
(pp. 77–99)

1. *Egyptian Gazette*, September 3, 1961; *Times of India*, June 14, 1961.

2. *Report on Indonesia*, VI, June, 1955, 12–13; *Hindustan Times* (overseas ed.), May 18, 1961; *Egyptian Mail*, September 2, 1961.

3. *Times of Indonesia*, July 7, 1960; Dj. Jerkovic, "Conference of the Uncommitted," *Review of International Affairs*, XII, June 20, 1961, 4.

4. For a detailed exposition of the neutralist conception of coexistence, see "Iraq at the Belgrade Conference," *Bulletin of the Republic of Iraq*, II, September, 1961, 1–2.

5. Iraq's Foreign Policy," *New Iraq*, No. 1, January, 1962, p. 3.

6. *Iraq Times*, September 14, 1961; *Asian Recorder*, III, July 6–12, 1957, 1530.

7. "A Decisive Action for Peace," *The Scribe*, II, May–June, 1961, 11.

8. *The New York Times*, April 4, 1959; *Times of Indonesia*, February 18, 1960.

9. See the excerpts from speeches at the Belgrade Conference, in *The New York Times*, September 2, 1961.

10. Election Campaign Speech by President Tito delivered on March 16, 1958; text supplied by the Information Service of Yugoslavia, Washington, D.C.

11. "Foreign Policy of the Republic of Iraq," *New Iraq*, January, 1961, p. 1.

12. *Egyptian Mail*, September 2, 1961, citing President Sukarno of Indonesia; and *Times of India*, June 12, 1961.

13. *Egyptian Gazette*, September 8, 1961; *The New York Herald Tribune*, December 6, 1961.

14. See: *Hindustan Times* (overseas ed.), June 9, 1955, and August 16, 1959; *Documents on American Foreign Relations: 1953* (New York: Harper & Bros., 1954), pp. 376, 379.

15. Our discussion of neutralist mediation efforts during the Himalayan conflict, and of Indian and Chinese reactions to them, is drawn from a variety of sources, including: "The Colombo Conference of the Six Non-Aligned Nations," *Forward* (Rangoon: Government of Burma), I, December 22, 1962, 2–3; *Ghana Today*, VI, December 5, 1962, 1; *Times of India*, March 14, 1963; *Indian Express*, November 9, 1962; *Hindustan Times*, January 14 and 21, 1963; *India News*, I, December 14, December 21, and December 28, 1962; *The New York Times*, February 19, 1964.

16. For diverse and continuing neutralist complaints about great-power animosity toward nonalignment, see: *The New York Times*, April 4, 1959; *Hindustan Times* (overseas ed.), March 6, 1958; *Times of India*, November 11, 1961; "Neutralist Leaders in Cairo," *The Scribe*, III, November–December, 1961, 14.

17. *News of Morocco*, III, November, 1960, p. 3.

18. *India News*, V, February 15, 1960, 2.

19. For these and other indications of a trend toward at least a modified form of nonalignment in Latin America, see *The New York Times*, September 15, and October 20, 1963, and January 23, and March 14, 1964.

20. *Times of India*, May 3, 1961.

21. For Indian opinion on efforts to "neutralize" Southeast Asia, particularly Laos, and on the failure of the ICC, see: *Survey of International Affairs: 1954* (London and New York: Oxford University Press, 1957), pp. 47, 287–88; *Times of India*, May 2, May 10, May 15, May 17, May 19, May 23, May 25, November 13, and December 8, 1961; *Asian Recorder*, VII, June 18–24, 1961, 4010; *The New York Times*, May 23, and June 3, 1964.

22. Quoted in *Times of India*, December 2, 1961.

23. *Egyptian Mail*, November 18, 1961; *Documents on International Affairs: 1957* (London and New York: Oxford University Press, 1960),

p. 257; *Hindustan Times* (overseas ed.), January 17, 1957, citing the views of Indian elder stateman Mr. Rajagopalachari.

24. *Egyptian Gazette*, March 16, 1961.

25. Quoted in "Under the American Shadow," *Eastern World*, XIII, April, 1959, 11.

26. "Americans Agree to Withdraw from Military Bases in Morocco," *News of Morocco*, II, November, 1959, 1.

27. See the editorial in *Egyptian Gazette*, July 25, 1961, citing the views of the nation's military commander in chief.

28. See the excerpt from the speech by Mr. Nyerere in *Africa Today*, VIII, December, 1961, 11.

Chapter 4. DISARMAMENT AND THE UNITED NATIONS
(pp. 100–133)

1. "Prime Minister Gives His Views on World Issues" (text of speech by Prime Minister Balewa of Nigeria on March 8, 1961, distributed by Embassy of Nigeria, Washington, D.C.), p. 1; Kwame Nkrumah, *I Speak of Freedom*, p. 116; editorial in *Hindustan Times* (overseas ed.), August 18, 1955; *Indonesian Spectator*, March 1, 1958, p. 21.

2. *India News*, II, March 6, 1964, 1.

3. "The Step by Step Policy," *Review of International Affairs*, XIII, March 5, 1962, 2; *Times of India*, September 3, 1961.

4. Quoted in *Egyptian Gazette*, November 23, 1961; "King Instructs U.N. Delegation," *News of Morocco*, III, October, 1960, 2; Djura Nincic, "On the Eve of the Disarmament Talks," *Review of International Affairs*, XIII, March 5, 1962, 9.

5. See the text of the declaration of the Belgrade Conference in *Documents on American Foreign Relations: 1961* (New York: Harper & Row, 1962), p. 471; *Times of India*, September 1, 1961; *The New York Times*, April 15, 1962.

6. "Burma's Views on Disarmament," *Forward*, I, January 7, 1963, 31; *Asian Recorder*, III, July 6–12, 1957, 1530.

7. *Times of India*, November 13, 1961.

8. "The U. S. Errs in Policy," *The Scribe*, III, October–November, 1961, 4.

9. *Documents on American Foreign Relations: 1961*, p. 471.

10. *Times of India*, May 26, 1961; *New Times of Burma*, March 11, 1960.

11. See the text of the resolutions adopted by this conference in *Ghana Today* (London: Embassy of Ghana, VII, June 5, 1963, 4–5.

12. See the discussions of the American viewpoint in *Egyptian Gazette*, November 10, 1961, and *Egyptian Mail*, November 25, 1961.

13. See: State Department report on the first phase of the Geneva disarmament talks, in *Documents on American Foreign Relations: 1962* (New York: Harper & Row, 1963), pp. 80–81; the remarks of Secretary Rusk in *Hearings, Nuclear Test Ban Treaty*, U.S. Senate Committee on Foreign Relations, 88th Cong., 1st sess. (Washington, D.C.: Government Printing Office, 1963), p. 55; *The United States in World Affairs: 1962* (New York: Harper & Row, 1963), p. 71; *The New York Times*, November 10, 1963.

14. See: Swadesh Mehta, "Asian-African Impact in the UN," *Indian and Foreign Review*, I, January 15, 1964, 29; text of speech by Prime Minister Balewa of Nigeria, July 26, 1961 (distributed by the Embassy of Nigeria, Washington, D.C.), p. 4; *Daily Times* (Lagos), August 8, 1961; "Burma at the U.N.," *Forward*, I, October 22, 1962, 15.

15. *Times of India*, September 8, 1961.

16. *New Times of Burma*, July 31, 1960; *Hindustan Times* (overseas ed.), April 24, 1952; *Iraq Times*, September 10, 1961.

17. "Sékou Touré in America," *Africa Special Report*, IV, November, 1959, 9; *Iraq Times*, October 3, 1961; L. Erven, "The United Nations and Anti-Colonialism," *Review of International Affairs*, XIII, February 20, 1962, 1–2.

18. *The New York Times*, August 12, 1962, dispatch by Thomas J. Hamilton.

19. *The New York Herald Tribune*, November 23, 1962, dispatch by Martin G. Berck.

20. Quoted in A. M. Rosenthal, "Africa Shouts to America: 'Choose!'" *The New York Times Magazine*, November 20, 1960, pp. 9, 134–41.

21. *The New York Times*, March 19 and June 11, 1961.

22. See *The United States in World Affairs: 1962*, pp. 315–17.

23. *Times of India*, September 12, 1961; *The New York Times*, September 21, 1963, dispatch by Juan de Onis.

24. See Andrew Boyd, *United Nations: Piety, Myth and Truth* (Baltimore: Penguin Books, 1962), pp. 72–73; and the definitions of "blocs" cited in Arend Lijphart, "The Analysis of Bloc Voting in the General Assembly," *American Political Science Review*, LVII, December, 1963, 902–3.

25. Quoted in *Asian Recorder*, VIII, September 24–30, 1962, 4802.

26. *Documents on American Foreign Relations: 1962*, pp. 42–43.

27. *Ibid.*, p. 438; and *ibid., 1961*, p. 491.

28. See: *Times of Indonesia*, September 22, 1960; *Times of India*, June 28, 1961; *Egyptian Mail*, September 2, 1961; *Egyptian Gazette*, September 21, 1961; "The Neutral Summit," *Eastern Economist*, XXXVII, September 8, 1961, 436–37; *Straits Times*, September 19, 1961; and "The United Nations Gropes for Hope," *The Economist*, XX, September 30, 1961, 1265.

29. *The New York Times*, August 25, 1962, dispatch by C. L. Sulzberger.

30. *The New York Times*, November 29, 1962.

31. Quoted in William R. Frye, "Man in the Path of a Troika," *The New York Times Magazine*, October 7, 1962, pp. 95–96.

Chapter 5. THE COMMUNIST BLOC AND THE NEUTRALIST ZONE
(pp. 134–67)

1. See the text of the 1961 Communist Party program in Harrison E. Salisbury (ed.), *Khrushchev's "Mein Kampf"* (New York: Belmont Books, 1961), pp. 74, 79, 80, 89, and 92.

2. *The New York Times*, May 1 and May 7, 1964.

3. See, respectively: *New Times of Burma,* July 23, 1960; and *Hearings, Review of Foreign Policy,* Part 1, p. 83.

4. *The New York Times,* July 6, 1964, dispatch by C. L. Sulzberger.

5. Léopold Senghor, *On African Socialism* (New York: Frederick A. Praeger, 1964), pp. 26–36; *The New York Times,* January 20, 1964.

6. For a detailed appraisal of Marxism from the Arab viewpoint, see Saadat Hasan, "Communism and the Arab World," in *Islam and Communism,* published for the Carnegie International Center (New York, 1960), pp. 38–46.

7. *India News,* VI, August 1, 1961, 1; *Hindustan Times* (overseas ed.), May 15, 1952; *ibid.,* March 21, 1957; *Times of India,* May 2, 1961; and *Hindustan Times* (overseas ed.), March 24, 1955.

8. U Maung Maung, "A Philosophy that Meets Both Material and Spiritual Needs," *Forward,* I, February 22, 1963, 22–23; *Asian Student,* XI, March 2, 1963, 7.

9. U Maung Maung, "Futility of the Armed Revolt," *Forward,* I, January 22, 1963, 28.

10. Quoted in Charles D. Cremeans, *The Arabs and the World* (New York: Frederick A. Praeger, 1963), pp. 291, 293; Hasan, *op. cit.,* p. 43.

11. *The New York Times,* June 28, 1964.

12. See the statement by the Indonesian Ambassador to Canada, in *New Times of Burma,* February 21, 1960; "Iraqi Foreign Minister Condemns Western Powers," *Mideast Mirror,* XII, December 31, 1960, 8; and *Asian Recorder,* VII, September 24–30, 1961, 4179.

13. Quoted in Fred B. Burke, *Africa's Quest for Order* (Englewood Cliffs, N.J.: Prentice-Hall, 1964), p. 150; quoted in Immanuel Wallerstein, *Africa: The Politics of Independence,* p. 150.

14. Quoted in Walter Goldschmidt (ed.), *The United States and Africa* (rev. ed.; Frederick A. Praeger, 1963), p. 74.

15. *Egyptian Mail,* December 16, 1961; "Arab Nationalism vs. Communism," *News of the United Arab Republic* (Washington, D.C.: UAR Embassy), VII, May, 1959, 1.

16. Quoted in Vernon McKay, *Africa in World Politics* (New York: Harper & Row, 1963), pp. 196–97.

17. *Ibid.,* pp. 197–99; Salisbury, *op. cit.,* p. 73.

18. *Hindustan Times,* March 15, 1963.

19. Abdel Nasser, "Where I Stand and Why"; and Cremeans, *op. cit.,* pp. 288–89.

20. Quoted in Ronald Segal, *African Profiles,* p. 271; quoted in Norman J. Padelford and Rupert Emerson, *Africa and World Order* (New York: Frederick A. Praeger, 1963), p. 42; and Wallerstein, *op. cit.,* p. 150.

21. *The Scribe,* II, May–June, 1961, 2–4; 93–94; and *ibid.,* July 23, 1961, 44.

22. *Arab Observer,* March 24, 1963, p. 24; and *Asian Recorder,* VIII, October 22–28, 1962, 4855; *The New York Times,* June 29, 1964.

23. Cited in the testimony of Mr. C. Douglas Dillon, in *Hearings, Review of Foreign Policy,* p. 294.

24. See: *The New York Times,* December 16, 1955; *Documents on International Affairs: 1955,* p. 484; *Times of Indonesia,* February 19, 29, and March 2, 1960; *African Recorder,* I, February 12–25, 1962, 91.

25. *The New York Times,* August 29, 1963.

26. *Egyptian Gazette,* January 1, 1961; Khalid I. Babaa, *Arab Positive Neutralism,* p. 45.

27. "Chou in Kabul," *Eastern World,* XI, February, 1957, 10.

28. See the statement by the Syrian Minister of State, Khalid al-Azm, in *Documents on International Affairs: 1957* (London and New York: Oxford University Press, 1960), p. 322.

29. For a detailed discussion of several prevalent American myths about Communist aid programs, see the testimony of Frank M. Coffin, an official of the Agency for International Development, in *Hearings, Foreign Assistance Act of 1962,* Part 2, pp. 332–33. For neutralist viewpoints on the advantages of Soviet aid, see *New Times of Burma,* March 10, 1960, and the editorial in *Eastern Economist,* XXVI, March 30, 1956, 514.

30. *The New York Times,* April 30, 1959.

31. Babaa, *op. cit.,* p. 7; Lt. Col. H. E. Crocker, "Afghanistan and Russia," *Eastern World,* X, January, 1956, 18; "Syria and the United States," *Arab World,* III, November, 1957, 3; Lorna Hahn, "Bizerte: Between Rounds," *Africa Today,* VIII, October, 1961, 6–8; *The New York Times,* May 2 and 4, 1964.

32. See the testimony of G. Lewis Jones in *Hearings, Mutual Security Act of 1960,* U.S. Senate Committee on Foreign Relations, 86th Cong., 2d sess. (Washington, D.C.: Government Printing Office, 1960), p. 288; and the testimony of Frank M. Coffin in *Hearings, Foreign Assistance Act of 1962,* Part 2, p. 331.

33. *The New York Times,* June 11, 1964, dispatch by Max Frankel.

34. *Hindustan Times* (overseas ed.), June 5, 1958; *Times of India,* March 18, 1963.

35. See *Times of Indonesia,* August 13, 1960.

36. See the views of Mr. Harry B. Ellis, as reported in *Christian Science Monitor,* November 2, 1962.

37. See the editorial in *Nation* (Rangoon), as reproduced in *India News,* I, April 12, 1963, 2.

38. *The New York Times,* June 22 and July 6, 1964.

39. See: Kamil A. Rahim, "Peace Through Strength," *Arab World,* I, November–December, 1955), 12; *Asian Recorder,* III, September 28–October 4, 1957, 1662; *The New York Times,* February 20, 1957; an undated dispatch from *Drum,* reproduced in *Times of Indonesia,* September 8, 1960.

Chapter 6. THE UNITED STATES AND THE NEUTRALIST MOVEMENT
(pp. 168–97)

1. See, respectively: *Documents on International Affairs: 1955,* p. 457; Secretary of State John Foster Dulles, "Confident of Our Future," Department of State *Bulletin,* XXXIII, October 24, 1955, 642; *Hearings, Mutual Security Appropriations for 1954,* p. 101; *Documents on American Foreign Relations: 1955* (New York: Harper & Bros., 1956), p. 18; *ibid.,* p. 355.

2. These and other examples of official and unofficial American skepticism about neutralism are presented in: *Times of India,* September 7, 1961; *ibid.,* November 23, 1961; *Morning News,* February 14, 1961; *In-*

dian Express, November 17, 1962; *Egyptian Gazette,* October 15, 1961; *ibid.,* October 29, 1961; *The New York Times,* November 19, 1961; "U.S. Aid Moves Awaited as Guinea Marks Eighth Month," *Africa Special Report,* IV, May, 1959, 4; Robert Murphy, "The Defense of Asia," Department of State *Bulletin,* XXXI, November 29, 1954, 800; George Bailey, "They Call Themselves Neutrals," *The Reporter,* XXV, September 28, 1961, 23; *Congressional Quarterly Almanac: 1951,* VII, 233.

3. *The New York Herald Tribune,* November 16, 1961.

4. See *The New York Times,* December 6, 1956 (italics added).

5. See the editorial in *Times of India,* November 11, 1961.

6. See the testimony of George Allen, in *Hearings, Mutual Security Act of 1956,* U.S.H.R. Committee on Foreign Affairs, 84th Cong., 2d sess. (Washington, D.C.: Government Printing Office, 1956), p. 542.

7. See the testimony of Harold Stassen, in *Hearings, Mutual Security Act of 1954,* U.S.H.R. Committee on Foreign Affairs, 83d Cong., 2d sess. (Washington, D.C.: Government Printing Office, 1954), p. 355; *Documents on American Foreign Relations: 1957* (New York: Harper & Bros., 1958), p. 40; *Documents on American Foreign Relations: 1951* (Boston: World Peace Foundation, 1953), p. 464.

8. See, respectively: *Foreign Policy and Mutual Security,* p. 17-R; *Hearings, Review of Foreign Policy,* p. 420; *Hearings, International Development and Security,* U.S. Senate Committee on Foreign Relations, 87th Cong., 1st sess. (Washington, D.C.: Government Printing Office, 1961), p. 650; Dulles, "Confident of Our Future," p. 641; *Hearings, Mutual Security Act of 1960,* p. 378; Charles E. Bohlen, "Key Characteristics of the Communist Threat," Department of State *Bulletin,* XLIII, October 24, 1960, 638–39.

9. Chester Bowles, "Three Frontiers that Divide the Communist World from Our Own," Department of State *Bulletin,* XLVII, July 9, 1962, 51; *The New York Times,* May 13, 1964; *Documents on International Affairs: 1957,* p. 328; *Hearings, Mutual Security Act of 1958,* U.S.H.R. Committee on Foreign Affairs, 85th Cong., 2d sess. (Washington, D.C.: Government Printing Office, 1958), p. 219; *Times of Indonesia,* September 26, 1960; *The New York Times,* October 19, 1958, dispatch by Thomas F. Brady.

10. See: *Survey of International Affairs: 1955–1956* (London and New York: Oxford University Press, 1960), p. 200; the quotation from President Eisenhower's speech in "Cambodia's Foreign Policy: Independent Neutrality and Non-Alignment," address by Mr. Nong Kimny, Cambodian Ambassador to the United States, on December 7, 1960 (text supplied by the Cambodian Embassy, Washington, D.C.), pp. 3–4; testimony of W. Averell Harriman in *Hearings, Mutual Security Act of 1959,* 3–4; testimony of W. Averell Harriman in *Hearings, Mutual Security Act of 1959,* U.S.H.R. Committee on Foreign Affairs, 86th Cong., 1st sess. (Washington, D.C.: Government Printing Office, 1959), p. 775; *Documents of American Foreign Relations: 1960* (New York: Harper & Row, 1961), pp. 97–98.

11. See: *Survey of International Affairs: 1955–1956,* p. 199; *Indonesian Spectator,* January 15, 1958; *Egyptian Gazette,* June 5, 1961; testimony of James P. Grant, in *Hearings, Foreign Assistance Act of 1963,* p. 396.

12. Quoted in *India News,* I, June 7, 1963, 1.

13. See, for example, "No Entry Again," *Eastern Economist,* XXXVII, December 22, 1961, 1167.

14. See the testimony of David E. Bell, in *Hearings, Foreign Assistance Act of 1963,* pp. 231–32; and the testimony of James P. Grant in *ibid.,* p. 415.

15. For these and other statements by executive policy-makers justifying cordial American relations with neutralist countries, see *Hearings, Mutual Security Act of 1958,* pp. 1709–70.

16. See Secretary Dulles' testimony in *Hearings, Mutual Security Appropriations for 1954,* p. 84; and *Hearings, Mutual Security Appropriations for 1957,* U.S.H.R. Committee on Appropriations, 84th Cong., 2d sess. (Washington, D.C.: Government Printing Office, 1956), p. 18.

17. See the testimony of W. W. Rostow in *Hearings, Review of Foreign Policy,* p. 273; Joseph C. Satterwaite, "The United States and the Continent of Africa," Department of State *Bulletin,* XLIII, November 14, 1960, 752; the testimony of James W. Riddleberger in *Hearings, Mutual Security Act of 1960,* p. 155; and the testimony of W. Averell Harriman in *Hearings, Foreign Assistance Act of 1962,* p. 670.

18. See the testimony of Walter P. McConaughy in *Hearings, International Development and Security,* p. 550; *ibid.,* p. 761; *Hearings, Mutual Security Act of 1960,* pp. 255–56; *Hearings, Foreign Assistance Act of 1962,* p. 230; and *Documents on American Foreign Relations: 1957,* p. 297; *The New York Times,* July 6, 1964.

19. *The New York Times,* June 12, 1963.

20. The author has explored these alternatives more fully in "American Diplomatic Tactics and Neutralism," *Political Science Quarterly,* LXXVIII, September, 1963, 418–44.

21. See the testimony of various executive officials in: *Hearings, Mutual Security Appropriations for 1959,* U.S. Senate Committee on Appropriations, 85th Cong., 2d sess. (Washington, D.C.: Government Printing Office, 1958), pp. 277, 284; *Hearings, Foreign Assistance Act of 1963,* p. 785; *Hearings, Mutual Security Act of 1958,* p. 625; *Hearings, Mutual Security Appropriations for 1960,* U.S. Senate Committee on Appropriations, 86th Cong., 1st sess. (Washington, D.C.: Government Printing Office, 1959), pp. 237–38; *Hearings, Foreign Assistance Act of 1963,* p. 404.

22. See, for example, the testimony of executive officials in *Hearings, Review of Foreign Policy,* pp. 305–20; and in *Hearings, Foreign Assistance Act of 1962,* p. 574.

23. *The New York Times,* December 17, 1954, and December 30, 1963.

24. See the testimony of Walter S. Robertson in *Hearings, Review of Foreign Policy,* p. 426; and the testimony of Rear Admiral E. B. Grantham in *Hearings, International Development and Security,* 87th Cong., 1st sess., 1961, p. 727.

25. *Documents on American Foreign Relations: 1952* (New York: Harper and Bros., 1953), p. 24.

26. See Secretary Dulles' testimony in Senate Foreign Relations Committee. *Review of Foreign Policy: 1958,* p. 792.

27. See the testimony of Secretary of State Rusk in *Hearings, International Development and Security Act,* U.S.H.R. Committee on Foreign

Affairs, 87th Cong., 1st sess. (Washington, D.C.: Government Printing Office, 1961), p. 27.

28. See the text of President Johnson's news conference in *The New York Times*, March 16, 1964.

29. Quoted by Mr. G. Mennen Williams in *Hearings, Foreign Assistance Act of 1962*, p. 614.

Chapter 7. THE FUTURE OF NONALIGNMENT
(pp. 198–218)

1. *The New York Times*, July 20, 1964.

2. For these and other expressions of neutralist sentiment in Latin America, see: *ibid.*, August 9, 1964, dispatch by Juan de Onis; "Pan Americanism Is Not Enough," from *Marcha*, cited in *Atlas*, VII, February, 1964, 105; "The U.S. Bores from Within," from *Marcha*, cited in *ibid.*, June, 1964, 351–52; Alvaro Martin, "Close Cultural Ties," from *Expreso*, cited in *ibid.*, 352–53.

3. See the text of Tito's address to the U.N. General Assembly, in *The New York Times*, October 23, 1963, and other statements by the Yugoslav leader in *ibid.*, October 18, and September 21, 1963.

4. *Ibid.*, May 31, 1964; and the letter to the editor of *The New York Times* by Mr. Orin Lehman, on June 18, 1964.

5. *Ibid.*, August 29, 1963.

6. *The New York Times*, March 24, 1964; *Indian Express*, November 29, 1962.

Index

Index

233